ABOUT THE AUTHOR

R J O'DONNELL is an award-winning journalist and author of *France, the Soul of a Journey.*

HOME PLACE, HEART PLACE

Journeys around Ireland

R J O'DONNELL

Matador
Unit E2 Airfield Business Park,
Harrison Road, Market Harborough,
Leicestershire. LE16 7UL
Tel: 0116 2792299
Email: books@troubador.co.uk
Web: www.troubador.co.uk/matador
Twitter: @matadorbooks

ISBN 978 1 80313 535 9

British Library Cataloguing in Publication Data.
A catalogue record for this book is available from the British Library.

Printed and bound by CPI Group (UK) Ltd, Croydon, CR0 4YY
Typeset in 11pt Minion Pro by Troubador Publishing Ltd, Leicester, UK

Matador is an imprint of Troubador Publishing Ltd

For the generous people who showed me the way on my journeys, and in memory of those no longer with us.

CONTENTS

FOREWORD

In these days of unyielding disquiet, and curbed lifestyles, there is certain joy in taking a book like *Home-place, heart-place* into your hands, and getting lost in the beauty and bounty of Ireland. We can cradle this book by our firesides and feel quietly excited to use it as a guide for making concrete escape plans. Elsewheres have always been seductive to those of us who love to travel and now the local elsewhere – the one that lies near us – is more alluring than ever. This volume by Róisín O'Donnell has the power to encourage less armchair travel and more movement of itchy feet to those quieter places, close and far-flung, that are lovingly and lyrically rendered in its pages.

O'Donnell brings Ireland to vivid life with a combination of personal reflection, gentle humour, reverence for the natural world, a concentration on art by the likes of Harry Clarke and the Yeats sisters, and a deep interest in the political and historical movements that formed this country. Reading this book in my East Galway home, I flew happily in O'Donnell's company to Croagh Patrick in County Mayo and, then, I was equally transported by a rove to an ancient abbey in County Louth. I found myself, too, enriched by the insider knowledge of the characters and history enthusiasts the author encountered on her travels, those generous guides who make this country such a hospitable, charming place to roam.

It is one thing to travel alone, it's even better to have a book like this one, a welcome manual to those Irish places we may have promised ourselves to visit one day – as well as ones that might be entirely new to us – presented with a gorgeous blend of wit, wisdom, folklore, and fact. I found myself pausing often to reflect on the narrative that details the turns of history that have brought Ireland to where it is today; on the invasions and colonisations that are reflected in some of our built heritage; and on the deep seam of creativity here that ensures the production of so much literature, music, and art. Here is a book to get you thinking as well as moving.

Pausing in a hilly corner of Kerry, O'Donnell writes, 'I drink in the raw localism and it feels like balm.' This is what the author celebrates in this fine book: the welcome solace to be found in the beauty and texture of all that lies around us on this island. Just as she says of a writer she admires, O'Donnell can make obscure places sing. I know other readers will be as captivated as I am by the locales described here, as much as the learned and anecdotal style of the book's narrator. *Home-place, heart-place* is as interesting as it is evocative and educational; poets and politicians people these pages, Raftery sits as surely here as Daniel O'Connell, but it is the places themselves that really glisten and that will lure readers from their homes, book in hand, and set them happily wandering.

Nuala O'Connor,
Ballinasloe, summer 2021

ONE

THE BURREN

The western coastal road of Ireland has meandered to its heart's content since time began though only recently has it got the name it deserves – the Wild Atlantic Way. Names are powerful. They touch a nerve. Wild Atlantic Way suits this path created by nature, compacted into place by the feet of jouneymen and the hooves and wheels of centuries.

From the Inishowen Peninsula in Donegal to Kinsale in Cork, it shifts and climbs over bays, ravines and jabbed headlands, winding its way along, thick with the tang of the Atlantic ocean.

I'm approaching Clare from the south Galway section of the Wild Atlantic Way, driving against the low January sun. A glimpse of a shoreline flashes into view.

'This is typical Clare white sand, look how the sun bounces off it,' says my friend, Treasa. I've invited her along to show me the county she was born in. She's 'breathing her native air,' as she puts it. Though she left her home-place for Dublin after she finished school she says. 'Clare never left me. It was only from afar that I started to realise what a rare place it was.'

Rare indeed. This is the Burren and you won't find terrain like it elsewhere in the world. Its bald hills and limestone pavements are strangely beautiful. I can see why it's called a lunar landscape.

Treasa says she'll never stop seeing home through the eyes of a child. It's this view of homeplace that I want to borrow for my journeys. So, for each location I visit, I bring along someone who was born there, just to recreate that youthful vision when horizons are unnamed, untamed and starry-eyed.

The rain of the previous week has vanished into the hills, disappeared into a honeycomb of calcium caves and fissures. Rains don't delay on the Burren high ground but wend their way into places invisible, to turn up later as wells, cures, spas and springs. And Clare has long welcomed people here to 'take the waters'.

'I remember freewheeling down slopes like these to school, the wind in my face, larking around with my brothers,' says Treasa. 'I can still hear the screech of the brakes that badly needed oiling.'

It was from one of her teachers that she got a love of Irish poets and poetry and in turn she passed that on to her own students when she became a teacher. Her memories are coming out in snatches of an Irish poem.

'I think it's the remoteness of Irish that's its charm,' she says. 'It was banned as the main language at a crucial time in history so it never got a chance to grow middle-aged and smug. Or maybe it's that you inherit a language that you've never spoken.'

No wonder we miss the turn for our planned Burren walk. 'No more reveries until we find this junction,' I warn her.

It's a left turn south of Kinvara, signposted Boston, but instead of going to Boston, we drive upwards on a road not important enough to be named. The walk is on the right and it takes us along the foot of a hill on a pathway with a grassy spine. It's a morning in good form, the light is at its best. The gods must have been up all night blending the colours to get it so perfect.

Shades of mauve, purple and blue are rising in the frosted air, mixing with sea and sky. To our left, one of the Burren hills is giving off a lavender hue. Its stones are sweeping uphill in terraces, scored by heavy lines making curves around the mound. Trees are scarce here and the odd one we see is bent and dishevelled by the Atlantic winds, stems gnarled like arthritic fingers.

Cows are balancing themselves on the slopes. Every winter they make the journey uphill, ambling their way in single file through the limestone rocks. I'm sure they know what they're doing, this winterage is following an ancient system of farming, but cows look too heavy for these shelving heights. Goats and sheep have better-built hooves to cling with.

The coastline below is broken, chopped and channelled, fields stitched together form a flat fertile plain, parading, slowing down and spilling into the sea. Through this collage on a lower shelf the Wild Atlantic Way cuts parallel to our road.

Beyond Galway Bay, Connemara's Twelve Pins peak like meringue. Treasa points across to the small island of Aughinish and tells me about childhood trips there – on summer Sunday afternoons when family and dogs were packed into the car for the day out. Aughinish was part of the coast of Clare until the great Lisbon earthquake of 1755 sent a tsunami our way that broke off forever its links with the mainland.

'It's still Clare's,' she says, 'but it can only be reached from County Galway, by a causeway. It was built by the British army in the early nineteenth century to move troops in and out of the Martello Tower when the tide was low.'

As we go over the brow of the hill a little chapel appears in the distance. Maybe it's the view from afar that makes it thrilling. It touches a memory of a place that once received a file of worshippers, crossing the fields to come together to pray. That was before life got so good that people realised they didn't have to pray.

It brings me back to the days when a group of us were regularly stopped by an old neighbour on our way home from school. He used to drone on about the Penal Laws (laws that denied Roman Catholics and dissenters an education, in an effort to make them accept the established Anglican Church), pointing out a Mass rock on a nearby hill where prayers were offered illegally. And he would tell us about that flat stone, still there, that they used as an altar, priests fleeing with chalices, getting hair-raisingly ahead of the authorities and sometimes dropping the communion host in a pool of water which, 'even on the hottest day of summer never dries up'. The chase sounded like the movies of the Wild West we were allowed go to on Sundays. 'Catholics and dissenters,' he used to say, 'weren't thought trustworthy enough to be educated.' And then came the advice that made us hide our smiles: 'You must never forget how privileged you are to be able to go to school. Your forebears had to do with education on the run, or without schooling at all.'

At the time I thought schooling on the run could be quite fun or better still, do without going to school at all. And I got little sympathy when I came home. My mother would back him up: 'You should listen to him. He has interesting things to say.'

My brother, who hated school too, would whisper, 'If he has, why doesn't he say them.'

Our brisk walk has warmed us up. Back in the car we throw our coats off and drive downhill to rejoin the Wild Atlantic Way.

Before we reach Ballyvaughan a left turn leads us into the old abbey of Corcomroe. This is Cistercian monasticism at its best. The monks sought out the wildest of places for their foundations. Cistercians were known for their skilled farming and reclaiming of waste land. They had their work cut out for them here.

Around 1195 when they founded this abbey, they were enjoying a wave of popularity. They dedicated it to Our Lady of the Fertile Rock (Sancta Maria de Petra Fertilis). Even the name is linked to Cistercian good husbandry, making rocks fertile. As well as draining, reclaiming and bridge building, they grew medicinal flowers and burned herbs to ward off plagues. (Pity we don't have them now.) The Burren has no shortage of healing herbs, wild garlic, haws and hazels.

I approach the narrow road at crawling speed. Farm animals and wildlife have right of way here. This must have been a thoughtful journey in the glory days when religious centres were seen as a little patch of heaven on earth. It's easy to mix up the skeletons of this monastery with the dolmens, stones and crags that dot the landscape.

Like all monasteries, obedience, piety and poverty were the guiding forces and prayers were shaped around the canonical hours of the day – psalms and communal singing for every shade of light. That was fitting because the light has a special quality here in the Burren, changing with the hours and the seasons, like an inner flame within the limestone. I can imagine the male voices of the monks echoing into these rocky hills. The Gloria in Excelsis would have been especially apt when the Burren flora burst into bloom in May and June. This rare flowering makes north Clare famous. Through the cracks and fissures of the pavements they erupt – multi-coloured orchids, deep blue gentian, mountain avens, stunted white and blackthorn, holly and ash. These rocks look fertile then.

The abbey is without a roof now, like all its companions in Ireland. They have stayed roofless since the 1530s, when King Henry Vlll stripped them. He couldn't feel sure of himself while the monasteries remained. They were rivals to his own power and the spread of Protestantism. And he needed their precious altar plate, candlesticks, mostly of gold and of course their land.

In the chancel we look at the effigy of Dónal Mór O'Brien, king of the Gaelic-Ireland territory of Thomond (present-day Clare, Limerick and part of Tipperary). He was a descendant of the founder. Though he's a bit mossy, he has survived well in spite of being out under the mists and rains of the west of Ireland. The O'Briens would feel chuffed to be remembered because to found a monastery in medieval times was something to brag about.

Corcomroe graveyard is still used. A woman is cleaning the family grave. She scrubs the stone and chats to us.

'Recently a grave was dug here and the digger slid against a pile of mussel shells that were here since the monks' time,' she tells us.

'Wouldn't the Cistercians be fairly and squarely caught out now if they had pretended they were strict vegetarians,' says Treasa. They only excluded four-legged animal flesh from their diet. Mussels didn't break that rule.

The woman points us in the direction of the well. Treasa wades in for a drink because she reckons the waters have healing properties.

'Back then people knew about these things – the ideal place to set up, beside a good water source,' she explains. But I talk her out of going in to drink it. Her feet might get stuck in the deep hoof marks. And no matter how curative the waters might be, I don't think it's advisable to share a pond with a herd of cattle. She takes my advice.

Walking back to the car, our footsteps echo in the gravel. The only other sound is the light scrubbing of the brush on the granite and the odd snort from the grazing beasts.

The poet William Butler Yeats, a man for evocative spots, made these ruins the setting of one of his plays. And you can well see why. There's a presence here that makes you want to stay in the moment. We avoid that temptation. The day is short in January and we have a lot to see.

Terraced hills stretch ahead of us as we drive southwards, channels of morning light bringing their smooth curves into creation. This part of the country was sacred to J R R Tolkien. Where better than among these hills could Tolkien find a parallel world for his creation, Middle-earth and its inhabitants, the elves and hobbits, who can vanish at will? Because inside this bare beauty is all the imagination can contain, a meshwork of caves and underground rivers that form springs and swallow-holes that appear and vanish overnight.

Tolkien loved language, from the folk tongues to the classics. He said himself that the appeal of Greek was its 'fluidity, punctuated by hardness, its surface glitter and its alien remoteness'. He must have found the same features in the Burren – the fluidity of its hills, the hardness of its rock, its dwarf woodland and its alien nature.

Alien because, in summer rare botanical species share space in the crevices of the rock pavements of the Burren – Arctic plants (normally only found in tundra), Alpine flora (their usual home is in the high Alps) and Mediterranean plants grow together. Because this strange mix goes against the natural order of botany, it shares the same sense of living legend as Tolkien's elves. They too are capable of achieving way beyond the power of nature.

Like many good things, the Burren, all 600 square kilometres of it, came about by chance, when Neolithic farmers here in what is now north-west Clare, cleared away the oaks and pines that thrived on the hills. That left the soil with nothing to anchor itself on to and it blew away and brought an end to the thick covering of grass and shrubs. Environmental hoodlums they may be, but the result is a treasure.

The hills are naked now and they bear their skeletons to the sun and the whip of the Atlantic winds. But some soil remains within the rock crevices and it's here that the rare flora that make the Burren famous, grow. They keep their faces well down to avoid the harsh sea breezes.

Just to follow Tolkien's footsteps, we drive in the long avenue to Gregan Castle. In the early fifties he used to stay here as a guest of the owner, Dr Frank Martyn. He had written *Lord of the Rings* at the time.

Simon Haden, the present owner of Gregan Castle, says, 'There's evidence that Tolkien had started *Lord of the Rings* before he came to the Burren. According to Professor Liam Campbell from the University of Ulster who is very interested in Tolkien, he revised it after his visits here. Pol na Gollum (which is said to have inspired Tolkien's Middle-earth) is very close to the hotel. It's the longest underground cave system in the Burren and it was very visited when Tolkien used to come here in the fifties.'

Growth is sparse. It was all very well for Tolkien's pen to be set aflowing by this landscape, but earning your keep was a different matter. The story goes that Oliver Cromwell's surveyor, Captain Ludlow, said that Clare had neither enough water to drown a man, tree to hang him nor soil to bury him.

This side of the story of the Burren landscape is driven home with feeling in Timothy O'Grady's book, *I Could Read the Sky*. Treasa recommended that I read it before our journey. It's a homage to the beauty, wisdom, skill of this part of the country but loneliness croons through the pages – the raw grief as people left their homeland to find work.

The young man of this story, on his way to England, opens over and over again the address his father has scribbled on a piece of paper, until the edges get worn away. And he keeps the two pounds his mother has given him separate for as long as possible until it finally gets mixed in with the rest. He can taste the brine in his mouth when he arrives, though he can't pretend to the other farm workers he has to share the loft of a shed with.

He lists off the talents that served him well in rural Clare but are useless in industrial England. He can mend nets, read the sky, make a basket from reeds, read the sea, read the wind and he knows the song to sing to a cow while milking. He can't take to English place-names because 'there isn't much movement in them and they're closed off at both ends'. Far from the comforting Clare place-names, they remind him of iron.

And when an uncle, who could cut a dash on a city street, is found dead from exposure in England, he reflects on what a fine farewell he would have got in his native Clare. Cromwell's scouts might have thought there wasn't enough soil to bury a man, but when it came to giving someone a send-off, Clare people did it in style. A lament on the flute by the grave where all the locals gather, keepers of tradition, who know the deceased seed, breed and generation. Because this was where roots defined a man, like the calcium deposits of the ages woven into the scape of the land around them.

Tolkien too must have known a thing or two about the taste of brine in the mouth – he and his young brother lost first their father, then their mother, at a young age.

'Oh I forgot to bring you to Kilmacduagh,' says Treasa suddenly.

'That's in Galway Treasa, that means going northwards again. We've already gone miles south.' I stop myself. She did warn me that the journey would be random.

'Drive wherever the day takes you' is her motto. And I decide I'm going to join in her lighthearted take on directions and follow the day.

We ask men on tractors, women carrying shopping bags, children with schoolbags. They're all hazy about Kilmacduagh which surprises me when I see this fine collection of monastic buildings. It's a young lad hopping a football who shows us where it is. It's on the Corofin Road from Gort. I make a note of that so that I won't ever have to ask so many people again. It's one of the finest monastic sites in the country, according to the leaflet which we pick up in the house opposite the site.

I ring the doorbell at the right moment. Two minutes later and the woman who sells the Kilmacduagh leaflets would have left for the funeral that's assembling. Like Corcomroe, the graveyard here is still in use.

When I ask her if she knows the names of the row of hills that Kilmacduagh is in the distant shelter of, she says it's the Burren but she can't identify them individually. As she quickens her step towards the funeral she passes on the question to a man who is striding heavily towards the house. He doesn't know either.

'They're locals,' says Treasa. 'They never pinned a label on the hills they grew up among.'

I shouldn't be delaying the woman. The hearse is already crawling up the narrow road to the cemetery, and walking mourners are following.

We keep a respectful distance. We look at the cathedral through the locked gate and the Glebe House, once the residence of the abbot. We have to wait until the crowd disperses to see the Round Tower. It's the tallest of its kind in the country.

'I've never seen a tower that doesn't distinguish itself in some way – the tallest, the smallest, the chubbiest or whatever,' says Treasa.

This one no doubt is different. It tilts startlingly, two feet off the vertical. It could be called Ireland's leaning tower. I shudder to think that one day it might tip itself into fragments because otherwise it's perfect.

Round towers were where monks climbed, using rope ladders, on to a doorway set at a safe height above ground to take their precious altar plate when they were in danger of a raid. So they say. Not everyone agrees that this was the purpose of the towers. I remember a tour guide once rubbishing that theory.

'The Vikings were hard men,' he said. 'They had made their way across rough seas through enemy territory, they had nagivated their narrow boats up the slimmest of rivers so it's unlikely that a few monks at the top of a tower would have scared them.'

A woman in the group didn't agree.

'That's to under-estimate local support which might be on its way,' she said. And the tour guide got a bit peeved when the rest of us agreed with her.

'Feel free to disagree with me,' he sniffed.

I'm on the lookout for the miraculous here in Kilmacduagh because the founder, the seventh century Saint Colman

MacDuagh, had a miraculous beginning. The local king, on hearing it foretold that this child's fame would outdo his own, had his pregnant mother cast into the river with a stone around her neck. Somehow she floated to safety and her child lived to be more famous than the king. He founded this monastery and his image is often shown with a rooster. The task of this bird was to crow to waken him for night office. A mouse helped him out too, kept him from falling asleep, and a fly marked his place on the page of his sacred book.

It's all so gentle, mythical, like a children's story, a man-animal sharing world, not like today when we've sprays and traps ready for these pests. But lovely though it is, I'm sticking to the alarm to waken me. I'm not a fan of mice in my bedroom watching me. I'd prefer to oversleep.

Treasa directs me by the village of Carran, through the heart of the Burren, by roads that wind tantalisingly around hills. At the viewing point of Fahee North a drove of young horses gallop down the hill, craning their necks over the fence to see what we're doing. When they see all that's of interest – not much, clearly – they turn, giddy with youth, manes floating, beating their hooves against the good bone-forming limestone and canter up the hill. They're like part of the landscape, silhouetted against the skyline.

Sparse and all as the Burren looks, the vegetation is rich in nutrients for the horses that are grazed here and that will turn them into future stars of the racecourse. The limestone keeps the hillsides warm so you have all-year-round growth.

Treasa talks to a couple who are on their way to the Burren Perfumery who recommend it as a nice place for lunch.

In the Burren Perfumery they've been mixing scents for nearly half a century. Alas, that's the only fragrance at this time of the year. They only serve lunch in summer time. Tea and biscuits are all they can offer which we help ourselves to in the little kitchen alongside the shop.

We fare no better in Cassidy's pub a few miles up the road. This is a family business dating back to 1830. They like tradition, judging from their website which lists natural remedies for common ailments. There's nothing for the more common ailment of hunger though. We take our drinks outside to catch a glimpse of the record-beating Carran polje. A polje is a flat-bottomed hollow, a feature of a limestone region. At 4.5 square kilometres, this one is the biggest in the British Isles. When it fills up, all eighty metres of it, it's part of the miracle of the rising and vanishing waters of turloughs that add zest to County Clare.

From Carran we go through a wilderness of limestone pavements that look like snowcaps. And there in the middle of it all, barely distinguishable from the rest of the stone, is the obelisk we're looking for – Poulnabrone dolmen. This flat capstone is supported by three standing portal stones. It looks like a vision from the past, of the neighbourly custom of carrying the dead. It dates from Neolithic times, between 4200 to 2900 BC.

By now day is closing into that serene time that spreads a winter's evening with a tranquil air. The fading light is bringing up the colour of the stony uplands. Greys and purples are crossing from hill to hill like secret codes, browns and russets rising from the ground.

Under a sky that bears a single streak of red, like the god of heaven has upturned his red ink bottle onto the blue canvas, we walk across the hilltop to view the dolmen. It seems the most natural thing in the world to find such a mighty structure on this windy spot. It must have been constructed for someone of serious importance. And the poor sods who had to carry the boulders must have been of serious unimportance.

'I wonder who singled out our generation for such preferential treatment, to live in such an age of comfort?' wonders Treasa. 'Or does God know each one of us, layer after layer?' But before I can gather an answer together (as if I have one) she hurries me along the jagged terrain. She has a nice viewing point from Corkscrew Hill to show me while it's still bright enough to see it.

'Take it easy,' I urge her. I can't think of a worse place to fall. There are only two of us against the rim of the earth, not a house in sight in this expanse of wilderness, nor a person, nor even an animal, though animals are little help these days.

The view from atop Corkscrew hill turns out to be worth the rush. There's something bewitching about this hour, it's not sure of itself, is it night or is it day? We watch Galway Bay vanishing into a shroud.

We drive on to beat the advancing darkness, leaving Lisdoonvarna to the twilight, a spa town I wouldn't mind seeing, or indeed sampling the waters that they've been taking here for three centuries. By the time we get to the Cliffs of Moher we have squeezed the last light out of the day and the only view we get of them is their black outline hunched against the sky.

If darkness doesn't serve us well getting here, it makes Vaughan's restaurant in Liscannor glow with cosiness. It's blissful to close the door on the January evening and draw up our chairs to the open fire. We haven't had something substantial to eat since breakfast.

Over dinner we talk about our plans for tomorrow. Treasa is going to show me, Feakle, in east Clare, to follow the trail of poet, Brian Merriman and herbalist and clairvoyant, Biddy Early.

TWO

FEAKLE

We approach Feakle by Killaloe, in east Clare, on the crossing of the River Shannon. There are no shortage of reminders that this was part of the heritage lands of Brian Bórama, Ireland's eleventh-century High King. He defeated the Danes in Clontarf in 1014, on April 23. It was a sunrise to sunset event and it went into the popular lore as the Irish freeing themselves from foreign dominance, which wasn't really true. No matter. The Battle of Clontarf and 1014 are as etched on the Irish mind as The Battle of Hastings and 1066 is on the English.

The road is narrow, more suited to slow-moving vehicles than the impatient driver in the jeep behind us. We take it easy and enjoy the grace of the rambling countryside by Tuamgraney. This was the home place of writer Edna O Brien, her childhood horizon. It's a landscape she loves. 'The ordinariness of its extraordinariness,' is what makes it, according to her. From here the road winds on by Scarriff, with the Shannon on our right.

'It feels like a place where there was a strong sense of community,' I say, and that sets Treasa talking.

'I remember a lot of that close-knit world. As children when we were sent to a local house on an errand, they always made tea for us and I can still recall the crusty bread spread with homemade jam. Food wasn't just about hunger, it was a way of being neighbourly,' she says. 'The bread in one house didn't taste the same as another, as if it fermented in a different way. In my head I linked each taste with a house. That was a time when they shook holy water until they nearly drenched us,' she laughs, 'when family rosaries were recited each evening. The only time I remember a rosary being said in the daytime was during a thunderstorm. And it always did the business, the storm shifted off somewhere else, to annoy someone further away and put them praying.'

The flow of a river must have cut through a lot of these tastes and customs. The River Shannon forms the east boundary of Clare. Across the border we can see the high ground patchwork of farmland in neighbouring County Tipperary. History is sewn into these fields. They remain in the size and shape that suited a time when ploughing was horse-drawn, or when seeds were scattered in handfuls. Back then they were measured in furlongs (length of the furrow), roods (a little over a thousand square metres) and perches (slightly more than five metres square). Dimensions like these have long since gone into the memory, like the sweat of the cultivators have seeped onto the hillsides. No two fields look the same colour from here. There are thousands of shades of green and beige but the haze from the river rises like a veil casting the same shimmer on all of them.

A left turn brings us by the River Graney. Further upstream it runs into Moy Graney. The road flows towards and away, losing and finding the river as we go towards Feakle. It's the graveyard we're heading for – the burial spot of two famous people, Brian Merriman and Biddy Early. Both upset the authorities, one with her herbal remedies, so curing that the clergy feared her power might rival theirs, though individual priests were said to consult her. The other offended with his bawdy, anti-clerical poetry. A memorial stone to Merriman stands outside. That's the first surprise to find it outside rather than inside the walls of the cemetery.

A local woman tending her grave explains, 'It couldn't be erected inside because no one knows the exact spot of his grave.' And she adds with a wink, 'if he's buried here at all.'

There's no doubt however that Biddy Early lies here though no one can tell the spot. 'My mother knew,' says the woman, 'but she would never say.'

When Early died in 1874 her funeral was poorly attended because people were afraid to be seen at the rites of a woman who was thought to have a direct link to a pagan power for her potions. She had been called a witch, hauled before a court in Ennis on the charge of witchcraft, but acquitted because there was no evidence. Now her burial spot is as unknown as the closely-guarded recipes of her mixtures.

To follow the other member of the banished pair brings us uphill in search of the hedge school in Kilclaren where Merriman taught. Hedge schools were a way of getting round the Penal Laws. These laws were strict, and not-so-strictly applied depending on which British monarch was on the throne. Schools breaking the rules had to stay well out of sight.

The fairies, those noble invisibles, were highly thought of in Ireland and they feature in both Early's and Merriman's lives. Biddy Early's lone childhood led her to chat to the fairies. Merriman's only surviving work, 'Cúirt an Mheán Oíche' (The Midnight Court), an *aisling,* or dream poem, featuring Aoibheal, Queen of the Fairies. It is 1,206 lines long and is considered the greatest comic poem in the history of the Irish language. It contains sharp social commentary, in the style of Frenchman François Rabelais, and just as bawdy. (Rabelais was a satirist, creator of grotesque jokes. The mere mention of his name in France provokes a laugh.)

'Cúirt an Mheán Oíche,' was remembered in oral form, not published until 1850, nearly half a century after Merriman's death. For generations it stayed safely out of reach, clapped inside the covers of old manuscripts, until the writer Frank O'Connor translated it in 1945. Ireland in the forties wasn't ready for some of the sexual directness it contained and it was quickly banned. It took years for the banning fraternity to agree to Merriman's commemoration with a plaque.

Treasa can recite '*Cúirt an Mheán Oíche*' and she launches into it:

Ba ghnáth mé ag siúl le ciumhais na habhann
ar bháinseach úr 's an drúcht go trom,
in aice na gcoillte, i gcoim an tsléibhe,
gan mhairg, gan mhoill, ar shoilse an lae.

Twas my pleasure to walk in the river meadows
In the thick of the dew and the morning shadows,
At the edge of the woods in a deep defile,
At peace with myself in the first sunshine.

She begins to talk again about her notion that a language lies dormant and that it takes poetry to enchant it into life, a bit like the Sleeping Beauty. I keep my eye firmly on the road. When Treasa meanders into these conversations it's easy to lose your way.

The poet Séamus Heaney unveiled a memorial to Merriman on the shores overlooking Lough Graney where the opening scene of 'The Midnight Court' is set. On the day of the unveiling, locals were able to point out the exact spot on the field where the hedge school was located and the place by the lough where the poet fell asleep and had his vision. We're not so lucky. There's no sight of anyone to give us directions.

Aisling poetry was born in the defeat and dispossession of the sixteenth, seventeenth and eighteenth centuries. The poet falls asleep, and out of the depths of slumber appears a *spéirbhean* – a beautiful woman – in a gust of musical lyrics. The poet wonders if she is Deirdre, Helen or maybe Venus? She's none of these. She's Éire (Ireland). And then, the phrases turn sour as the story of Ireland in colonial bondage is told.

It's the satirical twist that Merriman gives the *aisling* that makes it funny because the vision turns out not to be the enchanted maiden of otherworldly beauty typical of the *aisling* but a grotesque female giant with a warrant to arrest him. She sweeps him off to the court of Moy Graney to the fairy palace where Aoibheal, Queen of the Fairies, is presiding over a judicial enquiry. A *spéirbhean* is making a complaint about the grievances of women (mostly sexual) who are without husbands while Irishmen choose not to marry for as long as possible. She wonders why the clergy don't marry being that they are healthy. And wealthy.

The same year as Merriman wrote 'Cúirt an Mheán Oíche', 1781, in Germany the poet Friedrich von Schiller was writing his daring work, '*Die Rauber*' (The Robbers) which is also critical of the hypocrisy of religion and injustices like inequality.

We don't know much about Merriman, whether he ever read the works of Rabelais or Schiller. Though he lived for over twenty years after writing 'Cúirt an Mheán Oíche', he doesn't seem to have composed again. He died in poverty in English-speaking Limerick, where later in his life he taught Mathematics.

The annual Merriman summer school keeps up the Rabelasian rollicking tradition. The carousing that follows the learning and the debates is the best part of the event.

Looking for Merriman's hedge school makes the droning words of my old neighbour flash across my memory and I imagine I see fleeing priests with red-coated men hot on their heels scurrying across the landscape. His words echo: 'You must never forget how privileged you are to be able to go to school.' When you find yourself agreeing with something you once thought so boring, it's a sure sign you've grown boring yourself – or perhaps wiser.

As derelict houses pass us by I think of County Clare's strong tradition of music and house dancing. Few homes that hosted those capers are lived in now, and no modern dwelling is built with dancing in mind. These steps were mostly imported. The quadrille was a regimental dance, resembling war or indeed like a picture of the fields that many of the dancers ploughed by day. The movements were in a strict pattern of crossings and squares. These dances were brought back from the ballrooms of the continental gentry by soldiers who had fought in the Napoleonic wars. Wasn't that a lot nobler than killing one another on the battlefields?

The polka came from Bohemia, the Mazurka and the Varsovienne from Poland. When they turned up on Clare kitchen floors they were given local names – Clare sets, Shoe the Donkey, plain sets, barn dances, the Stack of Barley, names that made them their own and they became Ireland's great native art form. Others stuck to what they were originally called – highland schottisches, military two-steps, the Valet waltz.

The musicians' job was to power on the dancers, until music and dance flowed into one. Equally, they could go gently on the strings and let their notes turn tender for a slow air. Then for the sad tune, instruments were put piercing into a wail of half notes. These music makers were skilled and weren't conceited about their art either.

Music and dancing weren't to everyone's taste. Cardinal Cullen, Archbishop of Dublin, put a ban on the polka in the mid nineteenth century. He thought it was 'repugnant to the purity of Christian morals'. The polka seems harmless now, hardly a risk to either purity or morals.

Indeed the cardinal's legacy continued as late as 1935. The Dancehall Act, brought in by de Valera's government, targeted house dances, including the practice of celebrating the threshing of the corn with a party to thank the neighbours who had given a hand in the traditional *meithal*. Like the dances from faraway lands made their long journey to find a home in Ireland, de Valera, whose constituency was here in Clare, made the transition from radical young man to compliant head of government.

'I'll bring you to a traditional house,' says Treasa.

I can't wait. She directs me through a web of roads, minor and more minor still. I'm seriously wondering if we're going to get out of this labyrinth. When I suggest that maybe we should put the townland into the GPS or take a glance at a map, she waves away my worries: 'No need, I could reach this place with my eyes shut.' That bothers me. And just as I'm about to suggest that on this occasion it might be wise to keep them open, she says:

'Here we are. You can drive into the yard there.'

I'm expecting someone, with dog on tow, to emerge to ask us to move ourselves off. But the man who comes through the door smiles when he sees Treasa.

'Ah there you are, Jim,' she says as she pushes open the car door. While they're busy with loud talk of how great it is to see one another, I wonder if it's some homing device she tapped into to find her way on such a network of roads. Because, believe me, Treasa's sense of direction is not her strongest suit.

From inside come the tones of hearty welcomes from Jim's wife, Margot. Then Jim's mother, who has recently moved in to live with them, appears.

'You mean you got here with Treasa directing you?' Jim says to me with a wink.

'Ah stop that, Jim, teasing Treasa,' says his mother, with a reprimand as if they're children.

'Don't worry, Aunt Chris. I take no notice of him.'

Christmas festivities have not yet been put away. A tray of hot whiskies is put before us which as the driver, I can't indulge in, but I enjoy the pungent smell of cloves and lemon and watching them tipple their glasses of spiced booze in front of the crackling wood stove.

A string of relations is accounted for and I enjoy the crossing words, knowing nods, the local litanies of people and places – Ballynakill, Killafeen, Killeen, Killanena.

Chris takes out leather-bound photo albums. Some pictures look as if they date from shortly after the camera was invented. Older ancestors are in sepia, less far-into-the-distant relations are in black and white. There are photographs of them all when they were children, relatives in Australia, relatives in the United States, people playing accordions and fiddles. This gets us talking about the music and dancing of Clare.

Why did the tradition last longer here than elsewhere? Some say it's because it's an 'island' county hemmed in by sea on its west, hills to the north and the Shannon to the east that made it less porous than elsewhere. Chris doesn't agree, though she has no other reason to offer. Now in her eighties she remembers these dances.

'It was a different world,' she says. And glass in hand, she brings the allure of those nights to life: the tuning and humouring of the instruments, the thrill of the opening strains, the first draw of the bow on the fiddle string, the dragged note of the concertina. And the dancers – 'Some could twist in a saucer, as they used to say. Others needed half an acre for their wild footwork,' she laughs.

Chris recalls often going home in the early hours, having danced all night. She had met some of the towering names of Clare's music – Elizabeth Crotty, Junior Crehan, Willie Clancy. She talks about the early recordings.

'I preferred them, with their crackling and scratching. The ones done in the studios were too perfect, too polished. The old ones left more to the imagination. They had a touch of the half-heard about them.'

She sounds like Treasa. And it can't be put down to inheritance because Chris is related to Treasa only by marriage, her late uncle's wife.

I feel mean-spirited to spoil such an unhurried existence but when was there a stroke of work done? Chris herself was a teacher.

'We did it, we were young I suppose. You do these things when you're young – dance all night and still do a job next day.'

The banter is hard to leave. As we drive away from New Year wishes and waves of goodbye, Treasa suggests whirring around to the places where she was brought as a child.

That brings us by old houses, some in ruins, their former owners dispersed, others owned by people Treasa no longer knows, her own old home flattened. It brings us into the heart of Clare.

'When I'm here I feel in the mesh of grandparents, parents, uncles, aunts, all as real as the land around me. Most of them are dead now, *imithe ar shlí na* fírinne.' This Irish way of explaining death is so lyrical that translation spoils it – Gone on the path of Truth.

Bound up in the memory among the sweetly honed hills and broad valleys that unfold before us are the tones from which the music and dance of Clare took its vibration. And its pulse pierces into something pre-conceived. For music draws from a deep well and it whistles and bows among the percolated echo chambers of the limestone as we pass by. It recalls a world without boundaries, where everyone is kin, a night till morning affair. Songs, tunes, sets interminable, feet unstoppable, relays of dancers at the ready to replace the exhausted, like subs on a football pitch, musicians yielding to their instruments, bowing in long strokes, squeezing breath into the boxes, giving their best blow to the whistles, turning out tunes with names that bring the landscape on to the dance floor: The Grouse on the Bog, The Irish Washerwoman, The Heather Breeze, The Blackbird. These names were lifted from the land from which they had sprung.

No wonder Tolkien loved it here with his taste for magic rings, rendering characters invisible. It's easy to fall prey to the enchantment of this land and its rare topography where fairies play tricks of hide and seek, snatching the waters from the surface and bringing them through an unseen array of porous limestone, making stalactites and stalagmites along the way, reappearing as sacred wells and curing waters.

Maybe this invisibility guides Treasa too and renders her capable of finding the place of her childhood with her eyes shut, though elsewhere she can get lost with her eyes open.

As we negotiate our way out of a maze of minor routes I give thanks for our own unseen era, where maps appear before us from cameras located on far-off satellites guiding us on our way. Treasa's skill might impress me but I'm not yet ready to place my trust in her to get out of this place. So I use the GPS.

I'm going to invite her to my next planned tour, to Galway, my own native county. I hope I will be able to imbue the place with the same kindred spirit as she can. The bar is high.

THREE

GALWAY, HOME GROUND

This is Galway, the county I was born in. I invite an Australian friend, Karen to join myself and Treasa. We're driving past signs that point to places I often heard as a child – Loughrea, Abbeyknockmoy, Athenry, Corofin, Woodford, Ballyglunin, and they echo like incantations, calling up snatches of murmuring chat from the adult world of old, that passed over my young head at a mythical time, when I didn't have to work out if these words were places or people or events or things. As we passs by I get the fragrance of this dreamtime of my life.

We used to get letters from relations from these parts – Christmas cards from another parish, the tolls of whose bells would reach our place of an evening when the wind was blowing our way, spreading a holy breath across the fields. The older people knew which church each knell came from and in the twilight wonder of youth I used to think how intriguing those places were. Because that was a time when I thought faraway places were the colour of the rainbow. Little did I know that I would spend the other half of my life like a homing pigeon with a draw to my own horizon.

When I first left home I balked at the stride of urban life. My memories were of fields, not of pavements, and I had some juggling to do to unite the two. How can you explain the special sound of feet against the grass, that a farmer's pace is not the same as that of a city dweller, the early-morning dew, the customs, the dark spaces, the fairy trees, the respected superstitions.

In time I yielded to city life like a coastline takes on the shapely lap of the ocean. Visits home were caressed in warmth and handshakes. But there were the homecomings too that formed silent lines as hands were offered to say: 'I'm sorry for your trouble.'

Generations of my family left their print on the soil around Galway. The earth then folded the other way and left its print on them, in graves from Clonberne, Dunmore, Kilmoylan, Abbeyknockmoy. As the keens of their passing died down, they nurtured the land they had befriended, worked on, died on and let their spirits roam over it.

I'm sure in their time they wondered what the world was coming to. People always grumble about how outrageous changing times are. How many of them thought jazz and rock 'n' roll were shocking, or like Cardinal Cullen's horror, the polka. All I can say to the departed is that life has zipped well beyond jazz, rock 'n' roll and polkas.

In this Instagram age, we no longer have to wait for the afterlife for joy everlasting. We have a perpetual show here on earth streamed from Netflix, You Tube, and dozens of others.

The folks of old never knew the hyper connected world and were unacquainted with the web. For them the web was a mesh spun by a spider to trap flies. We know better, that's of course, unless we're the flies who have been trapped.

Karen was born in Penrith in New South Wales. One side of her family, convicts, arrived in Australia with the first fleet.

'Heroic rebels. It pleases me that my folks refused to obey unjust laws. If you're hungry, obedience is wimpish,' she says.

I tell her it's a fashion to say you hail from the exploited these days. It gives people a glow to bask in victimhood once they're safely beyond it.

'No, I'm not following a trend,' she assures me.

I'm going to show Karen and Treasa the south Galway route that goes from Coole Park (near Gort), to Doorus (also spelt Duras), Kinvara, Killeeneen, Ballylee to Loughrea. We begin with Coole Park, where as a child I was often brought on a family day trip. It was once the estate of Sir William and Lady Augusta Gregory and the place where the people who ushered in the most exciting period of Irish history in the late nineteenth, early twentieth century gathered.

In that stirring time before the first world war and the Easter Rising of 1916, Coole Park became the literary workshop of Ireland. It pulsed with the bustle of poetry, drama and myths. The spirit of the place is made eternal in poems like William Butler Yeats's 'The Wild Swans at Coole' and 'Coole Park'. But even if Yeats never put words on Coole, it's beguiling.

When I was first shown the copper beech tree in Coole Park where Ireland's literary giants carved their initials into the bark, I didn't know what the adults were talking about. And I didn't understand either how venerable the stone steps that once led to the front lawn of the house were. They now lead nowhere and are the only surviving part of the manor entrance on which so many famous feet climbed. W B Yeats, George Bernard Shaw, John Millington Synge, Edward Martyn, Douglas Hyde, George Russell, George Moore, Standish O'Grady, Katharine Tynan, Sean O'Casey were some of the guests Lady Gregory invited here, not only to enjoy the lively conversation but to work in adding to the literary output. Yeats put it like this:

They came like swallows and like swallows went,
And yet a woman's powerful character
Could keep a Swallow to its first intent.

We drive through the great gates into the car-park past the old dairy (a Visitors' Centre now), the laundry, the coach-house and one of the walled gardens. It's more wooded than I remember it, which is hardly surprising because many a tree has made its way towards the sky since my youthful trips here.

The trees in Coole were exotic. Some specimens were brought back from the east and this was what *Coillte* inherited when the Forestry Commission bought the estate in 1937. Eastern trees fitted well because it was Robert Gregory's eastern money that had bought this land in 1768 after making a fortune in the East India Company. Most of the ascendancy invested in trees. Robert Gregory also stocked the library with books and this collection was to have a big future in Coole.

We saunter along through the woodlands stepping on crunchy twigs, by oaks, ash, hazels, yews and elms and hidden leafy spaces that only God knows. This is where the tenants used to gather firewood. Generally, they were content on this estate. William Gregory's father had died of typhus which he caught when trying to help his tenants. And William himself was haunted by their suffering too. He was a good landlord. He used to say he never evicted a tenant, though you wouldn't have guessed it from the section of the Poor Law Act of 1847 which bore his name, the Gregory Clause. This article, inserted by MP William Gregory, excluded tenants who occupied a quarter of an acre or more from workhouse relief unless they first surrendered their lease. Though he stood firm behind his clause, he never used it against any tenant in arrears.

It was along here by the woods that Yeats and his friends found the charm for the séances that they found so alluring. Like a lot of their ascendancy friends in late nineteenth century Ireland, they were slightly obsessed by the occult. Many of them were members of the Hermetic Order of the Golden Dawn, a secret organisation which looked into metaphysics, the occult and the paranormal.

Lady Augusta Gregory's main interest was in fostering poetry and culture and it was really she who made it such a rare moment in time. Poets sang the names of these woods and waters and the words stayed preserved on the pages. Yeats wrote about the Seven Woods of Coole. In fact, there are more than seven woods in Coole. Maybe he was using poetic licence or maybe he chose it because the number seven is symbolic. It's a prime number divisible only by itself and in harmony with God's creation of the world in six days and resting on the seventh. It also ties in with the seven virtues (justice, temperance, fortitude, diligence, faith, hope and charity) or, for that matter, the seven deadly sins (pride, covetousness, lust, anger, gluttony, envy and sloth). Or maybe it was simply that Yeats miscounted the number of woods in Coole.

We're intent on seeing the turlough because it completes the haunting nature of this place. Turloughs are a kind of disappearing lake found in limestone areas and are almost unique to Ireland, especially this part of the country west of the Shannon. The turlough system in Coole-Garryland is said to be the most diverse in the country for its physical geography and its vegetation. It's also unusual because it's so close to woodland. It supplied the water for the Coole estate, brought by horse-drawn pump.

Turloughs show all the signs of being suspended between two worlds, rising and falling, fed and drained from underneath, through a honeycomb of limestone which swallows the waters, making them vanish overnight like ghosts. And that matches the interest in the supernatural and clairvoyant notions that fired the imagination of the Hermetic Order of the Golden Dawn. Treasa is especially moved by it all.

'I half expect to see Yeats, dressed in his usual black, walking around with his gang who couldn't resist a séance,' she laughs.

The part Lady Gregory played in the literary revival was her interest in collecting local folktales. She did what the Grimm Brothers,

Jacob and Wilhelm, had done in Germany nearly a century before. She drew stories from ordinary folk, from beggars to fish-women, from workhouse inmates to herbalists, and in doing this she placed herself like a hyphen between two worlds, the big house and the mud cabin.

An interest at the time among scholars was to delve into medieval manuscripts. Douglas Hyde, a regular guest here in Coole, had written *The Love Songs of Connacht*. W B Yeats's *Celtic Twilight* recorded stories from Sligo. Lady Gregory's cousin, Standish O'Grady, had translated ancient poetry and introduced a world of Gaelic scholarship.

But the ordinary people knew the raw power of these stories well before scholars set to work on the manuscripts. They knew the legends of Fionn and the Fianna, of the love story of Gráinne and Diarmuid, Cúchulainn (Ireland's epic hero of the *Táin Bó Cuailnge* – the Cattle Raid of Cooley, the war caused when the warrior-queen Medb led her forces against the Ulster armies led by Cúchulainn to steal the bull of Cooley in order to make her possessions equal to those of her husband, Ailill.) They told these tales with heart and colour around their hearthstones. Simple folktales were now being raised to greatness as they changed hands from the have-nots up the social line, and they were gathering into one burst of energy here in Coole.

Like the Grimms, Lady Gregory could see that these tales were the earliest and purest history. She liked how they opened up a simple world, a pagan past with links to dead generations. One thing that struck her was the contrast between the richness of the tales and the poverty of the tellers.

Here's a curious side of their ballads: they praised constancy and affection in marriage, yet marriage for love was out of the question (indeed as much for Lady Gregory as for them). But love of family, of God and most of all, of country – *tírghrá* – filled that gap. And that could get as hot as any romantic love.

Their version of *tírghrá* of course was at odds with Lady Gregory's. It spoke of repression, and worse, rebellion. That should have made them enemies. No matter. It was their words and the power of their language that stirred her.

Of all the guests in Coole Park my favorite is painter and visionary, George Russell. He went under the pseudonym Æ. He loved fairylore and the chivalry and love of truth that the old sagas contained. And he used to hold up to his countrymen the example of Cúchulainn, hero of the *Táin Bó Cuailnge*, and Ferdia pausing in their combat to embrace, or the warrior-queen Medb praising the magnificence of the enemies who were arrayed against her.

Of course none of this had a shred of the practical, but others were looking after what you might call the 'real world'. The industrial revolution was clipping along at a cracking pace in Britain. Smokestacks were rising from the mills, blotting out the skyline. Cash was exchanging like never before. The Victorian idea of self-improvement, that every era brings progress, held sway. But the people who assembled here in Coole thought that this fixation with money was blotting out a deeper Truth. Ireland had no such belching industry. It stayed poor and loyal to a mythical past.

I can sympathise with their ideas in my own small way, the loss of something essential amid plenty. I lived for a few years in Australia. That was where I met Karen. Her family owned the house we rented and we've stayed in touch since.

Australia is a country with a lot to offer – perpetual summer (bushfires apart), beaches lapping with surfing waters, bounding dolphins, barbies aplenty. But I missed home. When I said to an Australian colleague that I missed getting wrapped up to go out for a walk, he fixed his gaze on me for a second and sighed: 'It's amazing the mentality of some people.' So I didn't pretend about the other things that I missed – the shapes and sounds of my myths, my language, my hills, the lap of the Atlantic against the shore. You're never far from the sound of water in Ireland, not like the dried-out interior of Australia. I could imagine the reply if I had told him: 'Are the Indian and Pacific oceans not big enough for you?' or words to that effect.

I feel the people who gathered in Coole would have understood my plight, assuming for one far-fetched moment that I featured in their lives. It was the indifference towards their side of the story that got to them. Their language, their sagas, myths and folklore had got written out of the colonial script.

Irish, the tongue the natives spoke and thought in, was given no value. Official efforts were made to silence it, and by the nineteenth century this was complete. It was no longer used in the schools, in higher education, in the courts, so it became the language of illiteracy. By the mid nineteenth century even the Catholic Church, the religion of the majority, had forsaken it.

So, uncovering sagas and myths, heretofore unknown, pierced into a well of splendour. This rescue job was never more needed. By this time, the late nineteenth century, Ireland's political life had fallen into the doldrums after the death of Parnell and the split in the Irish Parliamentary Party. With the local language not written, and English history and brave deeds being the only stories on offer, it was easy to think that nothing of note had ever happened at home. But suddenly with the exciting discovery of the new-found literature, Ireland's past looked as vibrant as those of Greece or India. Indian scripture was written in poetry and the Hindu idea of a world soul, a single god for all mankind, caught the imagination, especially George Russell's, who had read it with relish. Ancient mythology merged all tongues into a kind of language of Eden.

The residue of that Eden still hangs around Coole. Lady Gregory saw her role as assembling people, nurturing talent and stringing together the many branches of literary revival. The signatures etched into the trunk of the copper beech are the main reminders now. The bark has expanded where it was carved, causing some of the initials to fall into the cracks and so aren't as easily made out as when I was young.

To pick up on the rest of the story we leave Coole and drive northwards on the Gort-Oranmore road, by Kiltartan, swinging to the left for Kinvara and the nearby townland of Doorus. Joggers are out in full force. They look as if they're training for a race. I don't want to be responsible for any of them missing it, or missing every race for evermore for that matter, so I keep well behind them as they don't seem a bit worried about running three abreast on the narrow road.

Doorus House is now a youth hostel, but in the period we're looking into it was owned by Frenchman, Florimond de Basterot, whose ancestors had once headed the *Parlement* in Bordeaux. In July during the wet summer of 1897 a meeting here turned out to have all the makings of a myth though it was a casual enough event at the time. De Basterot was the host and that day the seeds of an idea with a mighty future were sown.

He was an old man by then, big into his prayers. Paralysed from the waist down, after a high-flying youth, he liked the company of writers and artists. Among his friends were Guy de Maupassant and Maurice Barrès and on that day he was joined by his poet friends, William Butler Yeats and Arthur Symons. Also there was Edward Martyn from nearby Tillyra Castle who had just written his first play, 'Maeve'. And Lady Gregory dropped by too.

The elements had their secret plan that day and blessed was the drenching rain that held them indoors and at leisure to talk and expound on ideas, like the need for an Irish theatre to stage Irish plays such as Martyn's 'Maeve' which they were reading.

Lady Gregory took Yeats aside and over tea they gave vent to their shared interest in poems, folklore, myths and fairylore. What about a theatre in Dublin where Irish plays could be performed rather than taking them to London? Would that not restore the dignity of which Ireland was worthy and rescue her from the reputation as a land of buffoons (which the magazine *Punch* was illustrating in its cartoons)? Would this not be self-determination with a non-political twist?

Poet and critic, Arthur Symons grasped the moment when he said *La Strega* (Italian for witch) had put her terrible eye on Yeats that day with a long-lasting outcome.

It was all very informal, the unplanned birth of the Irish Literary Theatre, later to be called the Abbey, a national theatre. In 1925 it became the first state-endowed playhouse in the English-speaking world when the Irish government offered the directors £850 a year.

It's easy to feel the buzz of the weeks that followed during that rainy summer when the cultural pace quickened around south Galway – visiting one another's houses, like a travelling roadshow, from the stately Gregory house in Coole, to the more modest Doorus, to splendid castellated Tillyra on the Gort Road, with its Monets, Degas and Durers, and echoes of Palestrina played on the organ by their host in the Gothic hall among pillars of black marble. It's easy to get carried away with the commotion, the tapping of Lady Gregory's typewriter, the first ever Remington, on which she typed out lists of possible guarantors for the new project. They had plays. They needed a theatre, and money.

The dinner table at Coole pulsed with a mix of guests: painters, poets, mystics, historians, visionaries, bohemians and misfits. Lady Gregory had an eye for oddballs. She enjoyed the buzz of their banter. Yeats's conversation was especially glittering and he and Russell infused Coole with a touch of mysticism. Russell could talk about anything from dairy farming to the *Bhagavad Gita,* a Hindu sacred book. The Boer War was the topic of the time. Around the Coole dinner table they were pretty much all on the side of the Boers. These natural bastions of empire were not such staunch supporters after all, and that was a foretaste of what was to come.

'What's it about Galway that still has a draw for oddballs?' asks Treasa. 'From performance parades to Irish language theatre, has any other Irish city such a collection?' But before I get a chance to crow about the oddball nature of my county, Karen says,

'It's not just Galway? Is it not the Irish in general who claim to be dreamers and storytellers?'

It's true that in Ireland chat has always been a popular sport, from the jamborees in the great country houses to the stories around the hearthstones, to the present-day broadcasts of wall-to-wall chat-shows. It was this obsession with chatter that made Lady Gregory believe that Ireland was ripe for drama. 'Take any house in Ireland at the end of a rainy week,' she said, 'and the supply of conversation is quite inexhaustible though nothing has happened.'

Now, I ask, who would wait around for something to happen to have a bit of banter?

The gatherings at Coole were not just about conversation. Guests were expected to produce. Yeats was given the best room, and servants tiptoed past so as not to upset his inspiration. Douglas Hyde (author of *The Love Songs of Connacht*, and later first president of Ireland) was cloistered in one of the rooms to write a play. When he emerged, exhausted, with a one-act comedy, *Casadh an tSúgáin*, he was rewarded with Champagne.

George Moore brought a touch of the cosmopolitan to the group. He had picked up some writing skills in Parisian cafés where he hob-nobbed with the literati. The French writer Émile Zola was one of his acquaintances. He already had a string of novels and memoirs about his Bohemian life in Paris to his credit, or discredit more like, because libraries thought them too immoral to stock.

For some, Moore was the embodiment of the nineties, of 'anything goes' in sex or morals. Unlike the others, he had experience as a notable theatre critic, though he wasn't the most loved, and with good reason. He didn't mind sacrificing his friends to write them into his characters, most notably his cousin, Edward

Martyn or the Parish Priest of Labane (from which church he was banned by Edward Martyn's mother from going to Mass, much to his delight, until he heard he'd have to go to nearby Gort instead).

Light is fading as we head back to Kinvara where we stay the night.

FOUR

TRAIL OF A WANDERING BARD

Kinvara is wakening up to the day. Children are pouring out of a school bus and making their way up the hill in twos and threes, hitching their schoolbags and breathing billows into the frosty air. None of them I'd say are more than ten years old. They look happy but I'm stamping my own imprint of school days on them and feeling sorry for them. Back then when adults told me that school was the happiest part of my life I thought it was a grim prospect for what was to come. But looking back, school wasn't the worst.

Still, there's an enchantment about the little fishing village of Kinvara that would make a child not want to leave the day behind. Anchored boats are swaying in the harbour waiting for a boatman to loosen their ties and set them out to sea. The vessels show all the signs of pampering, painted with care in reds, greens, stripes of blue and black and you can see them again in the looking glass of the motionless water. The harbour stretches out towards Galway Bay, waiting to welcome the Galway hookers that will moor here later. Isn't that a lazy scene to swap a school day for?

We want to visit Reilig na bhFilí (graveyard of the poets), in Killeeneen. This is where the local and celebrated poet Anthony Raftery is buried. It's little known in its own home place.

There's hardly anyone to enquire from, and the few who are about can't help us. Even the locals have never heard of it. If we knew it would be so hard to find we could have asked two guys who were full of chat in the pub last evening. But we left them still knocking back pints. There's no chance they would be up this early.

Karen had asked them a question in the pub that set them talking.

'Is it true that Galway has a draw for eccentrics and oddballs?'

'It is,' said the scholarly looking fellow. 'That's why I'm here. I used to be a teacher. Now I write bits and pieces of poetry, not that that keeps me in a living but I get by. Teaching is a job you have to be cut out for and I wasn't so I gave it up.' But later, after a few more drinks he got less guarded and told us that it was teaching that gave him up. 'I lost it at times with the students. Once I called them a bunch of goons, though "goons" wasn't the word I used. They were asking for it. The principal took their side and I got shown the door. I called him a born-again moron. Maybe that had something to do with it.'

Treasa was laughing uncontrollably but he couldn't see why she thought it funny. The other guy, a self-styled character, told us joke after joke which we laughed at, heroically, though we had heard most of them before.

Their teaching or comedy skills might have been no great shakes but they would surely know how to find Reilig na bhFilí.

We drive north-east from Kinvara towards Clarenbridge, by frosted grass and flooded fields. Finally, we find someone who knows Killeeneen, a blow-in who has difficulty pronouncing the name.

'You've gone too far,' she tells us.

We turn back. This cemetery is niched into a spot so small that it's no wonder we drove past it. The poet Raftery lies here alongside his fellow poet and arch rival, Patsy Callanan, a local poet.

I expect to find the little gate padlocked and it stirs a thrill in me to push it open. This symbol of welcome revives a memory of a time when poets had the freedom of the unlocked doors around these parts. Raftery, the blind poet-musician was made welcome in the homes of the strong farmers around Gort and Kiltartan when he trudged around this area.

When I first was introduced to Raftery I used to wear my hair in braids and would hitch up my schoolbag like the children I saw getting off the bus. It all seems like the beginning of time now but I can still recite some of Raftery's *Cill Aodáin*:

Anois teacht an Earraigh beidh an lá ag dul chun síneadh,
Is tar éis na Féile Bríde ardófaidh mé mo sheol,
Ó chuir mé i mo cheann é, ní stopfaidh mé choíche,
Go seasfaidh mé síos i lár Chontae Mhaigh Eó.

Now comes the spring the day will be lengthening
and after Saint Brigit's day
I will raise my sail.
Since I got it into my head I won't stop
Until I stand in County Mayo

The sun is dappling through the gate railings as we pick our way on frosted grass by the ruins of a medieval church. Tall trees, elegant Victorian high crosses and more humble headstones are lying, standing, crushed together, slanting with age.

Raftery wrote some glum but moving stuff like *Anach Cuan*, a lament following a boat disaster in 1828 in Lough Corrib when twenty people were drowned at Annaghdown.

Karen thinks the Irish have a habit of keeping morose moments alive, singing about them into the early hours of morning. Treasa merrily admits we do, 'Why not?' We like our moroseness and why wouldn't we be let enjoy it?' she says.

'*Cill Aodáin*' is cheerful. Raftery lists the names like a mantra of places he is going to pass by on his wanderings. Its popularity is probably that it expresses the hope that comes with spring. Hope is a more driving sentiment than achievement. That's because we're fooled along by the promise of something great just ahead, always just ahead. And it ties in well with the time of year we're here – February. Already you can feel the days stretching their muscles after winter's sleep. Treasa says it's a pity we haven't come on the first day of February, Saint Brigit's day, the first official day of spring, when the sap is rising, to link in with the poem (she's a stickler for atmosphere). That may be all well for us but for Karen who has come from Australia, just to come to coincide with Raftery's wanderings, would be taking context a bit far

There's no trace of moroseness in the song Raftery wrote to the fair Mary Hynes, 'The Shining Flower of Ballylee', when he recalled that May morning when he first met her at Kiltartan Cross and she led him across the fields to her home in Ballylee.

> My star of beauty, my sun of autumn,
> My golden hair, O my share of life!
> Will you come with me this coming Sunday
> And tell the priest you will be my wife?

Though he was blind, she lit up his world. Her beauty, he claimed, outdid that of Deirdre, Venus or Helen of Troy.

Sweet verse could turn the other way too and when Raftery got vexed with life he whipped his tongue into action and sent words hissing at his enemies. He was deft at composing political anti-English reflections during the Tithe War (protests during the

1830s against paying tax to the established church) and you didn't need a poet to raise a hatred against paying to a church to which the majority didn't belong. The swipe of the poet's tongue has always been a powerful weapon in Ireland, like the curse of a saint. A poet's satire could unseat a king. In Raftery's time there was no king to dethrone because the rule of a foreign king was already unlawful in the minds of those who heard him.

We have Lady Gregory to thank for locating Raftery's grave. It was while collecting folklore that she first heard of him and he fired her with so much verve that she didn't rest until she had found out all about him. He represented the Irish oral bardic tradition which had been damaged by the Great Famine (he died in 1835, about a decade before the famine) and this is what Lady Gregory was trying single-mindedly to revive and record before it got wiped from memory.

So she loved Raftery, the last of the wandering bards. She loved him as the keeper of history and the guardian of memory. It thrilled her to talk to the older people who remembered him tramping the roads between Ballylee, Athenry, Kiltartan, Kinvara and Gort, carousing, playing the fiddle, singing songs, drinking, courting the girls, not knowing what the day would turn up. In his own words, 'Ag seinm ceóil do phócaibh folamh' (playing music to empty pockets).

Raftery liked to say he was abducted as a young boy by the sídhe (fairies) who taught him his music, leaving out, for effect, the part played by Mrs Taaffe, the wife of the landlord who adopted him and encouraged music in him when his family got wiped out by smallpox. Only the nine-year-old Anthony survived but his illness cost him his sight. He stayed with the Taaffes until one day he tried to ford a river with his master's favourite horse. The horse drowned and Frank Taaffe, in a fit of rage, threw him out, in spite of his wife's pleas.

On the road, penniless, all Raftery had were Mrs Taaffe's music lessons. I'm sure they made him a cut above the average wandering minstrel, but to say he had been taught by the *sídhe* gave him an even greater edge.

Lady Gregory first met Douglas Hyde one day as he wheeled his broken bicycle towards nearby Tillyra in search of information on Raftery. He had found the house where he had died, close to the nearby village of Craughwell. Now Lady Gregory wanted to know more.

So one hazy day she set off in her *phaeton* (open carriage) to make enquiries. Imagine her delight when she met two men who had been at Raftery's funeral. They showed her the spot where he was laid. To crown that find, a local woman gave her a handwritten book of his poems and in great elation she headed home to translate them. We have her and Hyde to thank for making Raftery's verses available.

She chose a single word for the headstone she commissioned. *Raifteiri,* echoing Homer, who was also a blind wanderer. And in the graveyard this morning I notice the grandeur of the headstone though he enjoyed little grandeur in life. This memorial stone was unveiled on August 26, 1900, one of those occasions when you'd have loved to have been there. Among the crowd that day were Douglas Hyde, Edward Martyn, painter Jack Butler Yeats and his patron, American John Quinn (a man who would play a part in Lady Gregory's love life).

Karen suggests that these men who claimed to be at Raftery's funeral might well have been playing a trick on Lady Gregory, sending a whole procession of people to kneel at the wrong shrine.

One famous person who came to kneel here about half a century after that inauguration day was American folksinger, Burl Ives. He wanted to pay homage to one whom he thought was the greatest of all the bards. He had good reason to hold him in high regard. He believed he himself was Raftery's reincarnation. He too was a wild spirit, a folksinger who had spent some time as a wandering labourer, hanging out with hobos and carousers. Then his career hit stride when he won an Oscar for his role in the film, *The Big Country*.

He first heard of Raftery from an Atlanta man, a collector of folk songs. He told him that one of the songs had been passed down from his Irish great-grandmother with language intact. She had come to the United States during the Great Famine. The song, sung in Irish, was called 'The Cream of the Blueberry Pie' and came from Raftery's poem 'The Shining Flower of Ballylee' – about the lovely Mary Hynes. It told the story of the May morning when on his way from church he met her at the crossroads at Kiltartan, and her beauty set him in a whirl.

Burl Ives was eager to retrace Raftery's steps and between stopping off for a few drinks on the way, wrong directions and other delays, it was the early hours of morning when he and his group arrived. By the light of a torch, they located a Raftery headstone. There was nothing for it but to sit on the grave and celebrate, open the bottle of poteen (a strong Irish moonshine) given to them by some locals. As day broke however, their spirits were dampened when they found they were sitting on the wrong Raftery grave.

Our visit isn't half so rousing. We arrive in daylight. We're not great fans of visiting graves in the dark. And exciting and all as we find it, we aren't up for celebrating with a drink this early although we would welcome something to warm up this cold morning.

From the grave we drive the short distance to Thoor Ballylee (near Gort), former home of W B Yeats and his family. This Norman tower couldn't look more bewitching. The water in the nearby turlough is brimming over, complete with swans. It must be a scene like this that inspired Yeats's poem, 'The Wild Swans at Coole'.

The flooding makes the road impassable so we park the car and walk. The waters are reflecting the crystalline winter sun, creating an upward sunshine from within the turlough, as if the sun, as well as the water, has come from underground. No wonder Yeats and his wife, George Hyde Lees, fell in love with this place and in 1917 moved to live in the tower.

It was the lingering of Raftery's lyrics around here that brought Yeats to Ballylee in the first place. His spirit was set aflowing with a recitation of the poem in praise of Mary Hynes by a local woman who could remember both Raftery and Hynes. So captivated was he that he recounted the story in his lecture to the Royal Academy of Sweden when he was presented with the Nobel Prize for Literature in 1923.

As we wade through the flood we meet a couple coming in the opposite direction. The flooding is nothing, they tell us, compared to other years.

'Take 2009 for instance. Up to there it was,' says the man, pointing out the top of an electricity pole with his stick.

The water only reaches half way up my wellington boots so we could have driven through after all. An oncoming van splashes his way into the water, taking no care to avoid wetting us. I'm glad we didn't know that the flood was driveable through. It's charming, wettings apart, walking up to the historic tower marooned in a flood of mystery.

The man with the stick turns to call back at us, to watch out for the scene from the *Quiet Man* where O'Hara and Wayne crossed on the stepping stones. He says a tree has grown on the spot since 1952 when the film was made. We can't identify it from the many others, and today neither is there a sign of stepping stones in the shifting waters near the tower.

That was wise advice that friends gave Yeats and his wife, not to settle here. But they ignored it. Today I can see both points of view, as the February winter sun lowers its angle to show up the underside of the sparse winter growth around the tower.

Yeats moved here after he finally married on October 20, 1917 (believing this to be the most astrologically auspicious time for him to marry) having first been turned down by the extremely beautiful and rebellious Maud Gonne, then rebuffed by her daughter, Iseult, thirty years his junior.

Here in Ballylee Yeats felt anchored to the things that charmed him – Raftery, the Gaelic past, the Irish language revival, romanticism so full of revolutionary daring. He must have seen a parallel in Raftery's hopeless pursuit of the beautiful Mary Hynes and his own fixation on Maud Gonne.

We could take a short cut from Ballylee to Loughrea, but I decide to go through Gort because there's something I love about the Gort-Loughrea road and I want to lengthen, not shorten it. Sometimes childhood visions can in no way resemble real places. That's part of their charm. So I'm glad when a rainbow hoops over us like a skipping rope. Arched across the road it is, its leg is planted in a medley of colour at the foot of the uplands of Slieve Aughty. It's like a foretaste of the spectacle of stained glass that we're on our way to see in Loughrea cathedral.

Wisps of mauves and purples cross the high ground around us and it makes me think of the time when on Saint John's eve, June 23, these hilltops lit up with bonfires as was the custom. Some landlords gave their tenants the fuel free of charge for the occasion, turf and bogwood. The turf burned steadily, but it was the bogwood that sent up the brilliant flames from hill to hill.

Just like there must have been some muse roaming around south Galway, there must also have been something exhilarating about the year 1897. That was when the foundation stone for Saint Brendan's cathedral was laid here in Loughrea – in October, just three months after that myth-making meeting in de Basterot's house in Doorus between Yeats, Lady Gregory and others, when the idea for the Abbey theatre was born.

The poetry and drama with a Celtic twist in nearby Coole, home of Lady Gregory, surely had a say in Loughrea too. While Coole sparked with words, Loughrea fired the spirit of the age in stone, mosaic and glass. Both shared the same sense of adventure. In Coole they wanted a theatre in Dublin where Irish plays could be performed rather than taking them to London. In Loughrea they wanted – in the words of Edward Martyn – 'to cut out the foreign art commercial traveller'.

The Martyn family, whose ancestor had accompanied Richard lll on crusade, paid the bill for the building of Saint Brendan's cathedral, along with a few other Catholic landlords around the Loughrea area. The total cost of the cathedral was £30,000. In today's value of over £4 million, it looks like a bargain.

This project put business pulsing in Irish studios. Artist, Sarah Purser revived the craft of stained glass in her studio, *An Túr Gloine* (the glass tower). Painter, Jack Butler Yeats was commissioned to do the sodality banners. Alfred Child, Michael Healy, Evie Hone, Ethel Mary Rhind, are some of the artists who left their mark here, in a show as to what heights art with an Irish aesthetic was capable of rising.

It's hard to know what to like most. Karen is taken with Michael Healy's window, the Ascension. With the sun lighting it up it looks like millions of stars flickering in awe at this take-off into paradise. My favourite is the Stations of the Cross. They're done in the subtlest of mosaic, in autumnal shades of blue and red by artist Ethel Mary Rhind, from Northern Ireland.

Loughrea cathedral is like the final outcome of Coole's literary enlightenment. It's all here – poetry, sagas, painting, stained glass, sculpture. On the opening day in 1902 the cathedral echoed with one more element – music from the male-voiced Palestrina choir from Dublin, founded and funded by Edward Martyn. Martyn took his musical inspiration from the revival of sixteenth century polyphonic music in the great cathedrals of Europe at the time.

Treasa goes to the office for the key of the little museum which houses the embroidered church banners. We touch them delicately with gloved hands. They're mostly processional and sodality banners to be hung at the end of the pews. They depict the who's who of Irish sainthood: Brendan, Colmcille, Colman, Brigit, Ita and Patrick, done by the who's who of Irish artists. The Yeats sisters, Lily and Lolly, did the embroidery and tapestry.

George Russell had a mischievous idea for the two tapestries he designed. He would disguise the Celtic gods and the *sidhe* (fairies) as angels, archangels and seraphin to make a fairy chapel with mystical figures so that Christians would be worshipping the *sidhe* without knowing it. The idea wasn't as roguish as it sounds because he believed that Ireland's natural religion was a version of druidism, and that modern Christianity fell far short of its pagan forebears.

One last sight to see before we leave is the Catholic church in the nearby village of Ardrahan which the Martin family also adorned with decorative art.

A man at the top of an electricity pole comes down the ladder to answer our call for directions.

'The Catholic church of Ardrahan is in Labane,' he tells us. 'It's about a mile or so further on.'

The priest at Labane must never get a thing done if he responds to every enquiry as willingly as he does to ours. The church was designed by architect W A Scott who had refashioned Martyn's castle, Tillyra. Edward Martyn's mother, Annie, donated the black Sicilian marbled high altar.

He shows us the Sarah Purser window to Saint Brigit behind the altar. It was commissioned after Annie Martyn died in 1898. The saint is said to bear a strong resemblance to Annie herself.

The most interesting structure of all in Labane church is the *baldachin* – canopy of stone – over the altar. It's thanks to the Martyn family that you have such a rare sight in a small country church. There is one (a bigger version, admittedly) over the tomb of Saint Peter on the high altar of the Basilica dedicated to him in the Vatican city (*Baldacchino di San Pietro*). It was designed in the seventeenth century by the Italian artist, Bernini.

The priest leaves us to look around the little church on our own. It's a nice contrast to Saint Brendan's in Loughrea. There's less awe-generating stuff here. It's more like a chapel, a place where you feel like praying or lighting a candle. Both done, we're ready to leave to head back to Dublin. That ties in with the next stage of Lady Gregory's literary group too when it spread its wings beyond Coole and joined the other forces that were criss-crossing the country. This was the late nineteenth century, a stirring time in Irish history. A flicker of light was sparking beyond the tunnel of colonisation. Revival, romanticism and a growing pride in Irishness swept the country. In a way it was a reaction to the mass culture that had been spreading since the 1850s, especially in urban areas where the English language was thriving. It was similar to the burst of romanticism that had hit mainland Europe, especially Germany a century earlier.

Two movements provided the wind behind the new awakening: the Gaelic Athletic Association and the Gaelic League. The GAA established in 1884 was reviving Irish local games (hurling, football, handball) that had fallen into disuse and mythologising the heights to which these games could rise. Hurling after all was the game of Cúchulainn.

The Gaelic League, founded by Douglas Hyde, Eoin MacNeill and Father Eugene O'Growney in 1893, was renewing native culture, language, folktales and getting them out to the rank and file. The Gaelic League had branches in the towns, the GAA had a network in the rural areas. Between the two they were putting a spring in the step of the whole country.

The theatre brainstorm in Doorus had reached Dublin, a city known for its conversation. In its own small way, the capital was going through the same ferment that Paris had a few decades earlier – a discussion for every night of the week. George Moore played host to Saturday nights in 4 Ely Place, W B Yeats hosted elite Monday nights in his house at 82 Merrion Square. But for egalitarianism it was George Russell's Sunday nights in his cottage-style house in 25 Coulson Avenue, Rathgar that stood out. Here the distinguished mingled with clerks and shop assistants, and the shy were drawn out to expound their ideas alongside the best of them.

When Lady Gregory brought the Abbey players to the United States in 1911 she met President Theodore Roosevelt. He was no stranger to Irish myths. He had read some of the writings produced in Coole. Four years before that meeting, he had written an article about Ireland's sagas in *Century* magazine with illustrations of Cúchulainn and Queen Medb by American artist, J C Leyendecker.

Really it was inevitable that all this literary and revivalist zeal would get caught up in a different current of *tírghrá*. Marching in the same step were those who thought politics should match the literary pace (despite Douglas Hyde's best efforts to keep the Gaelic League non political). A movement that looked with pride on the heroes and chivalry of the past had a punch in it that would call up red-blooded passion of nationalism and separatism. By Easter 1916 it had fed into a rebellion against British rule. The rebels were poets and intellectuals, many of whom were involved in the Abbey and other Dublin theatres.

It was a rising fired by a mix of myth and Christian inspiration, of redemption and self-sacrifice moved by heroes from Cúchulainn to Jesus. The rebels wanted to say Ireland was different and should be accepted as such and to stress their point, they seized buildings around Dublin and sought help from Britain's enemy, Germany. A little quotation from Cecil Rhodes, a staunch champion of British imperialism, 'To be born an Englishman is to win the lottery of life' gives an idea of how wide of the mark some thought the Irish rebels were. Turning down first prize in life's lottery? What? It's no wonder Winston Churchill believed: 'We've always found the Irish a bit odd. They refuse to be English.'

On the other side of the Atlantic Theodore Roosevelt, lover and all as he was of Ireland's sagas, complained that the Irish refused to conform to the American way (which was competing well with Rhode's life's lottery claim).

The ringleaders of the rising were hauled before a firing squad and that whipped the country into a patriotic frenzy. Yeats wrote: 'Did that play of mine send out/Certain men the English shot?'

The country changed from being under the light touch of Romanticism to falling under the heavy hand of Martial Law. Instead of bantering exchange of ideas in Coole and the Dublin salons, you had battering knocks on doors, blocked roads, ambushes, house burning, curfew and raids.

Guilty and not-guilty were rounded up and so the mythmaking began and the rebels became more popular in hindsight. Soon the soul of the nation was dreamed into the Easter Rising and it became the founding myth of the Irish Free State – Ireland's Storming of the Bastille, her Boston Tea Party.

As we head back to Loughrea and join the motorway to Dublin all mythical and sweet thoughts of localism are put to one side. Soon Coole, Raftery and south Galway, the little circuit of my childhood day out, fade behind us.

My next outing with be to view the Spring equinox from Loughcrew.

FIVE

LOUGHCREW

Loughcrew in County Meath is about an hour's drive from Dublin. To view the equinox sunrise in the passage chamber you had better be ready for an early start.

Punctuality is my strong point, though not Julie's. Instead of half past four, as arranged, I come to collect her at twenty past. Forgetting that I'm a few minutes before the arranged time, I text her from outside. I get no reply. I could have predicted this. She's still in bed. I knew she wouldn't wake up. I don't like ringing in case I disturb anyone else but I have to in the end. She answers the phone.

'Are you here already?' There's bad form in her voice, that tone that daughters reserve especially for their mothers. She was never good in the early hours. Normally we get on well but this time of morning would test any relationship.

'But I didn't even have breakfast yet,' she says.

'Breakfast, at this hour?'

I manage to wean her off the idea by promising that we can go for breakfast afterwards. It will be my treat, a return for early-morning disturbance.

We drive towards the M50, Dublin's circular motorway. In silence.

There's field-to-field fog that vaporises all boundaries. The moon has reached full round, and it accompanies us all the way.

'It's bigger than usual, because it's a super moon,' I explain. She makes no reply. But that doesn't spoil it for me. Fair and majestic it is, illuminating the west side of the sky. It looks as if it's posing for us alone (which is pretty true because we're the only people on the road). Every now and then it disappears behind a cloud, but for the most part it lights up our way. Though the poor visibility makes driving harder, it's doing wonders for the ethereal effect, for me anyway.

We join the M3 motorway, and at Kells go on to the much narrower Oldcastle Road, the R163. The fog is denser here. There's something thrilling about passing through while County Meath sleeps. Julie hasn't thawed enough into wakefulness to share my delight.

Nearing Loughcrew the moon gradually lowers itself under the rim of earth as it vanishes in an orangey hue. I have to check to confirm that it's moon-down not sun-up. Then pitch black engulfs her majesty, the royal county of Meath. I love the see-saw effect of this exchange of nature, the swapping of night for day. It's like birth and death – no mystery at all really. It takes place every day and humans are the only ones who sleep through this miracle, apart from other species in captivity.

We spot men in hi-vis jackets coming at us like apparitions from out of the darkness, guiding us into the final turn of the journey. The world is fully awake out here, a hive of activity as luminous torch-bearers pack us into place in the carpark,

We're ready for the climb, first up the steps then on to the mountainside. In pitch black we walk steeply up the hill. The darkness and the cold morning chill are testing, but I feel heady at the idea of beating the day to it. Our little torches are dim compared to the great beams others are holding, but they're well able to pick up the fluorescent stripes on the guiding posts along the path.

The occasional lowing of a beast and the distant bark of a dog echo in the silence. Julie walks sure-footed. For someone who earlier showed such hesitancy about her dawn date, she looks quite at home.

The climb is demanding, especially without breakfast. I'm not sure that I gave the best advice earlier. But it's all very bewitching and there's double joy when Julie says,

'I want to thank you for letting me come along. This is just wonderful.' You've changed your tune, I feel like saying. But I hold that remark back. 'Some mothers bring their daughters to get their nails done,' she laughs, 'others rout them out of bed in the middle of the night to climb a mountain.'

The man alongside us is having early-morning difficulties too. Clearly viewing the equinox sunrise wasn't his idea.

'I'm not dressed warmly enough,' he moans, yanking up the lapel of his thin jacket.

'I have to say you were very good to come, considering you appreciate this sort of thing so little,' says his companion.

'It's broadening my horizon,' he quips, nudging her on the elbow.

They join the queue for the chamber alongside us.

'Look it's facing east,' she says when she sees the chamber entrance. He laughs: 'I'm glad they got that one right.'

While we wait our turn the first shafts of light start to appear in the east and the world begins to transfigure into a two-sided vision of bright and dark. Then night peels away like a cloak unfolding across the sky. By now every second of the coming dawn is calculable.

We're allowed into the chamber in groups of six. It's easy to trip on the raised threshold or bang your head off the low stone lintel, which, considering our sleepy state, I think we should be warned more about.

The torch-holder from the Office of Public Works tells us this is the moment of sunrise. We're lucky to be in the chamber to witness it, relatively lucky. Today the sunrise doesn't perform the show for which they built this chamber so precisely to trap. The cloud has covered it, like a jealous rival. But even if it had been the perfect sunrise, the earth has shifted slightly since this chamber was built and it wouldn't have hit the bulls-eye spot that it used to focus on originally.

The woman who holds the torch shows us the engravings on the stones.

'These were farming people and the equinox marked the planting season,' she says.

A Spanish man asks her to pose for a photograph with this artwork in the background and she cheerfully agrees. When we emerge from the chamber it's bright. I appreciate light all the more, having witnessed every second of it. I nearly feel personally responsible for making the day dawn.

Modern-day druids are celebrating the moment on the hill, addressing whoever it is they address. Someone is beating a drum. But the guest of honour, the sun, hasn't yet come up above the rim of the earth, though the prelude is wonderful. Red streaks announce that it's on its way, like outriders signalling the arrival of an important dignitary. Another stripe forms across the sky, a jet. The aircraft is making a trail in a perfectly straight line. And, in a little show that looks like an arrangement between the man-made world and the world of nature, the streaks of aircraft exhaust fumes light up pink in the sunrise. Julie is sending pictures to her friends. If they're as sleepy as she was earlier they won't be thanking her for these early messages.

Hills, hillocks and drumlins are showing their forms now. Houses are coming into shape and villages begin to shimmer and flicker. A lone star remains in the sky, towards the east, standing sentry over the dawn.

The tops of trees and hedges are emerging out of their steam baths. The clumps of vapour, which earlier looked like an array of lakes, are getting easier to separate from the real lakes of neighbouring County Cavan. You can still make out the form of the fields, the grass throwing off its mist faster than the hedgerows. It's like seeing life through the haze of youth – all to discover, all to play for.

Sheep are stirring and shaking themselves. The sun gives them a glow on the dewy hillside. They need any spark of warmth they can get. Their every morning is like our once-in-a-lifetime chill of dawn.

Julie wonders if my car is blocking anyone in the carpark, but I'm not ready to go yet. I tell her that people who come to events like these are easy-going about having to wait. Later when we make our way down, in a blaze of sunshine, it turns out that it is we who can't get out. It's our turn to be easy-going now. A man advertising breakfast in a nearby café guides me out which involves moving forward and backward cautiously about twenty times. And after all his patience, coaxing our vehicle out of its parking trap, we don't even have breakfast in the place he's promoting. We go instead to the Headford Arms in Kells.

We eat with extra relish. Afterwards, it feels right to keep the morning on the not-so-ordinary footing with which it began. It would be a shame to let a dawn that began with such aplomb run into the routine of a regular day so we go to see the cottage where Meath's poet Francis Ledwidge was born. It's a museum now and not open at this hour but we can at least see what his youthful eyes once saw.

On the drive, from Kells to Slane, Meath's noble features – rich lands, awning trees, lush hedgerows – are enlarged by the early hour.

By now Julie is more keen than I am.

'This is wonderful,' she repeats, 'sorry if I was a bit cranky earlier this morning.'

Francis Ledwidge's home is about a quarter of a mile from Slane, in the townland of Janeville. It overlooks fields that tumble down the valley into the Boyne and rise into gentle heights on the far side of its banks.

Lord Dunsany, a writer along the lines of Tolkien, read Ledwidge's work and said he had stumbled on genius: 'I have the good fortune to have read many poems and stories sent to me, but in only two of them have I felt sure that I was reading the work of a master.' The other one was Mary Lavin. Both she and Ledwidge came from the banks of the same river Boyne.

The Ledwidge home (a Rural District cottage on half an acre) saw more than its share of trouble. Francis was four when his father Patrick died. That ended the fifteen shillings a week that he earned (a little above the wage of the average migrant labourer) and his mother, Annie, had to labour in the fields to feed her family of eight. The only allowance the state offered at the time was one shilling per child. The eldest, Patrick, got a job when he was old enough, and that took some pressure off. That was until he got tuberculosis, a disease that ostracised not just the sufferer but the whole family, more than Covid would today. The Ledwidges were saved from eviction from their two-roomed cottage when the local doctor spoke to the sheriff on their behalf. He said Patrick was too ill to be moved. More shame was heaped on them when his funeral had to be paid for by the parish, something that in a small community couldn't be hidden.

Francis had to leave school at twelve and that brought to an end the aspirations his family had for him. He described the despair – he thought God had forgotten them. To believe that fate has turned its back on you can make you feel powerless. At the time there was no shortage of folk descriptions for that particular difficulty – the evil eye, the curse, the scourge.

Francis's first job was in the kitchen of Slane Castle. One day he played a joke on the cook. He wiped out the menu on the kitchen slate and wrote Potatoes, Bacon and Cabbage instead. The joke wasn't well received and instead of sharing a laugh, the poor joker was shown the door. His next job was in Rathfarnham in Dublin, where at sixteen, he was to begin a grocery apprenticeship. He only served three days. He longed so much for home that he sneaked out in the middle of the night and in the dark walked the thirty miles (forty-eight kilometres) to Slane. We don't know what his mother made of it when she saw him. According to Francis, Annie Ledwidge never grumbled though this must have stretched her patience a little. After that Francis earned a living as a farm labourer, a road mender and other odd jobs before he joined the British army. It was from the trenches of Flanders he wrote to fellow poet Katharine Tynan: 'If you go to Tara (mound of the ancient kings of Ireland), go to Rath na Rí and look around you from the hills of Drumconrath in the north to the plains of Enfield on the south, where Allen bog begins and remember me to every hill and wood and ruin. For my heart is there. If it is a clear day you will see Slane blue and distant. Say I will come back again surely and maybe you will hear pipes in the grass or a fairy horn and the hounds of Finn – I have heard them often from Tara.'

Isn't there anguish in the words, even without knowing that his eyes might never again fix their gaze on the panorama that the Hill of Tara looks over.

If Ledwidge couldn't stand the homesickness of Rathfarnham, in Dublin, just forty-eight kilometres away from his home, what anguish must Flanders have caused him? He found some solace is writing 'A Lament for Thomas McDonagh', who was executed in May 1916 for his part in the Rising, when Ledwidge was home on leave.

> He shall not hear the bittern cry
> In the wild sky, where he is lain,
> Nor voices of the sweeter birds
> Above the wailing of the rain.

A year later Ledwidge himself was killed. It's hard to believe his body can rest easy in the second plot of Artillery Wood cemetery near Boesinghe in Belgium, in soil far from County Meath.

When I drop Julie home she says there's no way she can go back to bed as she had so sincerely planned when she left it in the early hours of morning. Me neither. I spend the rest of the day planning my next trip. I will go again to County Meath and see the Hill of Tara and locate the views from there that Ledwidge told Katharine Tynan to go and see on his behalf. And if I'm lucky I may hear 'pipes in the grass or a fairy horn'.

SIX

TARA

The breaks in the hedgerows and awnings open up pastureland and rolling hills where cattle fatten on the ample grass of County Meath. Pinholes of sun shine through leafy trees lining the way.

I can see why early farmers made their home here. And they left a heritage that gives Meath a lot to swagger about – clusters of passage tombs, burial mounds, sacred temples, along by the banks of the River Boyne – Newgrange, Knowth, Dowth, Loughcrew, Tara. This, the Irish Valley of the Kings, is archaeological heaven.

Every stone from large boulder to tiny pebble has been examined painstakingly for clues about prehistoric people. All the focus has been about how little we know about them – what they looked like, what names they gave the rocks they dragged to build their temples, what they called the hills or the grasslands. But, recent DNA examination has probed into a family secret and blown the cover of first-degree incestuous ties between them. Like the builders of the pyramids of Egypt, they kept power within the blood, breaking the taboo of marrying close relatives. This has shocked scholars.

I'm going to leave that controversy to the archaeologists, and follow Francis Ledwidge's view, to see what he saw from Tara or more vividly from Flanders. I want to look into the pull of a homeplace which was especially strong for him.

Even though his own family circumstances were dismal, Ledwidge lived in a time of hope. Around the late nineteenth early twentieth century the British government passed a series of land acts which introduced some measure of peasant proprietorship. The thinking was that owner-occupiers would lose interest in violent agitation for self rule.

Ledwidge used to play football and was interested in the growing pride in Irish culture that the Gaelic League and the Gaelic Athletic Association were creating. He wrote to an American professor: 'I am of a family who were ever soldiers and poets. I have heard my mother say many times that the Ledwidges were once a great people in the land...' This ties in with the new atmosphere of the time, of rooting up past glory, though his poetry doesn't reflect this much. A lot of it is about the simple things in life, more like a call to nature.

Ay soon the swallows will be flying south,
The wind wheel north to gather in the snow.
Even the roses spilt on youth's red mouth
Will soon blow down the road all roses go.

I arrive twenty minutes before the tour of Tara of the Kings is to begin. In the old church, which doubles as a Visitors' Centre, I watch a video on the royal site before I do the tour.

There's no shortage of trees around the church. They're fat in the limbs with age. Some look old enough to have witnessed the inauguration of the pre-historic kings, maybe of *Conn Cétchathach* (Conn of the Hundred Battles) who reigned here around the second century. He took power after killing his predecessor,

Cathair Mór (Cathair the Great). Or perhaps these trees remember the installation of *Niall Noígiallach* (Niall of the Nine Hostages) in the fourth century. Those kings wore their brave deeds in their names.

I spot a blackbird, mixing his lines with husky crows. This must be an omen. Ledwidge is called the 'poet of the blackbirds'.

The tour has already begun.

'The hill of Tara is surprisingly low,' the guide tells us. Her voice is blowing in the breeze. 'It's only 155 metres above sea level.'

'That explains why the climb hasn't left me breathless,' said a grey-haired man with a rucksack. 'And there I was congratulating myself on how fit I was.'

Exactly what I was thinking myself.

We're high enough for the wind to balloon out our jackets. The view is round and plentiful, light piled on light, sliding from blue into purple and the brown of the earth, twisting around the great circle of countryside, from hill to mountain to forest.

Meath people claim there's power in this view. If you turn towards the rising sun, they say, there's an energy that rises off the earth here that you don't find elsewhere – royal energy. This, the seat of our ancient high kings, roots us, they claim. It's where we come from.

Ah get away. Most of us don't hail from royalty and when you think of the ugly spats they got into for the crown, who wants to?

The guide doesn't get into anything like that. She points out the Mountains of Mourne, the Dublin mountains, the Wicklow mountains, the Slieve Bloom mountains, but that only accounts for some of the thirteen counties that are said to be visible from here.

According to what Francis Ledwidge penned to Katharine Tynan, we should see from Rath na Rí 'the hills of Drumconrath in the north to the plains of Enfield on the south, where Allen bog begins' A little more tricky is to hear the 'pipes in the grass or a fairy horn and the hounds of Finn' which he claimed to have often heard from Tara. The sadness of his words: 'Say I will come back again surely' feels like a swift stab in the stomach.

I bet visions like these are a whole lot more touched up in their absence because in memory, especially from far-off exile, it is always a clear day.

This spread of view was a requirement for all the ancient royal sites. Tara, Rathcroghan, Emain Macha, Dún Ailinne, Cashel, Uisneach all command a great circle of view. Power had to be visible, the king's fire had to light for all his subjects to see.

Of Ireland's six royal mounds, Tara is the country's most sacred, because it was the seat of the high kings. To say it's located off the present-day R147, in the townland of Castleboy about twelve kilometres from Navan is to rob it of all its mysticism, but bear with that if you want to get here. Today, Tara is on the route of Ireland's Ancient East. This road is the eastern equivalent of the Wild Atlantic Way. While the western way has the sea as its guide, the eastern follows the path of Ireland's antiquity.

But in the time of the High Kings, Tara was the starting and finishing point of five major roads that radiated across the country. Alas, there's no sign of ancient roads today. We only know of them from the *Annals of the Four Masters*, a manuscript compiled in the seventeenth century which covered Irish history since the Flood. It states that five *sligheanna* (roads) connected Tara with the north, west and south. It also says that these five roads, which had never been seen before, were discovered on the night of the birth of Conn of the Hundred Battles.

Ancient Ireland didn't use Roman road-building methods – they had their own techniques. The word *slighe* also means to fell or to cut and that suggests they cut the road through the forest, usually following rivers or dry esker ridges across bogs.

There's no surviving account of the inauguration ceremonies of pre-historic kings. If they had the know-how we have today, think about all the footage we'd have to save our guesswork. But maybe if we had, it would stop us from imagining. Heaven forbid. Most likely the hill retains the same rolling form as it had then and there's something satisfying about that much.

Chinese emperors justified their rule by 'the mandate of Heaven'. Elsewhere they found similar excuses for a power grab. The high king of Tara was a priestly office (a double *rath*, or fort, surrounds it, because it was the site of the high king). In prehistoric times and indeed a lot later, politics and religion were one function.

'The high king of Tara went through a ritual marriage with Medb, the goddess of the land and of sovereignty. So the story goes,' says the guide. 'More practically though, the candidate had to gain the support of kings from all over Ireland to make him worthy of office, like in modern presidential elections.' But there was another testing process which she leads us to, *Lia Fáil* (the stone of destiny), on the inauguration mound on the hill. 'This stone,' she says, 'used to cry out if a candidate who wasn't up to the priestly mark placed his foot on it, or his hands, or even drove his chariot over it.'

A useful giveaway, that. Pity it has fallen into disuse. The stone looks wonderful for its age, not mossy, its grey colour looking like new, good enough to test it out today, if anyone was interested in placing a foot on it.

The kind of king who wouldn't cause the stone to cry was generous, hospitable, just and truthful and he would oversee a reign of plenty. Animals would be fertile, crops would yield in abundance and the community would flourish. Equally, Heaven would note the disapproval of a bad king and send harsh times his way – crop failures, deaths of animals, floods and such like. This wasn't an unusual belief elsewhere either. In China the Yellow River catastrophe in 1887 was the clue that the Qing dynasty was losing its Mandate of Heaven.

Ireland's high kings were at the height of their power during the Iron Age, around the time of the birth of Christ. Indeed, in a way it was he who spoiled it all for them. Because around the time of the arrival of Christianity, Tara's heroic glory and Druidic influence went downhill.

The guide tells us how, in one of those nifty twists that Christianity managed to subvert itself from firstly needing the support of kings to ultimately making kings need its support.

'Saint Patrick damaged High King Laoghaire's authority when he lit a fire on the hill of Slane on the eve of Easter which fell on the same date as Tara's spring festival fires. No other fire was supposed to be lit, save that of the high king.'

We can take it that Patrick was a daring fellow if all this can be believed. Naturally, the high king saw the fire from Tara, it's only fifteen kilometres or so from Slane, as the crow flies. The guide points us in that direction. Nowadays, the view would more likely be of a crowd of gig goers. Slane is a major venue for hosting big concerts but today we're firmly planted in the fifth century. Indeed, Patrick's fire was said to have been seen throughout Ireland, though no one in the group seemed a bit convinced of that story. The High King assembled his warriors and druids, but Patrick out-smarted him. He warned the king to accept the new "faith" or else die.

And so, to make a very long story short and to skip over the great coup of conversion, a pagan landscape was changed into a Christian one. The new faith etched one more ring onto Tara's landscape. Sacred trees and wells were co-opted from one belief system into another.

This spreading of the word was a triumph, even if it involved some threats. It meant the Christian message had reached the furthest point of the earth. At least that was as far as they thought the earth stretched at the time, to Ireland, an otherworldly place at the edge of Europe. Ireland became a subject of Rome, of papal Rome, though it had long since sat on the doorstep of another Roman power, the empire, and managed to dodge its legions and taxes.

Now, let's take another leap over the centuries from Saint Patrick to the nineteenth century, to an equally smart operator, Daniel O'Connell. He too knew the value of a bit of theatre, and he held one of his monster rallies on Tara's summit, in 1843, when he was drumming up support for the Repeal of the Act of Union between Britain and Ireland. A ground-stirring crowd turned up, a million they say, to hear the great orator speak. Good propaganda it might be, but it didn't move the British. The Westminster government might have been ready to give in on Catholic Emancipation which O'Connell's agitation brought home in 1829, lighting up the country with bonfires. But repeal of the Act of Union was another matter entirely. Even Tara couldn't coax that one from the British.

As well as being the home of high kings, Tara is the site of a passage tomb, which the guide shows us, the Mound of the Hostages, built around 2,500BC. It overlooks and aligns with the clusters of passage tombs and satellite cairns along the banks of the Boyne – Newgrange, Knowth, Dowth, Loughcrew.

A river can make all the difference in how a civilisation ambles along. Meath's River Boyne holds its own in antique greatness with all the other pre-historic sites of this county. It appeared on the Graeco-Egyptian geographer, Ptolemy's map though he named it Buvinda (the name is thought to mean white cow, referring to fertility). The Boyne is not a highway of a river that rushes straight to sea but in a good-natured bow to the local landscape, it offers itself in bits and pieces, bending around in spirals, looping, doing the round trip through the plains of Meath, like a king on a royal progress, slowing its flow to serve many places, and meandering around the Neolithic sites.

These early farmers found the most auspicious locations for their homes and their burial sites, where the river coils and curls, a spot long-since known to be a strong energy point of the earth.

They can debate all they like about whether they built their structures in Tara, Newgrange, Knowth, Dowth, Loughcrew for astrological, spiritual or ceremonial reasons or if they were burial mounds, sacred temples or whatever. What tantalises me is their antiquity, their circles within circles, trapping solstices and equinoxes beneath their ringed mounds and noting the seasons since the dawn of time. Their dates are dizzying, arounsd 3200BC, older than the Pyramids of Egypt or Stonehenge. Some would say they're the world's oldest astronomical observatories. And they were built by people who knew neither metal tools nor wheels.

Like his ancient forebears, Francis Ledwidge was shaped by his native Meath and the Boyne. His love for his home makes his decision to join the British army surprising – a double surprise, because he had opposed John Redmond's (leader of the Irish Parliamentary Party) call to join the British army at Woodenbridge, County Wicklow, on Sunday, September 20, 1914.

On July 31, 1917 Ledwidge was blown to pieces by a shell in Liège, near Ypres, while drinking tea with his comrades. He was a few weeks short of his thirtieth birthday. His half-finished life leaves its mark in dashed hopes, unwritten poetry, longings unfulfilled, views from Tara unseen where he was to 'come back again surely'.

Instead he was scraped up from the earth and buried in soil he didn't belong to. His dust is absent from County Meath, the royal county, as royal as Annie Ledwidge told her son the family could trace its lineage to. But his words live on. He touched his homeplace with wonder and the sense of the sacredness of the land, a land he played a lowly part in. His first-hand acquaintance with rural hardship didn't spoil it for him, maybe it heightened it.

In his life he had lived the things that make a poet – the unattainable woman (Ellie, the daughter of a strong farmer whose family had bigger things in mind for her than Ledwidge, married another and died at the birth of her first child). He also knew the sadness of missing his clan and the torture of double allegiance – to the Easter rebels and to the British army.

He sang the names of the fields, the trees, the flowers and the birds. In a way his poetry fulfills a sense of duty, of care of his people, of his land, of his home-place, turning water into wine. He dedicated his first book of poems. 'To my mother, the first singer I knew.'

SEVEN

TÓCHAR PHÁDRAIG

From the moment I heard about the revived ancient route to Croagh Patrick in County Mayo, it filled me with such yearning that I couldn't wait to get into my boots and step it out. And here on Easter Monday, among the assembled crowd in Ballintubber Abbey I'm wondering if I'll be able for the seventeen-kilometre pilgrim walk. It might not be far for some, and I can spot the seasoned walkers at a glance. They're suitably shod, well clad with raingear and walking sticks. It's the longest walk I have ever undertaken.

This is the *Tóchar Phádraig,* Patrick's Causeway. The Easter Monday occasion is a kind of practice run, only half of the *tóchar.* The real event of Reek Sunday (the last Sunday of July) keeps you on your feet for thirty-five kilometres. I won't even think about that. For the moment, seventeen kilometres is enough to be frightened of.

When I was growing up in Galway the Reek made an occasional appearance to the west, like a magic moutain in a perfect triangle of blue. Today, I feel a quiver of memory that makes my mind shrink to just the amount of space my head contained at the time. Back then this faroff vision looked as perfect as one of the pyramids of

Egypt and, in those days of youth, it might well have been one of these structures, because in my small world, anything was possible. And, in the evening when the summer sun went down behind the mountain, in a blaze of red, it just could have been the Red Sea parting.

Reek Sunday caused a stir in our locality. That date stood alongside the Galway races in local importance. Of course, the races for all its claims, never said it was sacred. It was all about the thrill of the chase, the bets, the cries of the bookies, the nods and winks (later the cryptic language of the political parties and tents flowing with Champagne).

The Reek was about God. No nods, no winks. You prepared spiritually. The older people could remember when pilgrims went fasting and the really keen climbed bare-footed. It was one of those repeating stories like tales about bad winters or for our old neighbour, the story of the denial of education for Catholics during the Penal Laws.

Of course Reek Sunday wasn't without a bit of revelling too, its own thrill of the chase – getting up early to beat the day to it, the trial of the climb, getting to the top. All that called for a celebration afterwards. The questions when the pilgrims returned were typical of a country conversation: 'Did you get to the top? Was it slippery? Was there a big crowd this year?' when all the climbers wanted was to go home and rest their legs.

Then there was the witty neighbour's annual joke: 'Wasn't it far up he (Saint Patrick) went?'

I hope no one asks me questions today about how well I step out the seventeen kilometres.

The local priest-organiser, Father Frank Fahey puts us through some ground rules before we begin. He revitalised this route, negotiated with farmers to cross their land and wrote a book on the pathway, telling the story of every field and all thirteen stiles along the way.

'Rule one, you're not to complain. Instead, be grateful that you can do this pilgrim walk.' (I think it's premature being grateful when I don't yet know if I'm going to make it as far as the first stile.) 'If you get stuck in a bog-hole, be grateful.'

No one looks alarmed. I take this as a sign that it's unlikely to happen.

Rule two: 'Help each other out.'

This one sounds best.

We're invited to light a candle 'on the house' before setting off on the bus which is parked at the abbey gate. The bus driver is going to take us to Aughagower, the mid-point between Ballintubber and the Reek and we will walk back to the Abbey.

I read the brochure on Ballintubber Abbey. This monastery is located off the N84 Galway-Castlebar road. They claim it's the only church in Ireland where Mass has been celebrated without a break for 800 years. Of course 800 years of continuous piety is a mere trifle when we're talking about this ritual walk. Croagh Patrick, the cone-shaped mountain, in white quartzite, standing alone, had always called out for reverence. Even pre-Christians honoured it, before Patrick came on the scene at all.

In the course of the chat with the man who sits alongside me on the bus, I tell him I drove from Dublin.

'Don't tell me you came all the way from Dublin this morning,' he asks.

I have to admit I did, that there was something I had to go to last evening that I couldn't get out of, in spite of my best excuses. 'That's not the way to do this walk at all,' he says. 'You have to come and get into the atmosphere first, stay the night, feel the darkness of the country all around you, listen to the farm animals bleating, lowing... It's all part of getting into the spirit of the *tóchar*.'

I didn't know all that preparation was expected of me and I feel a bit boorish, not in tune with the deeper meaning of this event.

Out on the fields I meet people who think of this walk as a

stroll. Some have done the full thirty-five kilometres to the Reek, others have walked the *camino* or climbed the Reek, a few times on the same day. I have little to say for myself in return.

The blonde woman in the bright orange hoodie is so eager that she's nearly hitting off the heels of the two men who are leading the walk. You're not supposed to overtake the leaders, if you do they can't be accountable for you.

I first think it a shame to be walking with our backs to the Reek but, by the time I have stepped it out a few kilometres, I scarcely care what the view is. In any case I have to give my full attention to where I'm placing my foot and, even though Father Fahey has advised us to be grateful if we get stuck in a bog-hole, I'd prefer not to have to give thanks for that particular difficulty. So, I stick to hard ground. I get good at watching out for tufts of grass or bunches of rushes on which to launch my foot or follow where my eager predecessor has stepped and, if she hasn't sunk, there's a good chance that I won't disappear into the earth either.

We stop along the way, where the path crosses roads and someone meets us with a carbootful of refreshments. Boxes of chocolate bars are opened and containers of water are handed around. We're pointed in the direction of 'organic' toilets, acres of facilities, men on one side, women on the other, like a tridentine Mass.

If you feel weary and ready to give up the struggle, you can take a lift. Nobody does, but it's reassuring to know you can. These pauses give us a chance to take in the view. The Tourmakeady mountains to the left of the Reek spread, chopping up a long line of horizon and to the right lies the Nephin range. The bulk of Nephin itself is unmistakable. It has snow on its peak.

My father came from Mayo and his mother's name was Nephin and that made this mountain feel like a relative. She was dead before I was born, but I remember feeling that she was soaring like the mountain from somewhere beyond the rainbow.

From time to time our Mayo relations came to visit us. They would breeze in from the land of Nephin and the Reek and for a time our house would zing with loud chat, laughter, and a few heated arguments. They always brought the same kind of sweets with chocolate centres and green wrappers.

Today the Reek is showing a different view from the perfect, triangular vision of childhood. It's nearer, and its cone shape looks draped like a Lenten statue.

Soon we're trudging it out again. We walk along by the Aille river that flows from its source in the Partry mountains. We pass by the Aille caves where the river vanishes down a large sinkhole and flows for a time underground before it empties itself into Cloon Lough and then into Lough Mask. This is limestone country which makes water do magicians' tricks.

The *tóchar* is flat walking for the most part. I get in and out of conversation as I catch up with someone or fall behind. A man with a jumper buttoned up to his neck comments on what a trek it must have been for the people of old, badly fed and badly shod, if shod at all. That bit of complaining on behalf of someone else is allowed, I think.

We're instructed to close the gates and the message passes back to the end of the line. Urban folk need to be reminded that leaving gates swinging open can result in animals breaking into the wrong field. I served my gate-closing apprenticeship long ago. Growing up on a farm instils that into you.

Next resting point is where we can open our lunches. I've eaten mine already. I feel like on my first day at school when I wanted to eat my sandwiches five minutes after getting there.

Soon we're off again. Maybe I've grown fitter along the way but it comes as a big surprise to reach the N84, the main Galway-Castlebar road. That means our walk is nearly at an end. Seventeen kilometres feels a lot shorter than I expected.

It takes Ballintubber abbey a while to rise into view. Seeing it makes me feel wonderful about myself and my accomplishment, even if it is relatively modest.

Ballintubber Abbey has survived many an obstacle through its 800 years, from Cromwellian burnings, suppression and the notorious priest hunter John Mullowney known as *Seán na Sagart*, who came from around these parts.

The job of a priest hunter arose from the 1709 Penal Act which called for the clergy to take an oath of abjuration and recognise Queen Anne (who was especially harsh about enforcing these laws) as Supreme Head of the Church of England and Ireland, or face death.

Mullowney's credentials for the job included experience as a horse thief for which the gentlemen of the Grand Jury in nearby Castlebar struck a deal – hunt the priests and avoid the noose for past offences. The pay was tempting – £100 for the capture of a bishop or archbishop, £20 for a priest, £10 for a hedge-school teacher, £5 for a trainee priest. It would take a lot of stolen horses to match that kind of money.

You had to be resourceful to net a priest. One trick he used was to fake a deathbed confession, and then produce the knife. But he fell victim to his own game when a priest, dressed as a woman, tricked him.

A tree marking the unconsecrated spot near Ballintubber Abbey where he's buried never blossoms. It's hardly surprising that the earth rejects such a rogue.

My legs are sore and my boots heavy with mud when Cathal, a Donegal man with whom I'd exchanged a few words earlier, appears with a leaflet for another walk: *Siúlóid Thulach Beaglaigh* (Tullagh Begley Walk). 'Five hours of fairly challenging mountain walk following the old pilgrim burial route,' it reads. Am I up to it? I'll wait and see how my body falls into place before committing myself.

Tea, biscuits and fruitcake are spread out on a long table in the room above the abbey chapel. It's a reward for our penance. And a further prize is a signed certificate to confirm we have completed the *tóchar*. I wonder if the certificates are the same for those who took a lift. They should be a different colour for the warriors who lasted the pace. Or is this a case, as the bible says, that the last shall be first and the first last? I always thought that unfair.

It doesn't spoil my sense of exhilaration though, the sort people report after running a marathon. I want to tell everyone the details of my walk. Put out the flag folks, I've walked seventeen kilometres. What a pain I'd be if I walked the *camino*!

Before I leave I make myself a promise to come back to journey by the coast road that winds westwards from Mayo into Galway's Connemara.

EIGHT

SPUR OF BEAUTY

It's summer when I get to Renvyle Peninsula, one of the many spurs of land in west Galway that projects its beauty into the Atlantic Ocean. It was here Oliver St John Gogarty, writer, surgeon, and model for Buck Mulligan of Joyce's *Ulysses*, had his country house.

The journey takes me by Connemara National Park between two mountain ranges, the Twelve Pins and the Maumturks. Even in modern transport the road is bumpy. The trip must have been bone-shattering in Gogarty's time. No wonder when Lady Mary Heath, record-setter in altitude, flew her Avro Avian biplane into Renvyle in September 1928, Gogarty began to explore the idea of reaching Dublin by air. He was a daring spirit – sportsman, motorcyclist, archer, aviator. Air travel was in its very early stages at the time. Dublin by plane would have reduced the journey to one hour and served another purpose too – to view Connemara from the air which Lady Mary proclaimed was by far the best view of Galway.

A big crowd turned out to watch Lady Heath appear out of the sky in Renvyle. She had some record, the first woman to parachute out of an aircraft and the first pilot to fly an open cockpit plane from Capetown to London.

When, later that September day, she tried to land in Oranmore, further east into Galway, she couldn't because sheep were moving across the runway. Today I'm having the same problem, in my own down-to-earth way. Sheep still claim the same right here. Two of them are drowsily folded up in the midde of the road. They allow the car enough width to drive by. Others, distant into the fields, are barely distinguishable from the white stones.

On my left is Lough Eidhneach, and rising above the water are the mountains. Some are scored white with flowing limestone, their sinews, tendons and muscles exposed. They peak, they cluster, they level off, they chomp against the sky. They're wonderful. Hand in hand they form a line, arm in arm, separating just enough to allow the sky in, and sometimes blocking out the light entirely. The lake holds its mirror to them, giving them a chance to see how well they're looking, even with an upside-down view.

From the gate I drive in by a long avenue, to the edge of the world before Renvyle House hotel comes into view. Its architecture – high chimneys, attics, dormers and two projecting bays – goes with the grain of this region of choppy terrain and broken coasts.

When I meet owner Zoë Fitzgerald we wonder how Gogarty found this place at all. He must have been looking for some hideaway from his Dublin home and busy surgery. Zoë's family has owned it since 1952 when her grandfather, Derry businessman Dr Donny Coyle, bought it from Gogarty. Before that it was the home of the Blake family.

Gogarty kept paying guests here but he also loved to play host to his unpaying literary-artistic friends, W B Yeats, George Moore, George Russell, Welsh painter, Augustus John. When they stayed the ouiga board was never idle.

Zoë is eager to show me the Long Lounge, where Yeats' first Noh play *At The Hawks Well* was performed in 1917.

'It was a play loosely based on Cúchulainn, the warrior as a young man,' she says. 'He's in search of the life-giving waters and, at a well, he meets an embittered old man and a mysterious girl witch/hawk,' she explains. The Long Lounge looks just right for a small theatre and no great changes have been made since Gogarty's time. 'The flooring and two fireplaces are the same as they were on the night the play was performed. Some of the original furniture is here since Gogarty's time too.'

Zoë guides me to other memories kept alive here since the turn of the twentieth century.

'Here are two tapestries by Lily Yeats, of Saint Brendan and St Gobnait and a painting in black ink by Evie Hone. These were bought by my grandfather.'

They recall that splendid time of the new awakening in literature, art and stained glass, the heyday of Lady Gregory's Coole Park and Saint Brendan's Cathedral in Loughrea. We walk around the garden at the back and at the door, before I leave, she points to Diamond Hill, which looks like the house's own special view. Zoë recommends a climb: 'It's a lot easier to climb now. There's a pathway and I believe the view is wonderful.'

As good as the view from Lady Mary Heath's Avro Avian biplane, perhaps.

I leave Renvyle House and head east for nearby Kylemore Abbey which is just outside the surround of Renvyle Peninsula. At first glance I think this castle bears all the fingerprints of the corrupt landlord-tenant system. It was built in 1867 by Mitchell Henry, a Manchester cotton merchant and one of the richest men in the British Isles.

'It's true,' says Eithne O'Halloran, Kylemore Abbey's Experience Manager, 'he built a pleasure estate here but he wasn't one of those disinterested landlords. He became aware of the plight of tenants, their insecurity and high rents, and set about improving their lot.'

She leads me on a walk to show me what Henry created

here, Kylemore's showpiece, the walled garden where they once cultivated fruits of the tropics. It stands like a trophy, in the shelter of Diamond Hill, to Henry's ambitions. Here his gardeners tamed this wild land, coaxed it into fertility, creating a microclimate of tropical cultivation, defying the west Galway weather with hot pipes and greenhouses.

Standing with her back to the great hulk of mountain, Eithne tells me how they raised the temperature to equatorial level. 'Twenty-one glasshouses stood here, in a horseshoe shape so that they could reflect the heat off one another and hotwater pipes extended around the garden from a limekiln. The bricks for the wall came from Scotland and the granite from Dalkey. They grew vines here, bananas and other tropical fruits.'

It sounds like the Garden of Eden. Bananas must surely have been a strange-tasting food in Ireland at the time with famine ready to pounce at the slightest failure of the potato crop. The Royal Horticultural Society took a keen interest in the reclamation and drainage works that were going on here.

'When they awarded Mitchell Henry with the gold medal for drainage it was one of his proudest moments,' says Eithne. 'This work provided well-paid jobs and security for his tenants. Henry, as a Home Rule MP for West Galway, campaigned in Westminster for funding for land improvement. His argument was that not only would it be humanitarian – economic justice – but it would be viable as well. Only one of the original glasshouses now remains, and Kylemore's present goal is to restore the garden and forest to this past glory.'

On our way to the wood, *An Choill Mhór*, Eithne explains more about this plan.

'We're working along with the School of Natural Sciences in NUIG in a Biodiversity Stewardship Programme to bring back the Kylemore woodland to its full health. Mitchell Henry encouraged growing trees, native and imported, like monkeypuzzles and redwoods. In the first year he planted 200,000. It's now the largest area of mixed deciduous forest in County Galway and the habitat of a host of animals, birds and plant life.'

So Kylemore is once again a hive of activity, in a joint venture reminiscent of the nineteenth century.

'Clearing the rhododendrons is the biggest job,' Eithne says. 'Rhododendrons were tempting plants for Victorian gardens – evergreen leaf, ground cover and a spread of summer flowering. But they're invasive. And to get rid of them will probably mean digging them out and injecting each root stub, one by one, with a chemical. We're still looking into the most environmentally friendly way of doing it, but at least this method would prevent widespread spraying.'

The clearing of overgrown plants has unearthed some of the estate's history. A racecourse ran through the property along by the river and cricket and football fields. Mitchell Henry installed these delights to amuse his nine children.

Planet-friendly projects are not new in Kylemore. Already a wetland treatment system had been installed. Wetlands flora such as reeds are part of the ecosystem and are capable of absorbing and breaking down sewage better than any chemical.

'This is only part of the drive to keep clean the waters of the Dawros River which runs through the estate,' says Eithne. 'It's clean enough now to host the fresh-water pearl mussel, a mollusc that only thrives in the purest of water. In the past it was used for jewellery, but it's now one of Europe's most threatened species and protected by law.'

But let's return to the nineteenth century, to Mitchell Henry's benevolent landlordism. This is where Eithne makes the story her own, because her ancestors were among the people who worked here. She stops to show me her favourite spot.

'This is where my Uncle John (Joyce) used to fish and I've happy memories of it, sad ones too. We call it the pool but its real name is Lough Maladrolaun though no local calls it that. It's sometimes called MacMurrays or Bosomworths. Places were called after the family who lived in the nearest house so they changed with the residents. Uncle John was born in 1915. His father, my grandfather, was a gilly and a trapper on the estate. As a child John remembered his father carrying him on his back as early as five in the morning, to empty the traps.'

As we pass by where the gatelodge stood at the western entrance to the estate, she points out: 'May and Pat Nee lived there, and it was a house where everyone dropped in on the way home from Mass in the Abbey on a Sunday morning for a cup of tea before starting the journey home (those were the days when Mass-goers came fasting from the previous midnight before receiving the Eucharist). May and my grandmother sometimes acted as midwives to the babies born around the locality. Two women lived near the *srath* (a low crossing on a river) and when the river was in flood they ferried people across the water – on their backs.'

And now a pause to devote a moment to Kylemore's assembly of ghosts. A little problem here is that they're revered. From my small knowledge, I reckon that's not at all what ghosts want. They thrive on terrifying people, not on affection. My petrified reaction probably gives them a whole lot more satisfaction. I'm glad it's not night. But Eithne speaks of them as friends: 'Páidín Mór's bridge (opposite the racecourse) is said to be often visited by his ghost,' she explains as she points out the place where strange lights have been sighted. 'No one knows why Páidín Mór wants to haunt the place.' The ghost of Jack Harry has more reason for his night appearances. 'Jack worked in the gravel pit and when he was shovelling out the gravel one day the pit collapsed and he and his horse were killed. He still roams around Cnocán Jack Harry. People report hearing the noise of carriages along by the old road too. In Mitchell Henry's time this road was replaced by a new one.'

The local gentry paid regular visits here in Henry's time so it's no wonder that the rasping sounds of their wheels still echo. Lady Gregory from Coole was a regular guest, the Blakes came from Renvyle House, Sir William Wilde and his wife (Oscar's parents) made the trip from one or other of their two houses nearby (Lough Fee and Cross). And two Chief Secretaries for Ireland, Arthur Balfour and George Wyndham were frequent guests. In fact, these two did much to bring down the landlord system that their host had put such energy into improving. The land acts that Balfour and Wyndham passed provided good borrowing terms for tenants to buy out their holdings. This was the Conservative party policy, constructive unionism, and it cut the ground from under the landlords. Despite Mitchell Henry's benevolent intentions, this land-purchase scheme turned out to be more in tune with the tenants' thinking. More than anything else Irish tenants wanted a stake for themselves in the soil. They believed they had a right to it.

This wasn't unusual. Peasant-farmers from France, to Prussia, to Russia, to Irish tenant-farmers felt the land they worked rightfully belonged to them. The soil they cultivated and lived on was almost like the air they breathed. Generations of their families had worked the same plot, tended the land with their hands. Tenants-at-will often made wills indicating which son they wanted to pass on their plot to and the landlord usually respected their wish.

A light wind blows in our faces as Eithne leads the way along towards Primrose Hill, a little mound that bursts into yellow bloom in spring, then through rough terrain and rushes towards the stony field.

'I used to play here when I was a child,' she says, pointing to the heap of stones. Like everything in Kylemore they have a story to tell. They were piled up in a corner when they cleared the field to make way for the plough in the 1870s. 'It was the first field in Connemara to be ploughed. All the others around here were dug by spade. So, the horsedrawn plough was a big event. What I like about this field is that nothing has changed since, there's nothing at all modern here, not even a telegraph pole.'

Mitchell Henry spent less time here after his wife Margaret contracted a fever in Egypt and died at the age of forty-five. A mausoleum and a miniature Gothic cathedral still stand as a memorial to her.

An order of Benedictine nuns bought Kylemore Abbey in 1920. They had fled from wartime bombing in Ypres in Belgium in 1914. The site here had a problem though. One of the requirements of the Benedictine Rule was that a monastery be enclosed by a wall. Kylemore had none, but the nuns got over this technicality by the sheltering form of the mountains which stood in for a wall.

The nuns are still in Kylemore and continue farming and gardening. Eithne shows me a picture of their hands-on approach. They aren't afraid to roll up their sleeves and pin up the gowns, though the sisters use the garden for much more homely cultivation than their exotic predecessors.

Our final stop is to view where the Marconi receiver masts were placed high up on the hills. Eithne points up to where the cable went from hill to hill and to the heights the nuns went to, in 1932, to put their own 'receiver' here – a statue of the Sacred Heart of Jesus.

'It was a show of gratitude for having paid off their mortgage. Their abbey in Ypres was dedicated to the Sacred Heart,' she says.

We can only see the statue in miniature from where we're standing. They must have gone to a lot of trouble to install it because it looks half way up to heaven.

The nuns ran a girls' boarding school here, a posh one, mostly for overseas students. There was also a dayschool where the less wealthy locals came. Eithne, her sisters and their mother were educated here in the dayschool. As well as learning the school subjects, they learned a lesson in the different strata of society.

'Once my mother had to step in as a replacement in a drama competition (a French play translated into Irish) the school was entering for in the Taibhdhearc theatre in Galway city (eighty kilometres from Kylemore). The lead girl got tonsillitis and my mother was sick with worry about having to share a room in Galway with girls so different from herself. She didn't possess her own hairbrush, not even her own nightdress. Her older sister had to quickly make one up for her and a hairbrush had to be borrowed.'

Stage-fright was only secondary to social fright. But they won first prize.

We're running out of time in Kylemore. Eithne rushes me back to the carpark before the place shuts down for the night. I move along quickly. I don't want to be left alone among Kylemore's phantoms and the ghostly sounds of carriages.

I go out the gate with a changed view from that which I drove in with. I apologise to Mitchell Henry, builder of this great edifice, for my earlier severe assumptions. This benevolent landlord left but the locals stayed. They produced their progeny in this neck of the woods, their native place. And now it's fitting that Eithne, whose people tended the land here, is involved again in a new teamwork dream for Kylemore.

The next part of my journey will get me out of the car and on to a bike.

NINE

GREAT WESTERN GREENWAY

I take the long way round to Westport where I'm to meet my cousin and his wife, James and Nuala, to cycle the Great Western Greenway.

Approaching from the little village of Cross this sweep of land is full of treasure. I enquire in Cross post office for Ballymacgibbon cairn. The young woman who is sweeping the floor never heard of it. A man who lives in that direction overhears me and offers to show me in return for a lift home. I hesitate. But they seem to know him in the post office and no one makes warning signs behind his back so I take a chance.

He's very interesting. He points out Mount Gabriel and Moytura House, once the dwelling of Sir William Wilde.

'I've a book by Sir William,' he tells me. 'I guard it carefully. I nearly lost it once when I lent it to someone for research. Three years it took to get it back. Since then, I've an answer good and ready for anyone who asks for the loan of it – No.' He shows me the entrance to Ballymacgibbon cairn. 'I don't believe a word of the legend about it being the scene of a battle between the Tuatha Dé Danann and the Fir Bolg (the ancient fairy tribes of Ireland). It was William Wilde who came up with that story.'

I've dropped him off by the time I get a closer look at the cairn, an elaborate mound of limestone surrounded by a low mound. I would like to ask him, if not to commemorate a battle what was this complex structure built for. Seeing it more closely involves chancing my luck among a herd of cattle so I move on.

Next up is the village of Cong. You're never out of earshot of bubbling water in Cong. This village is built on an island between Lough Mask and Lough Corrib. It is well stocked with springs, underground rivers, sinkholes and lakes which accounts for the many bridges curving among the rich vegetation.

The ruins of a twelfth century abbey complete the picture and John Ford knew all about that background scene when he shot the Wayne and O'Hara film *The Quiet Man* here. Cong still taps into its sequel tourist business. A hotel keeps the name Danagher in memory of the famous Mary Kate Danagher of the film.

I go in search of the dry canal which has become the butt of many a joke. It was built in the 1840s as a famine relief scheme, to provide a link between Lough Mask and Lough Corrib designed by Scottish engineer Alexander Nimmo. The man in the bookshop is impatient with the jokers.

'The joke wasn't justified,' he tells me. 'It was all a lie that the engineers didn't understand what they were doing. That was a story spread by Sir William Wilde. The canal would have worked fine if they'd finished it with a clay lining, as they did with all canals, the part where it was lined worked fine.'

So much for canals, dry or otherwise. I'm about to leave Cong and take the road for Westport, heading into the sun, by Lough Mask, on the splendid route by Killary Harbour, Ireland's best example of a fjord, an Ice Age gift. Long and narrow it is – sixteen kilometres from the Atlantic to Aasleagh, its furthest point inland. Its deep blue waters are wedged between the Mweelrea mountains to the north and the Maumturks to the south. Outside of Norway you won't find a better sight. All it's missing is Viking longships sailing dragon-headed into the harbour. And further north is Delphi, part of the estate of the Marquis of Sligo of Westport House. He named his hunting lodge Delphi because during his grand tour, he felt homesick for these parts when the scenery around the real Delphi reminded him of his native land.

This might as well be a mythical tour, from the trolls of Norse lands to the gods of Greece. And the scene is worthy of the gods, with the Sheeffry Hills to the north alongside the peaks of Ben Creggan and Ben Gorm, though I must admit I can't distinguish either of them from their companions.

The winding road leads through wilderness and wonder, comely mountain followed by comely mountain. I've never seen such a drove of beauty. And they look as if they know they're good-lookin', strutting in a spectacular array of conceit, cascading in folds and pleats and wrapped in mists of purple and blue.

Mountains have a habit of following you around, making it hard to know one from the other. Yet you know every one of them has a name, like children in a family, all the same to the casual onlooker but strictly distinguishable to doting parents.

Even when a shower of rain hops off the windscreen and some mountains get hazed out of the picture, you know they're there, announcing their presence beyond visibility. And when the water flows down they look like snoozing elephants who sleep so soundly they don't notice the rivers rolling down their backs. Then the rain stops and they take on a different hue and exude new shades of blue all over again.

Under the spell of the hills I enjoy myself too much. I'm late for dinner in Knockranny House Hotel where I'm to meet James and

Nuala. They're patient with me and the hotel people don't mind that we're late either. They even give us the choice seat of the house, at the bay window, in full view of the Reek.

James and Nuala treat themselves to high-starred comfort holidays. They're not into roughing it on bikes but James is so excited about greenways that he's willing to make an extra effort. Nuala isn't sure.

'I'm nervous about going on a bike,' she says. 'It's ages since I cycled.'

I can't imagine anything to be afraid of from a bike. A plane, now that's different. Anytime I fly I want to ask a million questions. How experienced is the pilot? What made him choose this job, not a sense of adventure by any chance? What's the airline's record on maintenance? How do I put on a life jacket in the unlikely event…? I'm wondering does Nuala have similar questions about the bike.

It's a morning in good form as we walk to Westport town centre from the hotel where Gerry from Westport Bikes For Hire is waiting with a minibus to take a group of cyclists to Achill island. They provide this service knowing that most people find it enough to cycle the Great Western Greenway once and not to have to come back again with the bike. They recommend to begin at Achill and cycle northwards rather than the other way around as the breeze is more favourable. We take that advice. We need the most auspicious push we can get. As we get into the minibus heading for Achill a terrible shower hops off the windscreen. It's a bad start.

In Achill we're kitted out with helmets, hi-vis jackets, pumps and a puncture repair set. We're ready to face whatever the elements decide to spill on us. Going across the bridge in Achill, the breeze forces us off our bikes. But that's the end of the hardship.

Soon we're into our stride by wayside banks, uplands, sea, mountain, a lake and black-turned earth. This is the life, plunging through the air, the spokes humming as they catch the breeze. Even Nuala has relaxed out of her rigidity. There's a tang in the air and the sweet perfume of petals and greenery is coming from the earth. A plume of smoke is rising from a faroff chimney. The sky is blue and long puffy clouds float above us, some look like newly-shorn fleeces, others look more laden. I hope they hold back their moisture – they can release all they want once we reach Westport.

The Greenway has its own culture, a cyclist's etiquette, bowing to local friendliness. It's of great importance to Mayo people to talk to everyone: 'Hello, how are ye?' comes a voice from behind a hedge. It's a gardener, straightening her back from her weeding. Even those who aren't local have got into the Mayo way of greeting.

Because my father came from this county and we spent youthful holidays here I feel local. I recall to James that summer, which he too well remembers, when my sister was allowed to visit their house and I was brought to Angela, a cousin of my mother's. My trip wasn't near as exciting as hers and I felt envious about the great time she was having while I had to listen to my mother and Angela chatting, listing all the people who had died since they last met, or the fine details of jam-making or how many coils of wool it took to knit a jumper.

Angela even talked about an old boyfriend which sounded to me beyond understanding at the time, though he did sound a whole lot nicer than the grumpy so-and-so she was married to. When I tried to get away from their droning chat by running up and down the stairs (our house was single storey and their stairs was the only exciting part of my holiday) he said: 'Come down out of that, you'll fall and we'll have to go all over the place looking for a doctor for you.'

Angela tried to excuse his grumpiness. 'Joe is a bit nervous, he isn't used to children.'

So I played handball on the gable of the house. That didn't suit him either. He told me that the wall had been painted and that I would dirty it. When I called my mother's cousin Angela he said I should call her Aunt Angela. But I said she wasn't my aunt and he told me I was cheeky. Clearly I couldn't do a thing to please him.

Meanwhile, news from County Mayo was reaching us – a postcard telling us of swimming in the river, going to the cinema and meeting a nice-looking neighbour with hair the colour of chestnut. (My sister was thirteen, three years older than me and a whole lot more advanced. She had well moved on from running up and down the stairs to amuse herself.)

Along the greenway wild flowers light up the headlands and ridges. Nuala names them. She likes the wild ones more than cultivated flowers.

'They're extra special because they depend so much on chance.'

The cream-coloured meadowsweet which thrives on dampness has every excuse to flourish here. Its fragrance is rising towards us. The flower that purples up the verges she tells us is Wayside knapweed. And the red flower that peeps from underneath a tangle of stems is a dogrose. She even has a good word for the purple loosestrife.

'It's often called a gardener's curse, but let's enjoy it. It's not our garden it's invading.'

After our steep climb a view of the drowned drumlins of Mulranny Bay makes up for our panting and puffing. And now, for the real reward, a carefree spree of freewheeling downhill. But there's a sign asking cyclists to dismount. What spoilsport advice. We ignore it. Even Nuala doesn't get off her bike. Is it not this that we struggled uphill for? We have good brakes, front and back, and we're well helmeted. And it isn't exactly the Alps.

From time to time the peak of the Reek rears its lovely head. As we get closer to Westport it shifts to the other side of the Greenway. It's fuller now, showing off nearly all its conical body. We stop and turn around and there's Nephin beside it, both doing their twin show of quartzite beauty. A few miles further on Clare Island lines up for the snapshot beside them in a triptych of blue.

There isn't a sign of the rain that hit Gerry's windscreen earlier in the morning. It's like as if the sky has shed its allowance for the day and now it's happy to bask in blue for the afternoon.

When we give back the bikes in Westport, they tell us we're the first back. The others who came with us in the minibus this morning were younger than us so they should have cycled faster. Of course they don't say that to us. We'd never put another penny of business their way if they were that indiscreet.

We're all tired but well pleased with ourselves. In the morning James and Nuala go home while I drive to see Mayo's prize find, the Céide Fields, the first-farming landscape that was found underneath the blanket bog in Glenurla. This, a thousand acres, is the most extensive discovery of its kind ever uncovered.

TEN

GLENURLA

At one point a blanket of fog descends upon us. It's the speed at which it falls that surprises me but the guide talks on, shows no sign of wonder. I suppose here in Glenurla on the coast of County Mayo, by the Atlantic Ocean, you learn to take those changing weather moods in your stride. Only minutes ago we were enjoying a great view from the Céide Fields. The flat-topped hill fields, which is what céide means, were basking in sunshine over Belderg harbour.

The half-sunny sky (the other half is in a thick fog) is like a double-sided sight laid on especially to replicate the blanket bog that we're about to look into. A bog formed on these fields, after the Neolithic farmers who made the place famous, left. They were driven out by climate change, by colder and wetter weather. By then they had put in 500 years of farming on this spot on the rugged north coast of Mayo.

You can imagine the stir this find caused in the archaeological world in the 1970s when the home of the first layer of farmers after the hunter-gatherers was revealed. It's the oldest known and the most extensive field system in the world.

The remains of stone walls were the clue – field divisions preserved underneath the peat that stretches for several square miles. A local teacher, Patrick Caulfield, came upon them in the 1930s when he was cutting turf. He hit on a pile of stones that seemed too organised to be random. It wasn't until forty years later that the search began, when his son Séamus qualified as an archaeologist.

The discovery makes Mayo's Neolithic glory match that of County Meath where people of the same era left traces in Newgrange, Dowth, Nowth and Loughcrew.

'We don't know much about these people,' the guide tells us. 'It's thought they originally came by Europe from the Fertile Crescent, navigating their way across the seas and bringing their farming knowledge to this side of the world.'

We're told that they arrived to a continental climate, a lot warmer weather than that which greets the people who flee the same places today – Syria, Jordan, Egypt, the Middle East.

The new arrivals felled the pine forests which grew here, to make a clearing for their farming. This can be made out from traces of pollen. The designers of the Visitors' Centre copied the plan of the early timber houses where the people of Céide Fields lived. They were able to replicate them from the traces of posthole voids (a cut feature used to hold a surface timber or stone).

'These early farmers tried to team up with the sun, coax it so as to trap its heat,' the guide says. 'You have to remember how close the Ice Age would have been in their folklore so it was important to them to mark the seasons, solstices and equinoxes.'

The mapping of the fields was done by painstaking probing of the stones beneath the bog. Clues to where these Stone Age people lived and died came from pottery and charcoal. That was how their dwellings and tombs were located. And the shell of the fish they ate formed mounds of proof of their diet.

'Look around you,' the guide invites us. 'There's Maumakeogh,' he says pointing to a hill. 'In English that means a handful of fog.'

I love that pithy image. No wonder the sports writer and journalist, Con Houlihan called place-names 'a people's poetry' coined by primal poets.

By the time our tour is over it has turned cold and the fog has changed to a wetting drizzle. I take a quick look around the Visitors' Centre. Lovely and all as its architecture is, I find it an anticlimax after having looked at the real thing, the stones that were placed there by the hands of people who lived 3,500 years before Christ.

From Glenurla I drive westwards by the Wild Atlantic Way to the Mullet Peninsula. I'm on my way to see where they once traded in the colour purple, the colour of power, Inishkea north island, on the west side of the Mullet headland. I just want a glance at it, to recall its past. Admittedly, it doesn't trace its history anything like as far back as the Céide Fields, but far enough to stir up that sense of reminiscence of a long lost time.

From around 500 to 700 AD, Inishkea north supplied the purple pigment, extracted from the gland of dog whelk, that dyed the robes of none other than the Byzantine emperors. The islands of Inishkea were serious enough commercial centres to be shown on early European sea charts.

Driving along by the red-belled fuschia and orange montbretia that emblazon the roadsides, plants that thrive on the tang of the ocean, the poem by W B Yeats, 'Sailing to Byzantium' seems just right. It leaps over the great distance between this remote spot and the Golden Horn of Turkey, the land of ancient art and emperors.

Yeats fancied that by setting off on a voyage to Byzantium, he would dispel the curse of old age, and it would transport him to a kind of *Tír na* nÓg, The Land of Youth.

And therefore I have sailed the seas and come
To the holy city of Byzantium.

If only it were that simple. And it's all the easier nowadays than in Yeats' time, with cheap airline tickets and easy jetting. Faith has its limits though, and I'm satisfied to let the enchanted tailwind of his words speed me on as I head westwards.

Mullet's limb of land is bare and lovely. Exposed on all sides, few trees can bear up to the Atlantic winds. But that gives its grasses a greener effect. I must make sure I'm looking at the correct island, The man who answers the door of the house I enquire in knows it well. His grandmother came from the island.

'The residents were resettled on the mainland in 1927 and there's no one living there now, nothing except holiday homes. At low tide you can walk across the causeway, but no chance of that now with the tide in,' he says.

I'm not interested. I wouldn't undertake such a trek unless I looked carefully into the tidal knowledge of whoever was guiding me. I don't fancy meeting my end in an unexpected current. I'm happy for the moment to gaze across at this remote spot that dyed the fabric of authority.

I have to rush to the car to avoid the shower that has spoiled my plan to stay a while on the peninsula. You always have to be ready to take cover. The annual rainfall here is over 1.17m (46 inches). As I drive back inland the changing vegetation is noticeable, going from barren to sparse. The branches of the trees nearest the coast are windswept, like women whose hair is blown upwards from the nape of the neck. Further from the sea with better weather a tree can keep coiffured and well proportioned. The sun is shining again now, lighting up the subtle shadings of the curves of the uplands. I'm on my way to the little village of Straide.

ELEVEN

THE MAKING OF A REVOLUTIONARY

The name Mayo means 'land of the oak' and around here you get a sense of this deep rootedness. As I turn a corner on my way to Straide, Mount Nephin springs into view. I've never been so close to it before. I can see its roots, cuts and rough foliage. My blue vision of youth is turning to the yellowy-brown moorland colour of reality, breaking the spell of innocence.

For a minute I look at the landscape with rosy thoughts of a time gone by, the kind people indulge in when they don't have the hardship of trying to work the land and make it fertile. If the toilers of old could hear me now, they would smile at my soft urban fantasy, that I should envy them their savage existence.

Mayo was a county of large estates and absentee landlords, the county which suffered most (apart from Roscommon) during the decade of the Great Famine 1841-51. In 1871 most of the houses were one-roomed cabins. Nearly half of Mayo was under water, consisting of bog and mountain.

You had to be cute to survive here, to fight the landlords' hold. It was a Mayo man, who spoke with a Lancashire accent, who spearheaded the land agitation that would break down this hopelessly unequal system. His name was Michael Davitt and the land movement that he put his weight behind culminated in the Land League in 1879 (a moral force movement, according to its constitution, to settle the Irish land question). I'm heading for the museum in his honour.

I stop at a shop that has a full frontal view of Mount Nephin. As the man inside the counter reaches for the bottle of water I'm about to buy, he tells me how breathtaking the view is from the summit.

'On a clear day you can see Sligo Bay, Clew Bay, Galway Bay' With elbows on the counter, all set for a chat he's interrupted by another customer with a long list. Pity.

I approach Pontoon Bridge by Glen Nephin and squeeze across between the two lakes, Lough Conn and Lough Cullin, and into the little town of Foxford. Foxford's signature industry was the woollen mills, set up to alleviate poverty in 1892.

Nothing but Foxford blankets and rugs ever graced our beds when I was growing up. Today the thought of them feels warm, with comforting memories from the blanket bog of the Céide fields to the bedtime stories of childhood.

Now it's south to Michael Davitt's native village of Straide where I want to follow the path of this revolutionary. The seventeen kilometres of the tóchar is still on my mind when I arrive in the little church where Michael was baptised. It's now a museum and houses his memorabilia. My walk was a mere amble compared to what the Davitt family had to endure after they were evicted from their land. They just spent one hour in the workhouse in Swinford, because males over three years old had to be separated from their mother, and Catherine Davitt wouldn't part with young Michael. And so they trudged it out to Dublin.

Though not yet five, Michael had a clear memory of their house being pulled down and burned by the landlord's agent, the thatch catching fire and the furniture being flung out on to the road. Burning was a routine part of an eviction but to watch your home, your memories, dreams and stories, scatter in flames must have been recruiter-in-chief of a rebel. In his new home in Haslington near Manchester in Lancashire, Davitt, once he was old enough, joined the revolutionary Fenian movement (a body intent on freeing Ireland by revolution, led by thinkers, poets and scholars).

His family home in Straide had once been a 'visiting house', a place where neighbours gathered after a day's work. Many is the good story that was told and song that was sung around the hearth. Michael Davitt's father, Martin, had a good collection of Irish myths and legends. Stories of more recent events were recounted too, of Daniel O'Connell, or of that big day on August 22, 1798 when three French warships under General Jean-Joseph Humbert sailed into Kilalla, twenty-three miles (37 kilometres) from Straide. After the 1840s another layer got added to his stock of tales, those of famine, hunger and eviction.

The Davitt home was a place of learning too. Martin Davitt was a hedge-school teacher. He used to read for the illiterate and write their letters. And he continued that in his new home in Haslington.

The guide is local. Even without Davitt's great story to tell, he's enthralled by this place in the shadow of Mount Nephin. He shows me the graveyard on the slope of the hill where Davitt is buried with his grandparents. Their bodies lie alongside an old Franciscan-Dominican ruins. But the most gripping moment is when he points out where the family home once stood.

'There's the spot, on the slope of that hill.'

So much history rose from that plot of land. It's just a few fields from where we're standing. And today it's catching the sun in its curve, showing not a stone nor a piece of mud of its bygone homestead, nor a sign of its hardship.

'There's no doubt Davitt's parents, Martin and Catherine,

would have liked to be buried here in this graveyard too within sight of their own home and facing Mount Nephin. But they never got that chance to come back.'

'Would you like tea or coffee while you're watching the video?' the woman at the desk offers. The hospitality of the staff here reminds me of the welcoming nature of the Davitt visiting house.

After the film I take a look around at Davitt's personal things – his cigarette case, his two rosary beads. They're both special. One, painted cream, was presented by Pope Leo Xlll and attached at the end is a medal of that pope with the inscribed words, *Leo Xlll, Pont Massimo, Roma*. The paint is peeling off a little – from use maybe. The brown Rosary beads is wooden. Davitt brought this one from the Holy Land in 1885.

I read his letters. I value letters all the more these days because I know when the famous people of our era will be celebrated the delete button, the killer of modern mail will have reaped its sad harvest. Unless they keep the clouds of correspondence that lie in storage or the miles of footage that recall every move we make, no one will know what we were like. I'm sure no one will care what most of us were like but the odd few from every century have had lives worth looking into.

As a member of the Fenian movement Davitt was given the task of organising arms and for his trouble he got landed in prison in 1870. Englishmen at the time had a right to bear arms, but not Irishmen. On the year of his release from prison, famine struck – three bad harvests in a row came to a head in 1879.

With one side of my family from Mayo and the other from Galway, it's unlikely that some relation or other of mine wasn't among the crowd of 8,000 to 10,000 that turned up in Irishtown on the Mayo-Galway border on Sunday April 20, 1879, the coldest and wettest year on record. But I'll never know. James Daly, from nearby Castlebar, organised this meeting and it was to have a mighty future. It led to the founding of the powerful Land League, the biggest mass movement in Irish history, 'ranking among the most effective of rural agitation in nineteenth century Europe,' according to the historian J J Lee.

They came from miles, on horseback, in carts, on foot with a slamming slogan: 'The Land for the People'. This was something that had been already gained, peacefully in Prussia and, in France, violently.

The crowd in Irishtown was comparable to Daniel O'Connell's monster meetings for Catholic Emancipation. Land and religion, the two mighty grievances of Irish history, flowed together because the natives had been barred from both.

As Davitt addressed gatherings around the country, his own suffering was in full view. He had lost an arm in the buccaneering capitalism of the industrial revolution. That only supplied another romantic edge to his handsome looks.

Industrial accidents weren't unusual. Michael had three maimed friends on the street in Haslington where he lived, the casualties of poor working conditions. At seventeen it was his turn when one day he was ordered to replace an absentee machine minder in the cotton mill where he worked. He pointed out that he wasn't tall enough but the supervisor insisted. The use of physical force wasn't an unusual part of that insistence. Before Michael was half an hour into the job he had to remove an obstruction which meant stretching across the machine. He lost his balance and his arm got mangled and had to be amputated. The accident turned him to reading and education. It also made him sensitive to the suffering of others.

Some might call Davitt Mayo's Che Guevara. His red-hot socialism and interest in nationalisation of the land was too much for the conservative Irish farmer. But he had Gandhian instincts too, especially as he got older.

'A recent visitor we welcomed here to the museum was Gandhi's grandson,' the guide tells me. 'When Gandhi was studying law in

London in the 1880s and 1890s, he liked to go to the House of Commons and listen to the speakers. It was on one of those trips that he met Davitt (a member of the House) and they became friends.'

There's a lot here in the museum, between writings and memorabilia that recall the strident times of the 1870s and eighties. With MP Charles Stewart Parnell accepting Davitt's invitation to become President of the Land League, a daring energy swept the country. To nationalise the land might have been Davitt's ultimate aim but resisting evictions, not doffing the cap to the landlord, boycotting (ostracising someone who had bought land from which a tenant was evicted) would do for now. Behind Davitt and Parnell was the tailwind of the changing times and a growing awareness of injustice. Public opinion was moving apace and the ethics of the land system were being questioned. Into this stepped Davitt, an organiser with a grim memory and Parnell, a landlord who opposed the landlord system.

Parnell was three months younger than Davitt. Both were born in 1846, during the famine, one into a mud cabin at the mercy of the potato failure, the other into a medium sized mansion. In those heady days Parnell often dropped in to Davitt's lodgings in 83 Amiens Street, Dublin for a chat. The banter wasn't too unlike in the Davitt visiting house in Straide before the family eviction. All reserve was dropped as former Fenians and parliamentarians chatted and told yarns at their ease.

A lot of landlords – especially the ones who had looked out for their tenants – disliked the stridency of the Land League. Lady Gregory of Coole Park was one who didn't think much of Davitt's tactics or Parnell's for that matter. A local Mayo landlord, Lord Oranmore and Browne, thought the Irishtown meeting and the agitation that followed was communist in nature.

We don't know if Davitt ever read Marx's *Communist Manifesto* (though nationalising the land was Marxist and hopelessly misread the mind of the Irish tenant farmer). While in prison Davitt did read the work of John Stuart Mill. Mill favoured peasant proprietorship, and his writings became the bible of Irish land reformers. It must have been quite a thing for Davitt to get his hands on Mill's writings because the prison reading list was not so challenging: *Grandmother Betty, Naughty Fanny, Good Works, Leisure Hours, Sunday at Home.* These were unlikely to satisfy a man who we know liked Shakespeare, Coleridge, Wordsworth and the study of European languages.

I have another look around the museum as the guide tells me the story of the buzz that overcame the country during those few potent years with the Davitt-Parnell duo providing one rare moment in Irish history, when the forces of revolution and parliamentary democracy combined. It was enough to shift the tectonic plates of colonial history.

Just when the movement was at its peak, just when Parnell and Davitt together were giving peasants the leadership they so pitifully lacked during the Great Famine, the British government swooped. Davitt, considered too dangerous to be allowed to frolic around unchained, was picked up crossing Dublin's O'Connell Bridge one Thursday afternoon in February 1881. He was brought by train from Holyhead to London. And here's a good one – he was put in a first class compartment, escorted by a pilot engine, usually reserved for Queen Victoria. It must have amused him.

By October Parnell was clapped in prison as well. The agreement he came to with the British government in 1881, the Kilmainham Treaty brought an end to the most potent days of the land movement – 1879 to 1881. But it was the Land League that prompted the British government to reset Irish land policy and pass a series of reforming acts.

Before I drive home I record the mileage. From Straide to Dublin is 139 miles (223 kilometres), a long car drive, let alone on foot.

TWELVE

UMBILICUS HIBERNIA

Today I'm in Westmeath to see Uisneach Hill, the ancient heart of Ireland. The tour will begin at 12.30. While I'm waiting at the foot of the slope I think of how wonderfully lucky Ireland is to have been a latecomer to industry. It means that we have ancient royal showpieces like the one I'm about to climb, that would otherwise have been flattened under the bulldozers of progress. These mounds are still in the same form since antiquity, they hold within them history, pre-history, and tales of the past that dissolve into myth.

Uisneach is located on the Mullingar-Athlone road, in deep countryside. No Visitors' Centre, no elaborate signs announce it. An oasis of rural life dense with growth, it's tucked away from the roar of the highway.

From where I'm parked among the foothills, I can see the cows grazing and swishing their tails as they've always done, even going back to the days when they were used as a medium of exchange. This is the era I'm about to step into, the time when the Hill of Uisneach was the most significant of royal sites, placed in the same league as Tara's Iron-age mound or Emain Macha.

Whatever criticism you make of today's ways of doing business and there's no shortage to choose from – loyalty cards, valued-customer cards, credit cards, debit cards – you can't fault it for making commercial exchange a whole lot easier than using a cow as a currency.

I'm to link up with the guide, Marty Mulligan, in the car park. Other people who look like they've come for the tour begin to converge. Then Marty arrives, breezy and full of enthusiasm, and the crowd makes its way towards him.

'I grew up near here,' he tells us. 'First I didn't know Uisneach's significance, then as I got to know more, I started to cherish the place.'

Zeal is catching, not just Marty's but others in the group who have been here several times. Walking uphill towards the 2.5 square kilometres of plateau at the top, we're all sparking with the same fervour. Because Uisneach is part of a working farm, you can't turn up unannounced. Cattle have to be moved first into adjoining fields to let walkers go by.

'It's unusual to find this kind of high ground in the centre of the flat Irish midlands,' Marty tells us, as we follow uphill. He shows us the barrows (ancient burial places topped by a mound), cairns (mound of stones), wells, circular enclosures, a ring fort. Then there's the well-built and ventilated souterrain (this word comes from the French *sous terrain,* meaning under ground) invisible from the landscape and resistant to the changing temperature over ground. This was where pre-historic people stored food and took shelter from the enemy. Further uphill is the lake.

'All royal sites had lakes and if they didn't have a natural one, they built it.' Marty explains. 'The lake here Lough Lugh is on the hilltop. It's called after the Sun God, Lugh, and said to be the place where his mortal life ended. Ring forts predate the pyramids of Egypt. Some of them have run into trouble with the plans of road constructors.' When he says 'if you damage a ring fort you do so at your peril,' there's nodding agreement all around. I thought I was well versed in those things, but I'm nowhere as fluent as the others in the group. The conversation about energies is second nature to them, and they discuss Chinese feng shui (arranging living space so that the vitality flows to best benefit the dwellers) and the chakras (energy points) of the earth with the same ease as you would talk about the weather. They're all agreed about what luck Ireland has in having so many royal sites, rings forts, cairns and the like.

Marty says: 'I don't like to think of Uisneach as a royal site, because long before it was royal, I believe, it was sacred. The energy that rises off the place is like a giant battery – a living thing. The energies are very active at certain times of the year and the cattle know all about it. They place themselves in the line where they can best catch its flow.'

As we reach the summit he shows us the hawthorn, a tree native to Ireland. It was considered sacred, and its red berries fire up the place in autumn, in a scene that would rival the Neon world.

'Irish bonsai, I like to call it,' he says.

And then to a subject that enlivens him, the real fires for the feast of Bealtaine (the month of May) when the hilltops were once set ablaze, to summon up the earth's energies. Along with the druidical ceremonies, they coaxed the soil to warmth for the growing season.

'As youngsters we used to come here in Bealtaine and light a fire. We didn't know why then.' Now he knows all about why, and he talks about what a sight it must have been when all the fires were lit. 'You could nearly have seen the whole country as one hill after another went ablaze. And it's more or less the same view that the ancients laid their eyes on that we see today.'

Without fires at all the view from the Hill of Uisneach is astonishing. It's the perfect day to see virtually the whole country and some of the people who are familiar with the place, point out as far as the Burren in Clare, Galway and Sligo in the west, Tyrone to the north, Dublin and Wicklow mountains to the east and nearby Longford.

A man in the group says he saw on an ancient map that this spot connects with Croagh Patrick in County Mayo, by the prehistoric timber trackway found under the bog in Corlea, County Longford.

We turn our attention to the sacred ash tree, the Branching Tree of Uisneach, the Tree of Enchantment. Its roots are said to reach down to the underworld. Marty says the ash tree has long links with Uisneach. We can't get to it today because the cattle are fenced in there.

Just when I thought this was the climax of the tour, we're brought downhill to the real centre of Uisneach, and indeed the centre of Ireland: the great limestone rock: *Ail na Mireann* – the Stone of the Divisions.

'People call it the Cat Stone because they say it looks like a sitting cat,' says Marty. 'But to give you the names of this omphalos stone in all languages: Umbilicus Hibernia, the navel of Ireland. From the air they say it looks like a protruding navel and it's thought to have marked out the meeting of the five provinces: Leinster, Ulster, Munster, Connacht and Meath. Meath (which means middle) was the hub, the royal province where the High King dwelt, but it no longer exists as a province. Ireland's provinces have been cut back to four.'

One of the men in the group lists off eleven other omphalos stones in the world, so *Ail na Mireann* is in rare company. He says them so quickly I only catch Delphi, Ayres Rock, Jerusalem in the Church of the Holy Sepulchre.

'Legend has it that the stones at Stonehenge were taken from here in Uisneach, that King Arthur sent 15,000 men to Ireland to raise stones,' says Marty.

Those were the days when men were cheap and stones were precious.

He points to the quartz mound that rests on the hilltop plateau which has curative powers if you go around it seven times. We can't do the remedial rounds because the cattle are there. Pity, I was all set to test its reputation on my ample ailments. Insightful and all as the cattle are said to be, I don't notice them circling it.

As the two hour tour extends into four, the group, total strangers in the begining, gel into the glow of the day. There's a couple from Canada, an Irish couple, a man who sounds as if this is his umpteenth visit here, an Englishman and two women who have come separately.

When we part it feels like a farewell, fleeting friends for a time channelled in a common quest. Some pass around their business cards before we part, perhaps so as not to make it such a final goodbye.

'Do you mind if we hug you?' asks one of them And we all agree to that. We would be fine killjoys to refuse. But who could predict today that we would later be forced into following the Covid rules of turning down such a proposal?

Not to lose the momentum of royal mounds, two days later I'm on my way to Rathcroghan in County Roscommon, the seat of the mythical warrior Queen Medb.

I stop for lunch in Tarmonbarry, a crossing on the Shannon which features in the *Táin Bó Cuailgne* (The Cattle Raid of Cooley). I have come into Keenan's restaurant by the wrong door and a staff member unlocks it for me. He's very civil and assures me that my trying to break in through the bolted door is no trouble at all.

From the grey photo hanging on the pillar, which shows the original house before it was extended in all directions, I can see that Keenans has a long business history. They employed a large staff and in the picture they were all lined up outside the door for the snapshot in the full-length skirts worn at the time. It looks as if it dates from a time when the camera was a new gadget.

An air of the local abounds. Customers speak across tables,

addressing one another by first names. A young mother and daughter come in, and a grey-haired woman who is having tea and scones asks them how they had got on last Sunday. It's all a very lovely mingling of age groups, so typical of the country.

A man who has arrived after me is served before me. I suppose he's a regular, that's the downside of the local. It makes me uptight but I try not to get too tense about it. There are only a few minutes in it and those distresses over small things make the body lie in wait, taking its time to deliver its blow with a heart attack later on when you've long forgotton that day in Tarmonbarry when a customer was served two full minutes before you. Lunch is good, and the employees are friendly.

Rathcroghan, the royal site of Connacht, is in County Roscommon, about twenty-five miles west of the Tarmonbarry crossing of the Shannon. So enthusiastic is the guide about the mounds and myths of this piece of ancient territory, that before long the rest of us are sparking with his enthusiasm. His name is Eamon and he's from Rathcroghan Visitor Centre, in Tulsk, County Roscommon.

'I'm a local,' he says. 'I picked up a lot of the information about this place from my parents and my grandmother. This ancient territory is the spot where it all began, the tale of the *Táin Bó Cuailgne* (The Cattle Raid of Cooley).'

The *Táin* is sometimes called the Irish Iliad. It dates from pre-Christian Ireland, around the first century. Discovered in a few medieval manuscripts, it tells of a battle for a prized bull that would make the possessions of Queen Medh of Connacht equal to those of her husband's Ailill.

The tour of this ancient seat of power officially begins in the car park, but it doesn't look a worthy place to start such a mythical journey as the *Táin*. So Eamon brings us to the top of Rathcroghan mound.

'I reckon,' he says, 'this is where the pillow talk between Medb and her husband, Ailill, first took place, that led to the *Táin*. Ailill had become King of Connacht because of his marriage to this goddess queen. The row began when Ailill said to his wife that she was lucky to be married to him.'

Goddess she might be (some say she was the goddess of the land and of sovereignty brought to life) but she did what any of us would do if our men were such gits as to say that to us, assuming we had the resources. They compared ancestry, retainers, retinues, possessions, pedigrees and found they were equal in all things but one – Ailill's bull was superior. So, the queen set about finding a matching bull and such a beast was located in Ulster, the brown bull of Cooley. But she and her Connacht armies came up against a surprising opponent, the Irish mythological demigod of the Ulster cycle of tales, the incarnation of the Irish god, Lugh, young Cúchulainn and the boys of the Red Branch Knights of Ulster.

From atop the mound Eamon points out *Rath na dTarbh* (the mound of the bulls) where *Bealtaine* (May) was celebrated. He explains the ritual.

'This was where everyone came with a cow and a sod of turf which they threw into the fire. The cows were bled until the mound ran red. Back then cows were the value of your wealth, cows and slave girls were the units of currency. So, you could call this the reserve bank of the site. This archaeological site contains nearly a hundred monuments, covering about four square miles. Only a few of these are reachable because most are on private land. I'd love to see an over-ground walkway that would lead from site to site, because a ground view doesn't do them justice at all. From the air the collection of rings, burial mounds, enclosures, barrows and pillar stones are some sight.'

Some of these mounds are natural because this is a glacial region rich in limestone. Others are real burial places.

'I like to think of the mounds as the feminine side of the site, a version of the Chinese yin,' he says. 'And the pillar stones represent the masculine, the yang, giving the site balance. The top of the mound was once the site of the great circular timber structure, the royal home of Queen Medb. From the summit it would be hard to find a better place from which to spot an approaching enemy.'

Layers of fields spread out into infinity, getting smaller as they ebb further away from us, then crunching together into a single line. The only intrusions on the horizon's edge are the blue slopes of *Sliabh Bán* (White Mountain) and the Curlew Mountains of Sligo.

Eamon asks us to cast our minds backwards.

'Imagine the summit lit up with fires on the occasion of, say, the inauguration of a king. It was a way for so many people to witness the event.'

These people would have nothing to learn from today's hyper-connected world. Then he hurries us along to see what is for him the highlight of the visit – *Ownagat* (the Cave of the Cats), a cave and souterrain. His excitement about this, I have to disclose, is not catching. I suspect it's going to be scary when I'm told the space can't facilitate our small bags. They're better left outside. With some unease I throw mine on the grass. This is trusting country, nothing but farm animals in sight and they don't look a bit interested in chewing a bag.

Eamon hands me a torch and tells me to follow him. It involves crouching into the entrance under a hawthorn tree, the legendary entrance to the otherworld. To get in you have to go down on hunkers, place one hand on the low limestone lintel, the torch in the other, and edge forward. I'm not sure my zeal is up to it or that my body is fit for purpose.

'Once you're in it's plain sailing,' he says trying to encourage me out of my rigidity. Sure enough I can see he's standing, so the space evidently does get bigger. 'It's often said that Ownagat links up with the Kesh caves in Sligo,' he explains. I'll take their word for that. Or on second thoughts, to exit that way might be easier than going back the way I came in. Interesting and all as he tries to make it, the Druidic connection, the ogham lintel with the inscription: 'Fraoch, son of Medb', all I can think of is how I'm going to get out again without splitting my head in the process. I feel cold and claustrophic. I don't know how he manages to go on encouraging me.

'This is the birthplace of Hallowe'en,' he explains. (There are a few rival claims to the origin of this festival). 'Parents used to disguise their children in case the *púca* (an evil ghost that frightened us all until we grew out of believing in such threats) would take them. As children we were warned against going near this place.' He has clearly outgrown that advice.

People still worship here. You can see crystals placed where the stone forms a ledge inside the cave. They seem to enter this underworld to leave some object of ritual inside. Eamon offers to turn off the torches just to see the stream of light coming in from the entrance. I won't agree to that, however spectacular. My mind is elsewhere, recalling all the reports I've ever heard, of people getting trapped in caves where something moved that hadn't previously budged for millennia. It would be just my luck for some rock to decide to stir on my one adventurous outing. What would the neighbours say when they heard where I'd met my end?

I'm glad to pull myself out under the lintel and see daylight again. I'm full of the grime of the underworld. I clean my hands on the grass. That completes my journey to the home of the *púca*.

'What's it like?' asks the next person in the queue. I don't like to spoil it for him with my prejudiced view. 'It was ...different,' I say.

From now on my trips are going to be a whole lot more staid, no high-risk capers. Corlea trackway is the next stop on my list.

THIRTEEN

CORLEA

Kathleen, a former colleague, was born about three kilometres from Corlea trackway, near Keenagh in Longford. Today we're to meet her brother who is going to show us the local treasure. As we get nearer to her home place, she recalls her happy days growing up here.

'Both my mother's and father's families come from a long line of Longford people. My mother inherited the farm where we grew up between Keenagh and Ballymahon and her sister, my Aunt Catherine, lived with us. My father came from Newtown Cashel, towards the west of the county.'

A waterway influences the locality it runs through, even a manmade one. Kathleen's home was located along the banks of the Royal Canal, about twenty kilometres from where it disgorges into the River Shannon.

'The canal went through our land, dividing the farm in two,' she says. 'We used to swim in the canal and I remember sports days along its banks. One competition was the greasy pole where a competitor had to walk across a well-oiled pole. You had to be a good swimmer because your chances of slipping into the water were high.'

Kathleen's mother and aunt were both great singers, both devout women.

'Like a lot of that generation, prayer was a big part of life – my mother had devotion to Saint Anthony and my aunt to Saint Anne de Beaupré. Magazines used to come to our house, *The Annals of Saint Anne*, from Canada. Later, when I lived in Montréal, I made a special trip to Quebec to visit the church of Saint Anne de Beaupré.'

This small act of satisfying a kind of homesickness, transferred the faith and fields of Longford to Canada.

Today, we're going to be recalling an era well before saints or indeed Christianity – Corlea's Iron Age trackway or *togher* (causeway). Growing up, as she occasionally passed on her bike by this townland which was as unknown as the next back then, Kathleen was unaware of the treasure that lay hidden beneath the local home-ground. And so was everyone else at the time. Not until the nineteen eighties was the big find made – a trackway of large oak planks, the largest of its kind uncovered in Europe. In 1984 when turf-cutters accidently hit off it, they caused an archaeological stir.

Ahead of us, as we approach Ballymahon, *Slieve Bán* (White Mountain) is rising out into view. Nothing else interrupts our view to the horizon's edge. Longford is part of the flat midlands of Ireland.

Kathleen directs me towards a turn right after Ballymahon village which brings us over a hunched bridge, one of those sharp hills from whose summit you lose sight of the road beneath you for an instant. When I say how steep it is, she looks at me as if she never noticed that before. That's the thing about places you know from the ground level of childhood, their traits grow on you at such a living pace that you rarely stop to define them.

A few metres from the bridge is another turn right leading to the house where her brother and sister-in-law live. Its neat charm by an avenue lined with lime trees and timber fencing is like a scene from a story book. Even coming in by the back door of the house evokes a feeling of carefree youth. No ringing of bells, just a call to announce we're here. Kathleen's sister-in-law appears and leads us to the dining room where the table is set with patterned china.

Her brother, Jimmy, is waiting for us. Scones waft from the oven. Steaming tea is poured. We linger in the warmth. I laze in the drone of the crossing words, of stories, people and places lullingly unfamiliar – village events, houses built and sold, marriages, deaths. And when their son joins the table, more tea is poured, more scones, more chat.

We laugh as Kathleen recalls the things they got up to as children. That day when she went to her friend's house after school and left her mother and aunt worrying about her, she had an excuse good and ready.

'I told them that we sat by the canal and fell asleep and when we woke up we realised how late it was.' Or the day at Maths class when she got scolded for saying she knew a much easier way to do the sum that the teacher had illustrated on the blackboard. 'That would cause few waves in today's classroom,' she reckons.

Jimmy reminds us that it's time to go and the noisy dragging of chairs along the floor tiles replaces the banter.

Corlea is about three kilometres from the house by the bog of Ringdong where for generations the family has harvested turf. Farms close to bogs have turbary rights, historically granted by the landlord of the estate, to cut turf and remove it for fuel. Jimmy asks me to stop to take a look at where their parcel of bog is located. It's at the end of an access-way, and though all I can see is a pile of neatly-stacked turf, for an instant I feel I'm getting into the soul of Longford. The relationship with the bog in Ireland is deep in the primal memory. It has provided the heat of the hearth for generations.

The measured precision of turf-cutting, like roof thatching, is where craft meets art. With modern house construction and machinery both are in less demand now, but the hand-cutting of turf lasted longer in Ireland than elsewhere where heavy machinery was used. The result is that we now have a great spread of moorland. Today, using turf as fuel has reached its limit for health and environmental reasons but the bog is worth more than any forest for storing the earth's carbon.

The road is narrow. This is September, bringing-home-the-turf time of the year and the trailers are brimming with dark-brown peat. They have local knowledge and their great wheels have a better chance than mine of not sinking into the soft verges. Mine were made in Japan, following a formula that I bet never thought of a bog road.

We emerge at an intersection where the dome of the Visitor's Centre of Corlea Trackway rises into view. It looks as important now as it did when they laid this causeway in the Iron Age. The intriguing thing about the trackway is the absolute precision with which we know when these timbers were placed – between Autumn 148BC and Spring 147BC. Felling dates and tree ring analysts can be this accurate because they know that during that winter, two-hundred oaks were cut down to make a track across Ringdong bog to the drumlin island of Derryadd. The exactitude of such a remote event brings a quiver of time-elopement, pulls it from the depths of centuries of overgrowth, into the modern age, like a leakage of clues as to what our ancestors were up to.

Our guide is Noel Carberry. He's a local. Jimmy and he exchange a few neighbourly words before he begins the tour. Noel is casual about his great knowledge of this era, making it accessible even to those of us who aren't so clear on the dividing lines between the ages, Iron, Bronze, Stone or whatever. He knows how to dole out the information in installments, giving us a layman's guide, then when someone asks a more in-depth question, showing his great acquaintance with the era.

'Iron Age man lived in circular houses of wattle and daub, roofed with thatch. We know this from post-hole voids. We're familiar with their great skills from various hoards found, torcs and other fine artwork that you can see in the National Museum in Dublin,' he explains.

He directs us to the drawings of Iron Age man on the wall. For all you hear about not knowing what these people looked like, I think the men and women in the pictures look like any of us on the tour.

'You'll notice that some are dressed colourfully, in bright reds, this was a sign of wealth because dye was expensive. Another reason for our knowledge of Iron Age man is that we have two examples: Old Croghan man and Clonycavan man, dating from the Iron Age. Both were dug out of the bog preserved because the bog's chemical composition provides a natural mummification.'

These two men look no different from people of our own generation, even to the man bun that Clonycavan man was wearing when he was ritually killed and buried in the bog. They were vain back then too.

'The ingredients for his hair-gel came from either southern France or Spain. So overseas trade is no more a modern invention than a man bun,' says Noel.

I think it was worthy that it was the *sleán*, (turf-spade) of the turf-cutters that hit the stones of the Céide Fields in Mayo and the hard timber of the Corlea Trackway because turf-cutting has such a proud tradition in Ireland. In the soft bed of unripened peat something as hard as wood or stone raised immediate questions. The turf-cutters knew they were striking something that wasn't in its natural home.

Archaeologist and Celtic scholar, Barry Raftery was brought in to interpret the Corlea discovery. Noel brings us to the theatre where we watch a film on the painstaking work that was done when Raftery and his team meticulously unearthed the ancient oak planks, the ancient trackway. Finds like this have been made in Britain, Germany and Holland but none as big or with such heavy timber as this one.

An Australian woman in the group has a question for Noel when we emerge from the film: 'Why were they using a didgeridoo in the accompanying film score?'.

'It's not a didgeridoo, though it has a similar sound. It's an instrument found in *Loughnashade* (lake of the jewels) near the royal site of Emain Macha called the *trumpa créda*. It turned up in 1798 along with other finds and it's kept in the Treasury of the National Museum in Dublin. The instrument they used for the film was a reconstructed version of this ancient *trumpa créda* and it was played by Simon O'Dwyer, an explorer of ancient musical instruments.'

With the knowledge the film has given us, we go to see the result of the careful excavation. And there it is, an eighteen-metre stretch of the preserved oak planks, on the exact axis of the original trackway.

Noel explains: 'Because it's no longer in the natural preservation of the bog, it has to be kept at a careful temperature in suitable humidity so that no decay can touch it. Work has been carried out in the surrounding bog to ensure that it stays wet enough to preserve the remaining trackway that still lies conserved underneath the wetlands.'

To be immersed in such a distant time is enough to make you feel you've drunk a magic portion. It dates to before Jesus was born, the time of Tara's high kings, of Queen Medb, of the Celtic centre of power in Emain Macha, of Cúchulainn and the Red Branch Knights, of a time when history melts into myth.

Iron Age people didn't write, and the stories we have of the Celts are tales full of epics, feuds, honour and splendour. They were taken down from story-tellers long after the events, by the scribes in the monasteries. We know this because few others could write.

'Christianity is a religion of the book, so writing was a huge part of the monastic life,' says Noel. And when an American man in the group says, 'Who knows what spin they put on these tales? I'm sure they gave them a twist that brought out the superiority of Christianity over the pagan Celts,' there's nodding agreement around the group.

In the specially air-conditioned room of the trackway Noel prompts us into a bit of speculation: 'To what end, this road to God-knows-where?' And the guessing begins. 'Was it laid for a military expedition, a cattle road perhaps, or was it meant for horses to travel on, or for wheeled vehicles?'

We enjoy a relaxed few moments of your-guess-is-as-good-as-mine discussion about the trackway. Most agree that the surface is too uneven for horses, and too noisy. That leads someone to propose that there may have been a layer of peat over it to quieten it down. We know that this piece of trackway lines up with the royal sites of Uisneach and Rathcroghan. That gives us some bearing in this blind debate.

'The trackway dates from a time of great tribal activity,' says Noel. 'Bogs were natural divisions between tribes and later Christianity kept these boundary lines. These still mark out Christian parishes and dioceses.'

Jimmy, Kathleen and I go for a stroll on the board walk. This was especially constructed to view the artificial pools. They were created to make sure the water table is kept at a level in which the bog can hold on to its preserving power. A fresh breeze whispers over the boglands of County Longford. The pink-purple heather and the swaying bog cotton go off into the distance. Looking into the remoteness gives you a sense of floating into the mystery of the moorland. Its beauty is subtle, low key. It makes no drama about itself.

I want to stretch the moment, elongate it, all the way to the horizon. I glimpse into the edge of the universe to look for a hill but I can find none. A moving car glistens on a distant road and as we watch it, Jimmy says it's Keenagh Road. You need homegrown knowledge to know that, and it weaves into the scene a sweet sense of the local.

'You'll breathe no finer air than that of the moorland and a beach tan can't compare with the colour you get in a bog,' Kathleen says. 'And there's no better way for working up an appetite than the bog air.' But I think the appetite she has in mind involves rolling up the sleeves and doing a bit of work, not sauntering around like we are.

We make the return journey on a more main road, by the village of Keenagh. I'm relieved that I'm not going to be squeezed off the narrower road which took us here.

When we get to the house, dinner is in the air and we sit and eat it with relish. Afterwards we go to the old house where the family grew up. It's reconstructed now but it still holds on to its old charm. Kathleen and Jimmy point out the surrounding farm. They laugh as they recall what they called some of the fields – 'the convent', 'the lodge'. The names have a musicality about them and that fits well with this family of singers and accordion players. (Later when I talk to local historian, Paddy Egan, he confirms that these names have a sound historical foundation. 'There was a religious house in the "convent" field. The ruins are still there though it wasn't a nunnery as the name would suggest. It housed an order of Dominican priests who set up there after they had been run out of Longford town in the mid seventeenth century. "The Lodge" was a masonic lodge.')

We go back to Dublin by the slightly detoured route of Abbeyshrule, by the countryside of author, Oliver Goldsmith, the landscape he felt so homesick for when he was in London where he befriended some of the big names in literature.

In the picturesque village of Abbeyshrule we call on Kathleen's sister, Betty. She shows us around the village and the Royal Canal. This place has all the prettiness of a canal village and Betty is one of the volunteers who makes sure its beauty is maintained.

'You can cycle to Dublin from here on the towpath,' she tells us. I can think of nothing nicer to do than go on a bike along by the moored barges as they sway at their ease in the water. A group of girls are walking along by the bank and further up towards the end of the village teenagers in colourful life-jackets are getting a canoe ready to set sail.

Even though their commercial life was short-lived, canals transformed places they passed through. The horse-drawn barges dropped off goods and introduced industry to remote parts of the country during their heyday in the seventeenth century. The barges took emigrants on their return journey so they made leaving the countryside easier too.

In 1844 the Royal Canal was sold at a bargain price to The Midland and Great Western Railway. The rail company planned to fill it in. Mercifully, that didn't happen; they ran the rail track alongside it instead. The Royal Canal Amenity group is doing restoration work to reinstate the treasure days of the canals. They organise walks and cycles along the liner parkway.

The warmth of the day is enveloping me as we leave Abbeyshrule. Hospitality is an important part of Kathleen's family life and she keeps up the tradition in her home which is on the side of the Wicklow Way walking path. A few times strollers who have found themselves unsure of where they are, have sauntered in for directions. Some have been invited in, and one or two have even been given a bed for the night.

She tells me of two young Germans who once stumbled in when an unexpected fog descended on them. One of them was a music student and keen piano player.

'I never heard anyone make the piano sing like he did,' Kathleen muses. He fell into the right house. 'We played and sang that night into the early hours. And when they went back to Germany they wrote to me to say that evening was the highlight of their Irish holiday.'

'I'm not surprised,' I say. 'But maybe you shouldn't be so casual about letting people into your house.' She dismisses my caution with a wave of the hand. And, however sound my advice might be, I know at that moment I'm spoiling the mood of a dream world.

FOURTEEN

TULACH BEAGLAIGH

The mood of a dream world is still with me today as I drive by the gorse that's streaking down Donegal's mountains. It's more yellow than usual. Probably the cold start to the year made it hold back its petals and then release them in profusion. It is easing the hostility of the rugged terrain.

Beside me on the passenger seat lies the leaflet for the Tullagh Begley Walk (*Siúlóid Thulach Beaglaigh*) that Cathal gave me on Tóchar Day in Ballintubber. I'm bracing myself for the 'five hours of fairly challenging mountain walk following the old pilgrim burial route'.

It's Mayday, no day more marked out in the folk calendar than this, no date so lively in the fairy world or so full of superstitions and devilment, I mean genuine devilment, such as snatching away children or transforming yourself into an animal to take the milk from your neighbour's cow. Who could be bothered? But that belief once held weight, more in the dairy-farming south of Ireland. No worries for Donegal, this is mainly sheep country. Some of them are nimbly turning themselves at hazardous angles to nibble at a tuft of grass on the rocky high ground. They're mostly black-faced mountain sheep. Bleating lambs are looking for their mothers among rocks and curves.

The door of the Visitors' Centre in Falcarragh is open, though no one is around. I know I'm in the country – urban people would never leave a door unguarded like that.

When I see the crowd assembled alongside a bus, I realise that this, the twenty-fourth Tulach Beaglaigh mountain walk, is a big affair. The bus is already nearly full when I climb on. It's humming with chatter, in Irish and in English. The Irish language is hale and hearty here, spoken with a peninsular lilt. It feels like the Tower of Babel, but far from excluding anyone who doesn't understand, they change with ease from one language to another. The crowd is caught up in the fervour of a day out, like schoolchildren where lessons are suspended for a few hours.

The bus ride to Gweedore on the N56 coastal road takes about half an hour. At stops along the way other passengers pile in. A lot of them know one another and there's noisy recognition and laughter as each new person joins the crowd. A young man with a very full rucksack gets on, '*Bhfuil corp agat sa mhála?*' (Have you a body in the bag?) shouts some wag from the back seat.

Sometimes they complain in Donegal of being forgotten about because geography keeps them cut off, tucked up on the north-west corner, the sea to their north and west and the state of Northern Ireland to the east. Today I sense that exclusion is a mixed blessing, a chance to retain a distinctive culture. They speak Irish here with the same musicality as their mountains, a landscape of the mind as well as the terrain.

At our destination, where the walk is to begin, as we spill out of the bus, I spot Cathal. He's one of the organisers and he comes over to say hello to me.

We walk uphill. We're about to follow the footsteps of the burial party that took their dead across the mountain from the parish of

Gweedore to Tulach Beaglaigh – the most ancient burial site in this region and in bygone days, the only one within miles. Sixteen men used to rotate, in teams of four, to bear the remains. They must have been a whole lot fitter than I am. I find it testing to carry my rucksack which contains only a sandwich and a drink. They were at least spared the weight of a coffin because the bodies were not placed in anything so luxurious, but on a simple bier made of bog wood.

Inhaling the strong coconut perfume of the gorse keeps my mind off my weary limbs. Up here you're breathing the deepest mountain air. At times you get a gush of hope that the rising walkway is at an end, only to find that the path is concealing further steepness beyond the turn – like the twist of a sly snake.

Walkers come up alongside me and we exchange a few words. Some engage in longer chats, speaking as easily as if they're walking on the flat. I'm finding it challenging to answer them. I'm discovering depths in my lungs I never knew I had.

The leaders stop at intervals to give those falling behind a chance, but by the time we catch up, they hike off again. So the fittest, the very ones who need it least, get the longest rest.

Máire, one of the walkers, tells a few of us of a recent trip she made across the causeway to Inis Bó Finne, north of Falcarragh, when they got caught in an unexpected tide.

'It was very dangerous,' she laughs, enjoying the peril of it all.

I wonder if we're going to come up against anything so hazardous today. What have I signed myself up for? What kind of a crowd have I entrusted my life with?

We trudge on. A woman in the crowd says Rescue Remedy is good for these kinds of trials. I'll bet the bearers of old had no Rescue Remedy to lessen their pain.

Snippets of conversation show other signs of improved wealth. Some walkers say they have second homes in Donegal. The proof is all around us. In parts of this county, where the landscape slides along glens and hills, they're so well stocked with holiday housing that it looks as if it's suffering from an outbreak of measles. But it's a less painful disorder, the scar of affluence.

Soon we're on the summit, the site of the *Trí Leachta,* (three cairns) where *cúpla focal* (a few words) are called for. Cathal gives us some historic bearings.

'This is where the funeral parties rested and changed teams. Another resting point is *Seacht Leachta* (seven cairns) but we're not going to go this route today because it's a little more difficult.'

It's a relief to hear that. I'm not up for maximising my hardship.

The layers of loaded light from the summit make every step of the gasping and wheezing worth it. Lakes, sea, islands, mountains and streams are folding and flowing beneath us. They seem to be saying – 'You have to toil to get to feast your eyes on us.'

Away in the distance stretches Tory island and the smaller islands of Inis Beag, Oileán Dúiche and Inis Bó Finne (the latter is too distant to catch a glimpse of its hazardous causeway). It was on Tory that Donegal's loved saint, Colmcille, founded one of his early Christian churches when he was wresting the country from the grip of paganism. It was a hard sell and high-risk work, to get them to exchange their multiple gods for a single one.

To our right soars Mount Errigal. I was never so close to Donegal's venerable mountain before. Today, I'm nearly as tall as it. Its quartz is spilling downhill. A man alongside me mentions casually that he climbed it two days ago.

'You can always identify Errigal by the little dip on top,' he says.

He's not alone in his accomplishment. Some among the crowd have climbed Kilmanjaro and other peaks, which makes me wonder what I'm doing among such triumph. I imagine the nearest point I will ever get to those heights is on my way to heaven, if that's the direction I'll be sent.

To the left of Errigal is Muckish Mountain. I can hear someone saying it reminds her of the hipped roof of a long house. For me it's more like a mighty piece of earth shovelled into shape by giants.

Two men with flapping maps locate the townlands that come into view. The names ring out like poetry, noting their special place in the world: *Ceann na Ceathrúna, Baile na Creige Loch,* feisty names, because they survived the assault of the Ordnance Survey of the 1830s when Irish place-names were scoped out and anglified. Place-names tell the story of their spot on the earth. Built into language are notions of nations and identity so names can be threatening things. If you want to be a successful coloniser, you have to change them. I let the hum of the placenames that have survived croon around me. They touch a nerve, and I forget for one lovely instant all about life's boundaries and the humdrum of the everyday down at ground level.

When a man who is trying to rescue his map against the breeze, points out the townland of Carntraona, the moment feels too strong for me. The name *traonach* (corncrake) tells that this is a terrain where the corncrake sings, no birdsong so harsh but none so evocative. The sound of the corncrake coming from the meadow opposite our house crosses my childhood dreams. I hear its echo now and I let it sing through the years that divide me from a time when sounds went deeper than words and shaped a sense of mystery.

Half a dozen hands point to *Cró na hOlainn* (hillock of the wool) where farmers once brought their sheep for the three summer months to graze on the commons. One of the men recalls going there with his father as a boy to do the herding.

Up here you feel out of meaning's reach and yet it's loaded with meaning – the culture, the kinship, the neighbourliness, the history which consigned local names to a lowly role in their own story.

The Derryveagh chain of mountains stand in the distance, elbowing one another for attention. Lining up alongside them are Laracus, Aghla More, Aghla Beag. They don't need to be told they're lovely. Nature has no need of the compliments that humans crave.

Sliabh Snacht, a little further away, is visible between mountain tips. I'm familiar with this one because Sliabh Snacht has the distinction of being the first where limelight was used during the Ordnance Survey of Ireland in the 1830s. This bright form of lighting, invented just a decade earlier by Scottish engineer Thomas Drummond, was used, as the Argan lamps of the time were not powerful enough. Drummond proposed using limelight and the brilliant beam was visible against the night sky.

The Drummond influence didn't end there. During his survey work he got to know the locals and thought about their grievances. Later, when he was made Under Secretary to the Lord Lieutenant of Ireland, he reminded landlords that property had duties as well as rights. Today that wouldn't earn a line but back then, in the days before a basic standard was seen as a human right, he was up against a formidable block. Surprise, surprise, landlords disliked Drummond.

The wind is lively at this height. Our coats are smacking and billowing in the breeze. I have nothing to anchor myself to. I'm afraid I'll get carried away and crash against the stones and maybe disable other walkers on my way. This generous heap of stones that forms the cairn has come from the custom that each member of the funeral party took along a stone and placed them in ordered heaps.

Cathal and another man are still talking place-names and history as we make the descent. Compelling and all as the conversation is, I can't afford to listen in case I land head first down the hillside. My plan is not to arrive back on a stretcher. That would be taking the re-enactment too literally.

The descent is nearly as bad as the climb because my legs run away without being told to. We cross soft, slippery ground and black bogland. 'It was worse last year,' I hear a voice saying, so I don't complain. And just when we make it down with a sigh of relief, some joker calls out, 'We've gone the wrong way, we'll have to turn back.'

For one distressing second, I think it's not a joke.

We stop for lunch on the grass beside a stream. The murmur of chat gets louder. Donegal Irish has a different hum from my Galway dialect and I don't always catch what people are saying.

Soon we're on our feet again and after going over the brow of a hill, a road appears in the distance. This is the place where the exhausted can get a lift. I receive that bit of news with delight even if I can only see the stretch of road in miniature. It's good to know you can be rescued, though I hope I won't have to slink into a car in the presence of such fitness.

When we walk into the final piece of road, cars hoot as we pass. I imagine in the old days the locals bowed their heads before the funeral party. A woman is arranging drinks of chilled water on her garden wall. She does this every year, I'm told. It's a joy to drink the cool water. The drink that I took with me has long since gone.

Finally, it's uphill to the old graveyard of Tulach Beaglaigh. Prayers are recited over the dust of the dead, a requiem to a people and a time gone by. The duty of the day is over and now it's back to Falcarragh and into the Shamrock Bar where Irish stew awaits us. It's a regular treat for the walkers.

'Is it possible to have a shower and change before eating?' an Italian man enquires.

'Not unless a shower of rain,' quips one of the locals.

In the queue for the stew a woman asks the server just for potatoes, no stew and to make sure that the potatoes don't touch the stew because she's a strict vegetarian. I don't care for meat either. But I think what pampered toffs we are, commemorating such hardship and wanting a shower and vegetarian fare – the Rescue Remedy generation.

I'm not much company. I'm too exhausted to talk But I feel warm in the afterglow of effort rewarded, the same feeling of elation I had after doing the *Tóchar*, or when I finished an exam, or had a baby or some such hard slog.

FIFTEEN

FROM SINNER TO SAINT

Next morning I drive towards the southern part of Donegal. The mountains don't look nearly as daunting as they did yesterday. Errigal looks possible, having been so close to it less than twenty four hours ago. If I feel so freed from its power just from seeing it up close, I wonder how I'd feel if I'd climbed it.

Mountain-making took some throwing up, spewing out of lava, magma, molten rock, volcanic vomit. Yet, look at the beauty it froze into. A divine plan must have lay hidden behind it – heaven breaking loose disguised as hell.

Donegal doesn't ration its wild beauty in other ways either: untidy borders, headlands, swathes of scrubland, incisions and fault lines making valleys so robust that they almost slice the region in a south-westerly swipe.

During a brief holdup in traffic, I see what's causing the delay, a ewe suckling her curly lamb in the middle of the road. His tail is tremoring at the contents. I swerve to avoid disturbing him. I'm fond of my food, too, and I wouldn't like people mowing me down while I'm eating.

I'm on the road to Gartan, the birthplace of Saint Colmcille.

The landscape takes a gentler form around these parts. The view is of green hills stretching over the lake and on the far side a level track of countryside is dotted with more sheep, no scrubland in this part of Donegal.

This sixth century saint was of a regional royal house and his people gave him a site here for an abbey. It was to make up for a fit of pique in his youth that Colmcille was pushed towards sainthood. Holy books are full of cases of turning over new leafs. There's hope for us all. Think about Saul who used to stone Christians before his conscience caught up with him on the road to Damascus. He became Paul, the saint supreme. Colmcille threw his own stones, in a manner of speaking. When he visited Finian, Abbot of Clonard monastery (who too became a saint) he gave his guest the loan of a psalm in a psalter (a book of psalms). Colmcille liked it so much that he copied it without Finian's permission. As if that wasn't cheeky enough, when Finian asked for it back, Colmcille refused. Naturally, Finian got irate, as you would, and he finally took his case to Diarmuid, the High King in Tara.

This story would be long forgotten only for it turned out to have such a big future. It was the first case of what's now called copyright or for that matter, its more modern cousin, intellectual property. Brehon (early medieval Irish) law ruled that no matter where a lost calf was found, it belonged with its mother. High King Diarmuid took this as a guide and gave his verdict: *Le gach bain a bainín, le gach leabhar a leabhrán* which means 'to every cow its calf, to every book its copy'. (I'm sure the king intended no pun that the manuscript was written on calf skin vellum.)

Colmcille was having none of it, even the High King's decision couldn't persuade him to give back the book. His next move was to gather together an army. The battle that followed, the Battle of the Book, took place in Cúl Dreimhne (also known as Cooldrumman) in 561, near Drumcliff in County Sligo. It was no skirmish – about 3,000 died.

This manuscript now lies quietly in the Royal Irish Academy in Dublin showing no signs at all of all the trouble it caused.

We can take it from this story that God is forgiving, extremely so. But before taking God's mercy for granted, let me explain the amount of repentance it took for Colmcille to become a saint. Overcome with remorse for causing so many deaths, he sailed into exile in 563, along with twelve followers to the Island of Iona in Scotland. There he founded a monastery and converted the Picts and the Scots to Christianity.

On the eve of setting sail, he spent the night here in Gartan, on *Leac an Uaignis* (the flagstone of loneliness). And that set a trend for people emigrating to go on pilgrimage to this stone. To spend the night here before you left for a foreign land was believed to act as a balm for loneliness. It didn't do much for Colmcille – in Iona, we're told, he grieved for home.

Leac an Uaignis is well signposted. You'll find it on a narrow road off the N56. If it had sound, you would probably hear the keens of all who came here to offer up their grief. I'm surprised that it's not worn away with their knees, because Donegal has seen above average emigration numbers.

Those who left mostly headed for Scotland, a country of like-minded geography, of fault lines and slits sweeping in a south-westerly direction. Once the spring sowing was done, they set sail for the summer potato season. So, a tradition formed in Donegal, of looking to Glasgow as their 'capital' rather than to Dublin, or even Belfast.

But in their dreams they looked to home. The sweet pastoral labour of village life looked pleasant from factories and mines. Songs like 'The Hills of Donegal' and 'Cutting the Corn in Creeslough', touch up their home place with words of longing. They echo the old ways, the smell of newly-cut meadow, all-hands-on-deck for the harvest, the lowing herds and horse-drawn clouds of dust. Today, as the sun shines on the sloping hills I know I'm looking at a vision that occupied many emigrants' thoughts.

These images from afar were all very well but they provided no gold-plated existence. That's the trouble with great beauty, it often matches up with great poverty. Land ownership usually lies behind it. In the Visitors' Centre in Glenveagh National Park, close to Gartan, I watch a film that drives this message home. It's a shame there's only me and two others in the handsome theatre that would seat about fifty.

The camera pans and struts over the assembled grandeur of Glenveagh as a sad tale unfolds. Glenveagh lies along the Glen of the Gweebarra fault line. A gathering of highlands peeps over the valley: the Derryveagh mountains, Errigal and Slieve Snacht.

The film tells the story of John George Adair who bought Glenveagh in the late 1850s, about a decade after the Great Famine. Adair, from County Laois, had been a member of Young Ireland (a nationalist movement) and stood for election as a Tenant Rights candidate just five years before he bought this estate. At that point he was intent on making the world a better place for tenants, but he switched zeal from the rights of tenants to the rights of investors after he bought Glenveigh. Seismic shifts like these can occur, some going from sinners to saints, others making the opposite journey.

Adair paid for the land and he expected tenants to earn their keep. The large tenantry in the labour-intensive pre-famine days of tillage was no longer needed. Instead, a tidy sum could be made on black-faced mountain sheep that could be grazed on what had looked like a valueless mountain. This upset the tenants who had until then used it as commonage to graze their stock during summer. Adair slapped on a fine for trespass which on a fenceless mountain-side earned him a nice windfall – £368 in two years.

Justice was rough and ready then. All the property rights were on the landlord's side. Tenants had no security and no right to compensation for improvements they carried out on their plot. They felt sore about that. Land was sacred, like kin. As for commonage, that went back to the origins of man.

When sheep went missing Adair believed his tenants were stealing them, and he had the suspects arrested. Though cleared in court, they felt humiliated, and petitioned the Lord Lieutenant to investigate Adair's behavior. No surprise, their request was turned down.

Adair wasn't the only Donegal estate owner who saw the value of a mountain top. Landlords brought in Scottish shepherds to bypass the locals but sheep stealing continued. When eighty-five sheep disappeared from Adair's farm, his Scottish steward, James Murray claimed that this was the work of tenants, but police found the sheepskins in Murray's own cottage where he lived with his wife and child. Murray didn't make himself popular in other ways either, impounding stray animals and reporting brewers of the local moonshine, poteen. On Tuesday November 13, 1860 James Murray went missing. His dog came home late that night covered in bloodstains. Murray wasn't found until Thursday, lying on the ledge of a rock at the foot of a cliff, bludgeoned to death, his skull smashed. When they failed to pin the murder on anyone, Adair applied collective blame and evicted 244 tenants from the edge of his estate, some along by the shores of Lough Gartan, the birthplace of Saint Colmcille.

The sobs and wails rang through the valley as their cabins were pulled down. About half went to the workhouse. The younger tenants, one hundred and fifty of them, had to leave their home place and began the long journey to Australia, by Dublin, Liverpool and Plymouth.

Back in Glenveagh, Adair married a wealthy American woman Cornelia Ritchie and built Glenveagh Castle. It's a gem of a building. I walk uphill to see it and it matches the natural beauty of its surroundings, even if the price paid by the tenants dampens the enjoyment.

The walk is longer than I expect, but the scenic view makes it worth it. Just when I think the view has no more beauty left, another scene bursts forth like an amphitheatre – mountains, glens, a lake.

In the café, a robin has got in and wants to share my scone. He looks like a pet bird who has made the café his territory. I'm enjoying watching him hop around under the table, though I'm sure he doesn't enjoy much watching me scoffing and offering him nothing. In the end I give up and give him a few crumbs. I don't want to continue the harsh tradition of Glenveagh.

SIXTEEN

WHAT'S IN A NAME?

South-west of Glenveagh I find the village of Glenties crouching like a nestling bird by the Bluestack mountains. This was dramatist Brian Friel's fictionalised town of Ballybeg. It is huddled between two glens, at the junction of the Owenea and Stranaglough rivers. This town would have a special place in the world, even without Friel but with him, we get an extra slice of its personality. It became his home in 1939 when, at ten years old, he moved here with his family from near Omagh where he was born.

In his fiction he created a parallel world when he wrote about his own people and his own place. His pitch was as sharp as a musician's, reproducing home-spun words, grounding his writings in the local accents and rhythm. His characters were mostly villagers, people who grew with their own surroundings – farmers, priests, shopkeepers. And using them as a device, he juggled myths, memories, legends and pagan ritual alongside the new gospel of the modern world. Though some of Friel's characters don't think beyond the rim of their own horizon, others like Gar in *Philadelphia Here I Come* are tormented by the competing pull between home and away.

Wouldn't it be nice if the people of Glenties did what they did in France with their great literary figure, Marcel Proust, and his village of Combray. The French combined fiction and fact and renamed it, Illiers-Combray. What about Ballybeg-Glenties? That would make the place match its fiction.

Here among the hills it is easy to feel the echoes of Friel's play *Faith Healer*, where the enchanted sounds of words are used to stoke up a cure. Again in *Translations* words wend their way into the historic events of 1833 when the British military surveyors came to Ballybeg to create the new Ordnance Survey of Ireland. In a verbal powergrab the old placenames were uprooted and a new Anglicised version made its way into the landscape. An old sense of place got dislocated by the new masters of the word. This event coincided with the spread of the English-speaking national schools which replaced the Irish-speaking hedge schools and the Bardic tradition of Latin and Greek.

What's in a name? In the case of placenames, everything. They're sweet at heart, called after familiar things – a custom, a tree, a burial mound, where the sun rises, where the river bends. Their sounds echo as powerfully as the hypnotic chants bring about a cure in *Faith Healer*. In *Translations*, Friel grasps the troubling feeling of relearning the native map. He asks will they know 'how to go not from Lis na Muc to Poll na gCaorach but from Swinefort to Sheeprock.' The hedge schoolmaster character answers: 'It can happen that a civilisation can be imprisoned in a linguistic contour which no longer matches the landscape of fact.'

South from Glenties is Donegal town, the home-place of the *Annals of the four Masters*. By the time I get to the old Franciscan friary where the annals were written, the late afternoon sun is low-angled, sending its rays through the missing walls of this ruin above the banks of the River Eske. The water is a burst of light. People walking around the graves are casting long shadows among the headstones.

That the *Annals of the Four Masters*, were written in this abbey gives it heft because this work marks the climax of the Irish tradition of compiling chronicles. Put together by four scholars: Franciscan friar Micheál Ó Cléirigh, the chief compiler along with three collaborators; Peregrine Duignan, Peregrine O'Clery and Fearfeasa O' Mulconry, it was the largest literary undertaking ever carried out in Ireland.

What prompted it was the fear that the ancient records of Ireland would be lost forever. It gave an account of all that was known and guessed of Irish history since the earliest of times, and drew together sources from annals, chronicles, storytelling, poetry and hearsay. It would be called a 'national chronicle' had a nation existed when it was written in the seventeenth century. It was in line with the awareness of a homeland or a nation that was awakening in early modern England and continental Europe at the time.

The *Annals of the Four Masters* are held in four locations in Dublin: The Royal Irish Academy, University College Dublin, Trinity College and the National Archives. The dedication reads: 'On the 22nd of January 1632 this work was undertaken in the monastery in Donegal and was finished in the same place 16 August 1636'.

In fact, this is not quite true. Little of the work was done in the Franciscan friary at all. It was put together on the run as the monastery was largely destroyed in the Elizabethan wars.

From Donegal, next day, I turn north east to Stranorlar to call on the grave of Isaac Butt, nineteenth century politician and nationalist. I want to make this visit as a little pilgrimage to a man I think was passed over by history.

The Great Famine prompted Isaac Butt to turn his attention to the rights of tenant farmers and, unlike John George Adair, the owner of Glenveagh, he stuck with it. When he died, his obituary in the *New York Times* read that he was 'one of the most unselfish public men that Ireland had ever seen'.

Butt got caught in the fold of neglect that often happens when someone more colourful follows. His successor was Charles Stewart Parnell who was destined to be more linked with the movement that Butt created, Home Rule. Parnell flared across the nineteenth century until he came crashing, not so much for bedding a married woman as for being found out.

The neat and well-kept graveyard is on a grassy slope. I like its softness and its quiet dignity, a fitting resting-place for the gentlemanly Isaac Butt. Perhaps he was too gentlemanly. His respectful approach towards the parliamentary tradition of Westminster edged him out of popularity. Parnell's disruptive methods of filibustering earned him a lot more approval. This was a tactic that can be traced back to Roman times, but was revived in the 1870s by a group of MPs in the House of Commons – making boring speeches that went on for hours, reading out long passages from government reports, demanding endless votes to slow down the business of the house, dragging the Irish question into every debate.

It doesn't take long to find Butt's grave. It is under a tree where as a boy he used to sit and dream. His wish was to be buried here.

While I'm on the subject of under-appreciation I will next visit Monaghan, the homeplace of poet, Patrick Kavanagh. He was convinced himself that he wasn't nearly enough valued in his time.

SEVENTEEN

THE STONE THAT THE BUILDERS REJECTED...

Inniskeen in County Monaghan is a place that looked out for Patrick Kavanagh, ever-watching ever-forgiving, ever with its grip on him. A home place is like that, like a parent who goes on loving in spite of a fault-finding brood. The raw rhythm of its place-names became the foothold of his poetry. Kavanagh was niftier at taming words than cultivating soil and the black hostile earth which he couldn't wait to get away from, became the sacred stuff that would infuse his words with a soul. This was home and he didn't know, until he left, that Inniskeen had such power. At a safe distance he could elevate the places that had so tormented him, and immortalise them.

O stony grey soil of Monaghan
The laugh from my love you thieved;

Trees and bulky hedgerows make canopies over me. It doesn't

look like the kind of landscape that would thieve the laugh from a young man's love. It's drumlin country, tiny hills dot the fields that roll this way and that, fenced to the summit, widening as they make their journey downhill. But let me leave the best description of a drumlin to the man himself – a 'hanging hill'.

The Kavanagh museum in Inniskeen is a former church. Kavanagh was baptised here. This would have amused him, to have a holy building given over in his honour. They even have the original baptismal font, painted green because this was the colour older residents of the village remembered it to be.

These local museums run by fervent volunteers would often put to shame the official kind, backed with grants, staff and funding. Their fervour is usually driven by personal interest and they long to share it with you.

The guide shows me, on the largescale ordnance map under glass, the places that Kavanagh made famous: 'There's Mullahinsha, Drummeril, Black Shanco,' he says. It's Billy Brennan's Barn (from the poem 'Inniskeen Road: July Evening') I want to see and he brings me over to the wall where the framed photograph is hanging.

'You can't miss it,' he tells me, explaining where the actual barn is. And surely, it looks like a striking building, with its white walls and distinct red shutters. The dance in Billy Brennan's Barn where they were all cycling to in 'twos and threes' made Kavanagh aware of his moment of oddness. That evening he was an outsider to the local code – the 'wink-and-elbow language' of the other young men. It's an old theme, that many poets have put into words, the loneliness of standing out from the crowd, the personal price of poetry.

The Greek poet Constantine Cavafy believed that a poet should stand at a peculiar angle to the universe. A few hours in the Palace Bar or McDaid's pub where Dublin's vagrant poets and writers used to drink, chief among them Patrick Kavanagh and Brendan

Behan, would have left an onlooker in no doubt about their fidelity to that aspect of poetry.

Kavanagh believed in the priestly nature of a poet's function but, outspoken as he was about his opinions, he did little to draw patrons to support his noble calling. But he stuck with it, trying all means of enterprise to support himself, including building a still in his Pembroke Road flat in Dublin to make poteen. A little windfall came his way when a horse-drawn dray of the B & I Steampacket Company knocked him off his bike and he was awarded thirty-six pounds when he sued the shipping company for damages.

When in 1935 the *Irish Times* published four of his works, one of them – 'Spraying the Potatoes' – provoked a letter of complaint. A city newspaper, it read, should print something more uplifting than the 'warblings of a rural yokel'. The letter was written, maybe as a joke, by writer and satirist Brian O'Nolan (aka Flann O'Brien, aka Myles na Gopaleen).

Such was the dissent among Dublin's sparring literary brotherhood of the time, when jibes, taunts, insults mingled with pints and metaphors, exchanged across the bar floor or sometimes came out onto Grafton Street.

Brendan Lynch's book, *Prodigals & Geniuses* shows how great it was to be alive in that noble era, the forties, fifties and sixties, the Dublin of the struggling artists, of Parson's bookshop (on Baggot Street's Grand Canal bridge), McDaid's pub (in Harry Street), the Palace Bar (in Fleet Street) and Baggotonia (Baggot Street, Leeson Street and the Grand Canal) even though some of these carousers and self-styled 'characters' were only just alive. Because in those lean years of banned books and intellectual seclusion, it was a struggle to keep body and soul together. Some of these places are still there though the characters are absent.

I wander around the museum where the poems are exhibited on display boards. I watch a video on Kavanagh's life. And I think about his feat of making the transition from farming to poetry, not an easy change of career in the forties.

'It was George Russell, Æ (guest of Lady Gregory's whom we 'met' in Galway), who gave Kavanagh his first break when he published his poems in the *Irish Statesman*. By the time Kavanagh met Russell, just days before Christmas 1931, his poem 'Ploughman' had been included in the *Spectator's* anthology of the best poems of the year,' the guide tells me.

Kavanagh had walked the fifty-five miles to Dublin to see Russell. The tramp-like young man, even rougher looking than usual after a three-day walk, knocked on Æ's door in Rathgar. Better looking specimens have been cleared off middle class doorsteps. Not Russell's. He brought him in and talked long and expansively to him and read aloud from Emerson and Whitman.

If Mrs Russell had been there that day she might have noticed that Kavanagh was hungry. But she was in hospital and only lived until the following spring. Kavanagh left with a pile of books which he read in the Iveagh Hostel where he found a bed for the night. He wasn't the only hard-up artist who used this workmen's hostel. Novelist Liam O'Flaherty and poet and playwright Val Vousden availed themselves of this cheap accommodation too.

Nearly thirty years earlier Russell had done something similar for another late night literary caller, James Joyce.

From the video on Kavanagh's life you wouldn't think that he got such a kick out of contention. When he came to Dublin there was no shortage of others ready to join in – Behan versus Kavanagh, the prickly Flann O'Brien, the countryman set against the Dubliner. And Kavanagh was always up for a spat.

The poet Eavan Boland said of Kavanagh, that he was 'a beacon, above all, a man who knew who he was'. What she liked most about Kavanagh was 'he saw through the humbug'. And indeed, he didn't mind saying so.

The museum guide explains, 'Kavanagh wasn't educated if you

think about it in the narrow sense of schooling. He said himself that he left school when he knew more than the teachers. But it was while he was there that he heard the recitation of a poem by James Clarence Mangan by one of the senior pupils that set his imagination going. We can suppose at that stage he still knew less than the teacher.'

A neighbour lent the sixteen-year-old Kavanagh some of his books, works like Byron, Shelley, Goldsmith, and he immersed himself in them, hiding them in hedges so that he could read them while working in the fields.

The guide brings me once again to the map. He points out the local River Fane.

'In times gone by, this made Inniskeen an island. Not anymore. The southern side of the river has long since dried up and brought it into the mainland with mud and silt. When it was cut off, there was a monastery there. Older history still traces this area to Celtic myths. Kavanagh would have been well aware of the legend that Cúchulainn watered his horses in the River Fane, before continuing his pursuit of the Connaught army in the *Táin Bó Cuailgne* (the Cattle Raid of Cooley). His battle and duel with his adored foster brother Ferdia, the most moving episode of the *Táin*, took place in Ardee, at the ford of the River Dee. It's just eighteen kilometres south of Inniskeen.'

It took someone handy with words to subvert the world he thought so tedious into such a lofty flight. Here in the museum what strikes me about that is that anything is possible. This transformation is at its best in his poem 'Pegasus'. I read it on the display board in the centre of the floor. Kavanagh unites the idea of selling a working horse and selling his soul or taking flight as in the Greek myth, breaking away from local halters: controlling churchmen, petty politicians and shopkeepers and growing wings on his back.

My soul was an old horse
Offered for sale in twenty fairs.

I offered him to the Church – the buyers
Were little men who feared his unusual airs…

When these wings brought Kavanagh to Dublin it didn't turn out to be the promised land that he thought would sweep away the anguish that farming had caused him. He found out that the artificial culture of the capital had little to teach Inniskeen. He was like most people stricken with the pull of home and away, wanting to be here when he was there and there when he was here. Memory, that touched-up gap between reality and longing, allowed him to transform the life he had rejected into the strange and the wonderful. There was raw elemental truth in its dunghills and primal labour. Absence made them all the more potent, and they rose on the road with him to take their place alongside the best of them as he turned his mundane world into words of splendour. (I'm sure, well acquainted that he was with scripture, he saw a parallel with the line – The stone that the builders rejected has become the cornerstone: Psalm 118.)

He had laughed at the previous generations of poets, like Yeats, who had elevated the peasant into something noble, but he did the same himself. There was a difference though because he, unlike Yeats, was of that stock. Much as he gave out about parochialism he knew the value of the parish. He knew that when the membrane around the parish dissolves it becomes the universal. He wrote:

Parochialism is universal; it deals with the fundamentals…
To know fully even one field or one land is a lifetime's
experience. In the world of poetic experience it is depth that
counts, not width. A gap in a hedge, a smooth rock surfacing
a narrow lane, a view of a woody meadow, the stream at the
junction of four small fields – these are as much as a man can
fully experience

The poem 'The Great Hunger' 1942, gave Kavanagh the status of a major poet and finally brought him some financial reward, though he stuck with the idea that he was underappreciated.

Some say his great contribution was to free up poetry from the highbrow world of academia. And for that, as much as for his work, he should be celebrated.

In spite of copious guidance in the museum about how to find Billy Brennan's barn, I get no sighting of it. I spot a man watering flowers outside his workshop and stop to ask him. He leaves down his watering can and leans on the ledge of the open window, all set for a chat. He recalls some of Kavanagh's poems and shows me a triangular field at the back of the workshop that the Kavanagh family owned which featured in his work, 'Shancoduff'. When I tell him I can't find Billy Brennan's barn he says he'll hop into the car and show me. It's all very impromptu, very local, very lovely. The very man we need – the present owner – is driving his tractor up the laneway that leads to the barn.

'Ah there he is, I'll ask him,' says my helpful passenger, and he hops out and has a few words with him. No worries about permission to drive up the gravel laneway. And there it is, Billy Brennan's barn, the red paint of the shutters faded into an off-red since the photograph that hangs in the museum wall was taken, but unmistakable otherwise.

'That's the house, Billy Brennan's,' he says. The windows are still curtained but it's showing all the signs of a place abandoned. In a strange reversal the barn in this case is more important than the house. I drive my guide back to his workshop. He has left it open and that makes it feel like a moment in a time gone by, of rural trust and casual friendship.

He gives me directions for Kavanagh's birthplace in the townland of Mucker.

'Won't you make sure to look out for Cassidy's hanging hill

from 'A Christmas Childhood'. Do you know the poem?' he asks. He starts to recite it. And then he reveals the punchline. 'Ours was one of the families that got a mention in that poem, Lennons.'

My father played the melodion
Outside at our gate;
There were stars in the morning east
And they danced to his music.

Across the wild bogs his melodion called
To Lennons and Callans

I'm on my way to Mucker and I do, as I promised Patrick Lennon, watch out for Cassidy's hanging hill. What a magical way to paint a picture of a drumlin. The fenced field slopes steeply, hanging out to dry. It's enough to make you feel suspended between two worlds.

EIGHTEEN

SLIEVE GULLION

With this feeling of inter-worlds I'm ready to leave Inniskeen and head towards Newry in County Down, to see Slieve Gullion from Bernish viewing point on the slopes of Camlough mountain. Bernish knows its history. It soars over some proud exploits. The world of ancient myths is deeply scored into this great saucer of landscape and the circle of hills that surround it – the Ring of Gullion. Horizons spread out beyond horizons and the clouds come down to caress the mountain tops in the distance, covering them with the misty drool of their kisses.

Some scenes just sit there waiting for a legend to be plonked on them. Looking down on Gullion's immense ring dyke (an Ice Age residue) which spreads out like a great amphitheatre, a home for a legend doesn't come much better.

I don't know if it's the height that's going to my head but it's easy to feel part of the heroic continuity. This was the scene of the action played out in Ireland's Iliad, the *Táin Bó Cuailnge*. It was here in Slieve Gullion that the armies went in different directions in search of the brown bull of Cooley.

The *Táin* gives the opening for a description of this dramatic confluence of valleys and it solders it together in heroic action. Like the battle, this scene is brutal and gentle. It came into being when continents shifted and convulsed in the great volcanic shake-up millions of years ago.

In her search for the bull Queen Medb moved along the Slighe Mhidhluachra, one of the five great roads of ancient Ireland that radiated from the mound of Tara. You can still see this *slighe* (road) – the modern version of it at least – the Dublin-Newry road.

The Kilnasaggart pillar stone also lies along the *slighe* and that brings me back down to ground level and on towards Kilnasaggart Road. It's so narrow that the growth on both sides brush against the car.

I have difficulty finding the pillar stone. I'm glad when I spot a teenage girl, the only sign of humanity around here. She tells me it's on the right though she's pointing to the left. When it fails to turn up on either, left or right, I go into a house where I can hear the sounds of hammering. A dust-covered man emerges from a half-constructed building. He's talkative. Not only do I get directions but a whole history of his family and the locality. He must have been longing for a break from his hammering. He points out the eyeful of countryside, showing me different houses and the stories of the occupants.

'This place has a long tradition of boot-legging,' he winks. 'Bandit country, south Armagh.' And I get the story of clandestine capers and cross-border farming. Just a glance is enough to see how ideal it is for banditry, a spread of countryside that takes some knowing – every hollow where you could lie low, every sandbank, every gap on the staggered border with the Republic of Ireland is visible. He has never visited the pillar stone.

'It's too near,' he says merrily. Then as I'm pulling off he shouts: 'Don't leave the locality without seeing Faughart where Saint Brigit was born.'

That gives rise to another story. He's a non-believer, he tells me.

'I don't believe in anything, apart from what's before my eyes. This world is enough for me,' he says in a satisfied tone as I drive away.

The pillar stone is on private land. I'm nervous about crossing. There's plenty of cow dung though no sign of its owners. Even cows can leave you for dead, if they take it into their head to dislike you. I'll look as inoffensive as possible.

Three men are working with a digger and nothing has attacked them, so here goes. As I walk by I ask them where the pillar stone is. They point in the direction of a little gate. I just walk as if it's public space which must look cheeky. It only strikes me afterwards that one of them could be the owner.

The pillar stone is nestling in the hills, like an animal crouching in the shelter of the hedgerows or an outlaw hiding his or her goods. I know I must be in the townland of Edenappa or to be precise in an antique sense, in the pass through the Slieve Gullion ringdyke. The early cemetery in which it was sited, on one of Ireland's five great *slighe*, the Slighe Mhidhluachra, is said to have connected Tara to the northern royal site of Emain Macha. This alignment between important sites gives it a new reality, though no sign of it remains now. But the dust from the feet of the walkers of old must be somewhere buried beneath the lower surface.

This pillar dates from around 700 AD and is thought to be the earliest historically dated inscribed stone in Ireland. The inscription translates, *This place dedicated by Ternóc son of Cerán Bec under the patronage of Peter the Apostle.* A large Latin cross is carved above it, and beneath is another more ornate cross enclosed in a circle.

And so, to Faughart, the birthplace of Brigit. The road grows wider now, and a vista expands from the brow of the hill (like the legend that surrounds Brigit). What a range of landscape the young saint awoke to every morning. This miracle of a scene must have put to the test how much her eye could contain, a half sphere of compressed landscape all the way to the mountains. It's all the more powerful when you consider that it hasn't changed since her time.

This was the sight of a still more ancient scene, the spot where the Connacht armies of Queen Medb regrouped in the *Táin*. The ancient sagas would never have arranged for them to regroup in an unworthy spot. Medb arranged the meeting here, supposedly to ask for a truce at Faughart Hill, but it was a trick. However, her opponent, young Cúchulainn survived against fourteen opponents that Medh set against him.

As I rest later on, before my visit to Armagh, I let the legend of Saint Brigit run into my dreams. She was smart. She pulled off a trick that a modern-day developer could only dream of. She asked the King of Leinster for a site for her monastery, for just as much land as her cloak would cover. Seeing her tiny cloak, the king agreed. Then as she placed it on the ground the cloak grew, not stopping until it had covered several acres. The King of Leinster was so enthralled that he became a Christian.

NINETEEN

LAND OF LILLIPUT

Near the little town of Market Hill in County Armagh I ask at the gate of Gosford Forest Park where to find Dean Swift's chair and Dean Swift's well but the young man tells me he could find these places himself but to explain where they are is a bit trickier. He directs me to the map in the carpark. This estate was once the property of Sir Arthur Acheson, a friend of Dean Jonathan Swift. It's now in the ownership of the Forestry Department.

Swift was a cantankerous fellow and he had no shortage of reasons – deafness, vertigo and other complaints. But his hosts here must have had patience in spadefuls. He used to come to the Achesons and stay eight months at a time and spend shorter bouts here as well, lasting a few months. Sir Arthur first invited Swift in 1728.

Between dreary Sir Arthur (he was, by all accounts, very boring) and cranky Swift it's amazing that they lasted in one another's company for such an open-ended stay. Maybe it was Lady Anne Acheson, his wife, who made up for the dullness. She was said to be great company, and good looking.

But one good thing about Swift's contrariness was he turned his ire on society. His satire dug into the ills of what he saw around him. After two centuries he still has instant recognition. That would have gratified him. It was his work on the Land of Lilliput that made him memorable. *Gulliver's Travels* is often thought to be for children, but that's to miss its biting satire.

Swift spent some of his time helping the Achesons with – or as someone put it, 'bullying them into' – gardening projects to his own liking and at their expense. There's no shortage of scope for gardening in this vast acreage. There's no shortage of opportunity either for the long walks through briars and bog-land on which Swift dragged Lady Acheson.

Swift liked to swap banter with the workmen and he picked up some Irish at the same time. It's not clear who looked after his cathedral in Dublin while he was away for such long spells.

I find the map showing Dean Swift's Well and Chair but I can't get my bearings to find the real places. I can see why the fellow at the gate found it hard to give me directions. In the end I give up altogether and head towards Armagh.

In contrast to Gosford, all you have to do in Armagh is to glance at the tops of its many hills to find whatever monument you're looking for. It looks like Montmartre in Paris with Sacré Coeur on its highest point. Armagh has two hilltop cathedrals, Catholic and Protestant, both dedicated to Saint Patrick. The Protestant one is on the site of the original Christian church founded by Patrick in 444.

I first visit the Catholic cathedral. Like Sacré Coeur it was built in hard times. The French basilica went up at a time of national humiliation, following the Franco-Prussian war in 1870, a defeat that was seen as much a blow for Catholicism as for France. Building work in Armagh cathedral predated Sacré Coeur by about thirty years – starting on Saint Patrick's Day 1840. It was halted by the Great Famine, delaying its opening until 1904.

A woman who is lighting candles has dropped her purse and

her money has reeled along the marble floor, making the only noise in this great building.

I look around at the stained glass and the profusion of mosaic. Some of these tiny pieces must have stretched the tedium of the tilers. Outside on a plaque is a story that tells of Saint Patrick saving a fawn from his gluttonous companions who wanted to kill and eat the little animal. He carried him on his shoulders to *Tealach na Licci* (Sandy Hill) to be reunited with his mother – the site on which the Catholic cathedral is built.

This tale comes from the *Book of Armagh* (Codex Ardmachanus), one of the treasures created during Armagh's long ecclesiastical history. It was compiled in the ninth century. It is small, and a lot less ornamental than, say, the *Book of Kells*, but it's a gem, by far the most important of Ireland's manuscripts and contains the earliest copy of the *Confessions of Saint Patrick*. An Abbot of Armagh, Torbach Mac Gormáin, with the scribe Ferdomnach, compiled it.

It was nearly lost around 1680 when its hereditary keeper, Florence Macmoor pawned it for a fiver to pay for his trip to London to testify against Oliver Plunkett, the archbishop (later made a saint) who was being tried and was executed for high treason. It is now held in Trinity College, Dublin.

The walk to the Protestant cathedral brings me down and steeply uphill again. The Robinson library which shares the hill at a lower level, is at the end of one of the terrace of houses that encloses the cathedral grounds and famous gardens.

When I ring the doorbell of what I think is the library entrance, I disturb a clergyman. He's very agreeable. He's eager to ease my embarrassment for ringing the wrong doorbell.

'If you had come here in 1771,' (the year it was founded), he explains jovially, 'this would indeed have been the right door.' He accompanies me around the curve to the present-day doorbell. Maybe he's afraid to leave me alone in case I wander off course again and set off alarm bells somewhere else.

Inside the library is like stepping into another age. The collection of old tomes against the dark wood panelling is a place that fills you with foreboding as to where to begin. But I know exactly where to start. I have come to look at the first edition of *Gulliver's Travels*. Kept under glass casing, it's one of two copies. The publisher had altered the first one, dated October 28, 1726. That took some nerve, and Swift was having none of it. The text would read precisely as he wanted. The second is exactly as Swift planned. And when it came to publishing his next book, the Dean made sure he found another publishing house.

Another treasure here is an early edition of Handel's Messiah and I'm allowed to turn a few pages with gloved hands.

'What fascinates me about it,' says the librarian, "is how little music notation has changed since its first ever performance.' (Handel's Messiah was first performed in the Great Music Hall in Fishamble Street in Dublin in 1741.) That's certainly true; it looks no different from modern sheet music. Dean Swift grudgingly lent some of his choir boys and musicians from Saint Patrick's cathedral for this great occasion.

The Protestant cathedral is nearby and I go and rest a while in the calming twilight of stained glass. Outside I take a look at the famous gardens. They slope slightly downhill on the south east corner of the grounds, following the curve of Castle Street.

At the entrance is the herb garden where two colourful mosaic plaques have been added since my last visit here. The circular one contains some useful sayings – 'People who live in glasshouses should not throw stones. Keep calm and carry on. Don't judge the book by the cover. Live life to the full.'

I know them all. They're like New Year resolutions that, if they're lucky, last as far as February. I resolve to follow them all. That lasts a full three minutes when I'm provoked into breaking the 'keep calm' rule. A dog jumps up at me and dirties my coat with his grubby paws. He's only trying to be friendly, the dog parent explains. I smile suitably at the cute little animal which proves the truth that you can't judge the book by the cover.

Next is the orchard garden where the slope downhill gets more pronounced. Adjoining that is the parterre and then the place I like best, the contemplative garden. It's cut off by a high wall and 'rooms' are created by hedging so you can be alone, or at least feel you are, to do your meditation or clear your head. I try, but I find it hard to settle and take advantage of what the creators have in mind. I can't fall into a trance just anywhere, especially with a dog of a friendly dispostition ready to round the corner.

I head for the northern end of the cathedral to see the resting place of High King, Brian Bórama. According to the *Annals of Ulster*, this is where he's buried. It was a special tribute to the High King, who defeated the Vikings in the Battle of Clontarf in 1014 (though he was killed himself after the battle by a group from the retreating Vikings), to bring him to the apostolic city of Ireland rather than to his native Killaloe in County Clare. Because, by the time of his death, Armagh had established itself as head of the Irish church. This bold claim was for much the same reason as Rome had claimed preeminence over Constantinople around the seventh century.

Rome was the custodian of the body of Saint Peter and they used it to good advantage. Armagh likewise staked its claim to Patrick because it was the custodian of the insignia (badge) of Saint Patrick, convertor of the Irish.

Back then, the Bishop of Armagh made sure to have the insignia and other relics with him when he and his retinue travelled the country imposing tribute and lands from secular lords. As in the rest of Europe at the time, bishops on visitations like these were a common sight. They threatened the authority of kings. The consequence for people not opening their house to them was severe – render seven female slaves and do seven years penance. Insulting the insignia earned you the loss of four female slaves.

A tiny decorated house-shaped shrine, a container for relics, and the remnants of a satchel were discovered beside the River Blackwater at Clonmore, Armagh, proof of these travelling relics.

Armagh's closeness to the most sacred Iron-age mound and ceremonial capital of Emain Macha (Navan Fort), capital of the kings of the Red Branch of Ulster, must also have had something to do with the claim for Armagh's primacy. Both churches claim it as their ecclesiastical capital. The Catholic cathedral is the Rome of the Irish Catholic Church, and the Protestant cathedral is the Canterbury of the Church of Ireland.

When in the Visitors' Centre in Emain Macha a few miles west of Armagh, a woman approaches me and asks.

'Have you come far?' I think it's a serious question. That's a bit slow of me considering she's dressed in Iron Age costume. When she follows with the next question, 'Have you come in peace?' I cotton on that it's a reenactment of the time when Navan Fort was in its heyday. The couple alongside me, who came from the coast are much faster to pick up on the drama.

'Have you brought salt?' she says to them.

'We did, but we were robbed on the way,' one of the men answers.

'Pity,' she explains. 'Salt is important. We use it as a medium of exchange.'

She leads us to the Stone Age dwelling and explains that they're wealthy, that they own seventeen cattle. The circular dwelling is realistic with a roof of river reeds and animal skins on the floor. Inside are items that show off their skills of weaving, stone-grinding and weapons for hunting.

'We pass on our learning,' says one of the men. 'We don't write like the Romans.'

Some of the skills they pass on are how to do battle with a wild boar – clearly a waste of time for some of us who can just about protect ourselves from doing battle with a crowd in a shopping centre, or an over-friendly dog. Put us up against a wild boar and we would probably reach for our smartphones for solutions and in the meantime he would show his superior smartness by devouring us.

'Boars have extraordinary memories,' he explains. 'If you stole one of their young and crossed their path again, you would live to regret it.'

I expect it would be the last path you would cross.

We're led outside to the medicinal herb beds of sorrel, spring onions, parsnip and the herb most sacred to druids, meadowsweet. I know meadowsweet was a favourite of Queen Elizabeth 1, but I hold back that forward knowledge. How could I possibly know about this queen when I'm firmly planted in the Iron Age.

Around the corner is the fire over which hangs an iron pot, with soup or stew at the ready – Iron-Age fast food, for when you're hungry, rather than at mealtimes. The rule is, you have to replace what you take. Beside it is a pit where you can cook with water and hot stones, for day-long cooking.

The re-enactment is cut short because the tour of the mound is about to begin. We regroup in the lobby where the guide is waiting. Now we're free to unfold out of our Iron-age roles. The guide leads us along: 'We're walking along Saint Patrick's Way,' he tells us. 'It's an eighty-two-mile walk but we're going to branch off and up the hill to a mound thought to be the dwelling place of the High Kings of Ulster, King Conchobar Mac Nessa. It dates from the era of the Ulster cycle of tales – the *Táin Bó Cuailgne*, Deirdre of the Sorrows, Naoise, Cúchulainn and the Red Branch Knights. But in the sixties a find here changed the nature of knowledge of this site,' he tells us.

This was the discovery of an early Iron Age structure, a series of figure-of-eight buildings and a forty-metre timber ringed structure dating from 95 BC. The circular construct was not domestic but thought to be a ceremonial temple, the largest known in any region of later prehistoric, pre-Roman northern Europe.

'Here's the biggest mystery,' he says. 'It was built to burn and they duly torched it. An event like this has not been recorded elsewhere. Then they covered it with earth and formed a mound. After all that effort they abandoned the site. Excavators found the centre post of the structure and tree-dating experts in Queen's University in Belfast were able to trace the burning to 95BC.'

What were they at? The unhelpful answer is no one knows. It could have been for reasons ritual, to appease the gods, and there's some evidence from pollen counts that the gods needed appeasing around then. It was a time of crop failures.

The kings of Ulster went downhill, around 300 AD, and not long after that Patrick arrived with a daring message, a single god. What was so much more wonderful about a single god I can't say, but the worship of multiple gods soon became the sin of idolatry.

'Like all the royal sites of Ireland, Navan fort or Emain Macha overlooks a great spread of view.' The guide points directly east to the Church of Ireland cathedral of Armagh, on the site of the original Patrician church. 'That it lines up directly east of Navan fort is no coincidence,' he believes. 'Ever so slightly to the north is the double spire of the Catholic cathedral. And there's Slemish,' he says, pointing north at Slieve Mish. 'That hill in distant blue is where Patrick came as a slave and where he found God during his six years as a shepherd.'

I feel a wave of a picture completed, like the satisfaction you get from working out some complicated puzzle, the story from start to finish, the great changeover of power as the Iron Age went into retreat and the Christian age stepped into the breach. Before the group disperses, the guide has one more splinter to add to the archaeological jigsaw: 'An ancient *slighe* (road) was unearthed from under the present-day Navan Fort Road on the far side of the mound. This, it seems, was part of the Slighe Mhidhluachra, one of the five great roads of ancient Ireland that spread out from the mound of Tara, and passed by the Kilnasaggart pillar stone in the townland of Edenappa.'

Easing myself gently out of the Iron Age I head for the Glens of Antrim.

TWENTY

GLENS OF DREAMS

Glenarm, Glenaan, Glenariff, Glencloy, Glentaisie, Glenshesk, Glendun, Glencorp, Glenballyeamon, the names roll like bells. These are the nine Glens of Antrim and their sound matches this landscape that God has gifted with such grace. Words come easy here in The Glens and poets weren't found wanting – John Hewitt, Moira O'Neill, Siobhán Ní Luain, Anne-Marie Fyfe. Some were drawn here, others were of here. Siobhán Ní Luain (Johanna O'Loan, her birthname) came from the tenth glen, Glenravel, and her poetry gives a childhood glimpse of the idioms, secret codes, and the native knowledge of her people.

I'm going to get some insights on her today. I'm meeting up with her relations – Maura Ó Loan, Paula Tumelty and local historian Donnell O'Loan. We link up in the little village of Martinstown and I follow them downhill to the cemetery where Siobhán is buried. Maura and Paula are her grandnieces and Donnell is a more distant relative. They're going to introduce me to her homeplace which is their homeplace too. Maura and Donnell were born in Glenravel.

Some glenspeople think Glenravel is not part of The Glens

proper and so they relegate it to tenth place, the tenth Glen of Antrim. It's an inland glen unlike the nine which face out to sea. It's a spot with its own sense of place, its own community, its own dialect though, unlike some others, it never was an Irish-speaking area.

Glenravel graveyard is nestling on the slope of a hill. Half way up the incline, a bell tower stands protectively over the tombs, like a bird guarding her clutch. It's placed in a spot where it can best sing out its chimes and let them resound through the glen. It was always separate from the ill-fated church that stood further downhill on the same site – the church was blown up during The Troubles in the seventies.

I can see from the inscriptions on the headstones that O'Loan is a common name here. It's Donnell's and Maura's name and Paula's grandmother's name. There are other repeating family names too – Higgins, McQuillan, Carey, Scullion – and they tell something of Glenravel, that it's a place of large progenies where families mixed and intermarried. The result is, when you're looking for directions around these parts and mention a family name, you have to narrow it down – several times – before you get the right people.

Siobhán Ní Luain is often described as a poet who transmits the story of her special place in the world, of a way of life, of a place with a strong sense of that small farming community from which she hailed. But Paula thinks that gives an image of a family who didn't know beyond the rim of the glen.

'Siobhán would have been very aware of the far-off world. Her parents married in New Zealand in 1870. Her four elder siblings were born in Australia, though they'd settled in Glenravel by the time she was born.'

At the graveside Maura reads Siobhán's poem, 'The Thatcher'.

'I'm choosing this, because I imagine it was there the thatcher stood when he looked along the glen,' she says, pointing to the bridge.

I talked with him upon the bridge,
A thin man bent and old,
"I crowned the roofs with gold," he said,
"I crowned the roofs with gold."

The water, darkening at the bridge,
Flowed at its sleepy will,
And half-way up the mountain side
The oats were golden still.

Maura's Glenravel accent is floating into the air as she recreates the vision of the thatcher, like an echo of her great-aunt's memories.

We're ready to go to the nearby townland of Ballsallagh, to the house where the poet was born. This is where she spent her childhood and we get to see the surrounding scene that inspired the words. It was Maura's birthplace too and she loves that shared closeness with her great-aunt, though two generations separate them.

'I remember as a child, waking up during the night and seeing that same 'fairyland' as Siobhán describes in her poem, 'Moonlight on the Rowan Tree'.

Who's sleeping in the end room now?
What child looks out on mystery,
A garden like a painted set,
And moonlight on the rowan tree?

The house is a traditional two-storey farmhouse, with chimneys on both gables. The main door leads to a front garden though the back entrance facing the farmyard, looks like the one that's most used. One alteration since the poet's time is the slated roof, no longer the 'golden thatch' that warmed and coloured Siobhán's poetry.

A distant relative, Declan Scullion lives here now. He too has poetic connections. His great grandfather, Patrick McQuillan, wrote the poem 'The Tenth Glen'. So, it's a day for poets and their offspring. With an unhurried air he shows us a framed picture of how the house looked when Siobhán lived here.

And here in the slightly dipped landscape in the shelter of the trees and a nearby hill, by the sound of the River Ravel, Maura and Paula talk grandmothers, granduncles, cousins, grandfathers until relations ravel into a medley that resonates like the name of the glen itself. I can't follow the family lines, there are too many grands and greats and, in the end, I stop trying, and soak in the local delight. The words pass over my head, codes of meshing heredity, echoes of ancestry, of people and places unknown, bringing me back to my own childhood comfort, of sounds not yet understood, of people talking, of people knowing, while I listen, a small person whose knowledge hasn't got off the ground.

Maura reads 'The Sally Patch' with words stretching and tumbling on the farming terrain it overlooks:

This was my sally patch, my childhood through,
When I was free from school and free to play
In its lithe greenness the whole summer long.
A path went through it. I could run that way
From road to river, from the house concealed;
A winding path that no one else could find.
I made of it a veiled, green secret place
For playmates that lived only in my mind.

I want to locate 'the patch between the river and the road' from the same poem, where the 'ragged sallies' took root, and mentions in other poems like 'the haunted house', '…a ghost that was known as Ben'. When I say it looks exactly as I expected it to be, a small area of grass, of manageable size for a child's eyes, Paula says: 'That's a compliment to her skill in transmitting the scene.'

Maura explains the ghost known as Ben.

'Two brothers, George and Edward Benn, were the landlords of this area. They weren't popular. Someone took a shotgun at one of them but missed. They threatened to haunt the place after their death. This became an excuse for young lads to escort the girls home in the evening, in case the Benn ghost might get them.'

The Benns made the train loop into a detour in case it would spoil their aspect.

'It was the first narrow-gauge line in Ireland and it was constructed in 1870 to transport iron ore from the mines. Later it took passengers until it closed in the 1930s,' explains Donnell.

It might have been a blot on the Benn's landscape but for Siobhán it held the ready-made wistfulness that found its way into 'The Narrow Gauge Line'.

When I was a child I'd have said that forever
The train would endure just the same as the river.

Maura points to the hill opposite the house about a field and a half away from where we're standing and tells a story that was passed down the family, of just how slowly it took that slope.

'There the train had the steepest gradient to climb in all of Ireland and it crawled up the glen. When Aunt Hannah (Siobhán was known as Hannah to the family) came home on her visits from Dublin someone used to be given the job of standing by the railway line, to look into the passenger carriage to see if she was on the train. If she missed the connection it would mean they would have to go to Ballymena to collect her, if they could see her in the carriage, they would just have to pick her up at the local station in the village of Cargan.'

The River Ravel flows along at quite a clip. Its waters are blackish from the iron-ore mine in Dungonnell. Roll back the centuries and this little river had a critical job to do:

'Though it seems minor, it was an important boundary between the Celtic kingdoms and battles along by its banks were recorded in the Annals. Even today it is a dividing line between civil parishes,' explains Donnell.

We've other places to see so we move along.

When Donnell asks Maura and Paula if they're staying for the rest of the tour, they answer eagerly. 'Oh yes, we're here for the day.'

Enthusiasm is catching.

We leave Ballsallagh to the echo of Siobhán Ní Luain's poetry, her words became custodians of this townland, keepers of its memory – thatching, churning, walking the ducks – heirlooms of the quiet tasks of her people.

I follow Donnell's car by roads that are narrow, uphill and downhill, in spots catching up with the old route of the narrow-gauge line. It's late summer and already the day has a feel of autumn. White clouds are hurrying along, shifting the light in front of them. The restless sky makes the hills look all the more solid. Antrim sheep graze nimbly on the shoulder of the mountain, unfazed by the passing traffic. The more vertiginous minded higher up look like white dots. Nearer to Glenariff Forest Park the highground is hued from end to end in a purple flower, like a veil spread downwards to the roadside.

'It's called Rosebay willowherb,' Donnell tells me. And when he says that Glenariff is called the Queen of the Glens I think how well the purple of this flower, the colour of power, ties in with the royal name. From the summit Donnell picks out some places from the ample view, where the landlord once lived, though nothing remains now except the dark leaves of the forest plantation and the lighter green of bare fields.

'That's where the Dobbs house stood. He was the landlord. They had no family and his wife either sold or bequeathed the land to the Northern Ireland Government Forestry Service.'

That makes me feel a whole lot better, kind of makes my day, that some wealthy people were eager to share their view and their great spread of property with the rest of us. Donnell sweeps a hand across winding trails, and the route he took on a recent walk. Walkways crisscross and intersect on the slopes. And now a look into a more testing saunter – Waterfall Walk. This cuts deep into Glenariff, which shows off its proud name, Queen of the Glens – in precipices, ravines and chasms as it gorges its way to the sea.

'It's U-shaped, where 10,000 years ago the ice gouged out this shape. Beneath the feet is basalt, further down towards the coast it's a limestone area,' Donnell explains.

The land is wild in the glen compared to the fertile plains on the higher slopes. Sheep have to pin themselves to the steep sides of the valley for some pickings. Far into the depths houses in sculpted miniature blend in as if they're part of the natural scene.

'Of course the title Queen of the Glens is arguable,' says Donnell, showing no favouritism. I don't know what the competitors look like but, at this moment, there's no argument. I feel I'm floating on air up here with the highground rotating around me like a carousel. Then Donnell tells the story of the early days of tourism, in the late nineteenth century when the idea of down-time was born, an idea with a big future, when city people started to come here to share this landscape.

'Around the turn of the nineteenth century when the mines closed, the train was used to draw tourists here. They boarded the train in Belfast, then took the narrow-gauge line from Ballymena, on to the main station of Parkmore before continuing along the left fork where tourists were met by jaunting car to take them to the Waterfall Walk.'

He explains the historic reason most of the homes visible from here are inhabited by Catholics: 'The Glens weren't part of the Plantation of Ulster (the seventeenth century colonisation of Ulster when English and Scottish Protestants were settled on land confiscated from the Gaelic Irish after the Flight of the Earls).

It didn't include Antrim or Down. At the end of the fourteenth century The Glens came into the possession of the McDonnells, a Scottish clan, and they became the Earls of Antrim.'

But clans like empires rise and fall.

'During the English Civil War, McDonnell backed Charles 1, and paid the price. When the Cromwellians came to power he had to forfeit his possessions though he managed to get them back when Charles ll became king.'

The narrow glimpse of sea that's visible between the verticles of the valley has a look of faraway yearning about it. Donnell points to where Scotland is visible on a clear day, a handy sight for McDonnell to view his other possessions across the North Channel. But you need clear weather. We get no sighting of it today.

I follow Donnell's car downhill towards the foot of Glenariff, on a road which doesn't allow brakes a single minute's rest. At an elbow turn, I follow sharp right into the carpark where the old teahouse once stood. It's now Laragh Lodge restaurant. The view has that postcard look about it and, in my mind, I imagine another scene, of tea being graciously poured, in china cups to portentious ladies and gentlemen. The great love of sipping tea that people developed back then made its importers rich.

Maura and Paula are already at a table. Paula spreads out the sepia pictures of Siobhán.

'Before the publication of her two books, Siobhán's work appeared in newspapers and magazines, mostly *Dublin Opinion* (a satirical magazine). And right up to the end of the long run of Ciarán MacMathúna's radio programme *Mo Cheol Thú*, they were regularly read aloud. Listeners asked for them over and over again. I think their appeal was the nostalgia and the rural depiction of events and the countryside of her youth.'

Lunch over, we stroll along by the waterfall. From the heights of the Forest Park we had looked down on Glenariff as it descended. From this end we see The Waterfall Walk on its way up.

'Stairway pathways cut into the near vertical sides of the gorge and boardwalks on stilts on the river', so reads the brochure Donnell hands me. We have to raise our voices to be heard above the noise of the pendant of water called Ess na Crub (the fall of the hoof). Further up, where the Inver River joins the Glenariff River, it gets harder to hear a conversation.

Our next stop is Cushendall, a two-mile drive by the coast, at the foot of Glenballyeamon. Sometimes Cushendall is called the capital of The Glens, more because of its cultural heritage than its size. Francis Turnly, merchant and philanthropist, bought it in the early nineteenth century with the money he made in the East India Company in China. It overlooks the waters of the Dall which was especially diverted to make way for the town's design and in 1975 it was made an area of conservation. The red hue of the town's proudest building, the Curfew Tower, knows it belongs here – Cushendall, like most of The Glens, is a place of sandstone formation. Squarely standing to attention, the soldierly shape of the tower befits the role of sentry duty that it was given. Turnly had a watchman armed with musket and pike guard it. Tea money might have funded its construction but it's the new wealth of rock music that powers it now. Musician Bill Drummond owns it.

West of the town centre is the cemetery. We've come to see the grave of Margaret Emmeline Dobbs. She was an Irish language enthusiast who took with delight to the Gaelic revival around the turn of the twentieth century. This heady time still calls up a frisson of excitement, this new brand of nationalism, driven by the Gaelic League and the Gaelic Athletic Association.

What makes the story of this *scoláire Gaeilge* (Irish scholar) worth telling was she was one of a number of privileged women, from the Protestant-Unionist tradition who grouped up with the women of The Glens, an Irish-speaking area. She was the daughter of Edward Conway Dobbs, High Sheriff of Carrickfergus. Though the ordinary Gaelic-speaking women of the Glens (if anyone can be called ordinary) might sound like odd companions for Miss Margaret Emmeline Dobbs, that was only half the oddity. Her brother, James Dobbs had partaken in the Larne gunrunning in April 1914 to use force if necessary to resist Home Rule and maintain the union with Britain. Yet she was a close friend of Irish nationalist, Roger Casement and she donated £600 for the Casement Defence fund in 1916 when he was charged with high treason for gunrunning for the opposite cause, Irish freedom.

It was here in the town of Cushendall that a meeting was held in the schoolhouse on February 28, 1904 which led to the first announcement of *Feis na nGleann* (a Gaelic League cultural carnival). Margaret Emmeline was one of its founder members. Maura tells us of her own special interest in this *Feis*. Her great uncle, Hugh Flatley, a schoolteacher, was also a founder member of *Feis na nGleann*.

Roger Casement was brought up in Antrim. He was a fervent follower of *Feis na nGleann*. He hired a steamer to bring a crowd of two hundred or so from Rathlin Island to the Red Bay in Glenariff where they landed to attend the first *Feis* and he led a procession from Cushendall to Waterfoot. About two-thousand people turned up in Glenariff that day. It was a memorable event – singing, dancing, music, games, the *poc fada* contest, storytelling and the echoes of that special tone of Irish spoken in The Glens. (The *poc fada,* or the long-stroke is where competitors strike the *sliotar* or hurley ball. The winner is the player who drives it to the furthest point.)

The *Feis* wasn't to everyone's liking. In 1906 a landlord of the Turnly family threatened to penalise his tenants for offering to lend a field to the *feis* committee. But he was up against a defiant lot. They were determined to make it the great success it turned out to be. Casement rolled up the sleeves and cleared Turnly's field of its high-growing weeds and thistles with a scythe.

Margaret Emmeline kept up her strong interest in the Irish

language until her death in 1962 at the age of 91. Her funeral, meant to be private, turned out very public indeed when hundreds from The Glens turned out.

What glowing days these were, the most exciting of modern Irish history I reckon, with cultural currents crossing divides, from Lady Gregory's Coole to the salons of Dublin, from Gaeltacht Donegal to the wives and daughters of Belfast's big industrialists, high sheriffs and staunch unionists, from Synge's Aran islands to the Glens of Antrim.

We're inclined to dawdle. Donnell reminds us that the day is moving on. We've more to see in Cushendun, the grave of Ada McNeill of Cushendun Lodge, another *scoláire* Ulster Protestant lady.

The road from Cushendall to Cushendun is about a ten-minute journey. I lose and find my two guiding cars, Donnell's and Maura's, as the road bends and straightens out. Cushendun means 'the foot of the brown river' – the River Dun – the colour brown flows down from the peat and boggy hills. We follow Donnell to Glenmona House, the home of Ada's cousin Ronald McNeill, Lord Cushendun.

Donnell tells a yarn about him: 'The story goes that one evening the IRA called on Lord Cushendun to tell him they were about to bomb his house. When he opened the door, he asked them if they could come back another time perhaps, that he was giving a dinner party. And they agreed. The original house was burned by the IRA and the one we see today is a rebuild.'

So, it seems they did come back at another time.

We stroll to the grave of Ronald's cousin Ada. She too looked to the women of The Glens, to gather their legends and get the voice of Irish from the living Gaeltacht. Her grave lies quietly by the sandstone church in Cushendun (now used for secular events. One is about to arrive, a posh affair by the looks of it).

Ada McNeill and Margaret Emmeline Dobbs were only some of the enthusiasts of the Celtic revival. Others were Rose Maud

Young of Galgorm Castle, Gertrude Parry of the Casement family, Barbara McDonnell of Glenariff and Margaret Hutton, the wife of a Belfast industrialist and friend of Patrick Pearse, executed for his part in the 1916 rebellion against British rule. Hutton's house on Belfast's Malone Road was a hive of cultural gatherings and she donated money to Pearse's Irish school in Rathfarnham in Dublin.

Paula explains: 'Irish wasn't such a political statement back then as it's now perceived in the North of Ireland.'

Donnell agrees. 'These women saw no difficutly in celebrating Irish culture and sticking with their own political tradition. They remained staunch unionists and had no problem keeping politics to one side of culture.'

Exactly what Douglas Hyde, the co-founder of the Gaelic League wanted – that the organisation be kept out of politics. (He failed in the end.) His idea was a Celtic revival, native culture, language, folktales and sagas to be shared by all. He himself, the son of a Protestant clergyman, had learned Irish from the locals in his home in County Roscommon.

What followed was like a love affair, up and down the country, people were stricken with this interest in new-found culture and games. To find a spot, like The Glens, where the language was the everyday tongue was nearly as exciting as finding the ancient sagas in the manuscripts. No wonder they sought them out and teamed up with them. In the year of the founding of the Gaelic League, 1893, Irish was hail and hearty in The Glens, especially Glenarm, Cary and Glenariff.

We know from the daily entries of Rose Maud Young, as keen a diarist as she was a *scoláire Gaeilge,* exactly how smoothly the Protestant enthusiasts kept their cultural interest separate from politics. Rose Maud was the daughter of John Young, Chief Sheriff and Deputy Lieutenant of Antrim. Her diaries show her celebrating events of parallel worlds – attending *Feis na nGleann*, going to Irish classes in Donegal, celebrating UVF (Ulster Volunteer Force) parades, attending a party in her home (Galgorm castle, an estate of two thousand acres near Ballymena) for the coronation of George V, enjoying the bonfires in Galgorm for the Royal Jubilee and travelling to Dublin for the inauguration of her friend Douglas Hyde as President of Ireland.

But let's give Rose Maud her *scoláire Gaeilge* name as it's written on the plaque of her home in Galgorm, Róis Ní Ógáin, unveiled in February 1996 when her anthology of Irish verse, published in three volumes in the nineteen twenties, *Duanaire Gaedhilge,* was launched by her grand niece Rosemary Lady Brookeborough.

Rose Maud's interest was first stirred by Bishop William Reeves, Rector of Ballymena, an Irish speaker and a frequent visitor to Galgorm. He had collected some old Irish manuscripts. And then, in 1891, when studying in England she visited Oxford and when she came across other old Irish manuscripts in the Bodleian library – *The Annals of Tighernach and The Life of Colmcille* – they struck a familiar chord.

Our day's tour has come to an end and we part here in the carpark. But before we go, Donnell has one more sight to point to, the house of poet Moira O'Neill on Cushendun's water's edge.

Her real name was Agnes Nesta Shakespeare Higginson. She got inside the lore of The Glens by adopting a local name and dialect. When she died poet laureate, John Masefield (a regular visitor to Cushendun) wrote that the charm of her poems was her deep feeling for place, as in 'Lookin' Back.'

Wathers o' Moyle I hear ye callin'
Clearer for half o' the world between,
Antrim hills an' the wet rain fallin' ...
Whiles ye are nearer than snow-tops keen:

What a day it has been. As our car doors clap shut and we wave one another goodbye, I drive away in a glow of the sweet warmth of place, of a day that called out goodness from start to finish, of The Glens from first to ninth – and, most of all, tenth – of times present and times past, churnings, thatchings, linguistic meshing, cultural exchanging, flowing into one stream, like the two rivers, the Inver and the Glenariff, cascaded into one another earlier today, in the Queen of the Glens.

Turning southwards, driving home by the Antrim coast, the Causeway Coastal Road, I look out for the changing layers of rock of The Glens – limestone here, sandstone there, black basalt. But why am I measuring rock formation in this unmeasured beauty. I let the Antrim plateau scroll against the sky at its ease. Between the mountains, The Glens pass by, calm and mysterious, sheltered against the crystal sealight on my left. This highground has no peeks but carries fields on its back pushing their way upwards as far as they can go. Others stand, rugged and unkempt, barren in spots, bearing their stoney edges like teeth to the sea.

I watch out for the great feat of engineering that Donnell talked about earlier today, when this road was constructed in the 1830s. There wasn't a natural road here so one had to be implanted – at great cost.

'They used techniques that hadn't been tried before. There was no tunnelling, like in later road building. A new road was pressing. Hills were steep. The mountains were boggy and the roads muddy. The gentry had to regularly get out of their carriages to push them uphill.'

So, the County Grand Jury, made up of landlords responsible for the administration of the county, understood the hardship of their fellow gentlemen and got funding from the Board of Works (which dealt with public works). Scottish engineer William Bald came up with an idea that had never been tried before, in Donnell's words, 'to bring down the edge of the headlands to sea level.'

Groundbreaking and all as this project was, it was minor

compared to its social effect. It opened up The Glens. Before, each glen lived in its own world, nestled like an animal in its lair. Hunkered between high ground, the nine glens looked out to sea. At nighttime when their lamps burned, and marked them out of their remoteness, they must have looked like the separate worlds they were, each valley twinkling with its own sprit of place. Back then the easiest way to visit a neighbouring glen was to take your boat and loop in from the sea.

'It was easier to go the twelve miles to Scotland than to go the seventeen or eighteen miles to the local town of Ballymena, by Glenravel on a rutted road,' says storyteller, Liz Weir. Liz has made The Glens her home, making the journey the other way around, from Ballymena where she was born, to Glenballyeamon, a remote spot on a remote glen, a thousand feet up the mountain.

She believes that the Antrim coast road, penetrating and all as it was, didn't shake The Glens entirely out of their folds. They still guard their legends and folklore and she keeps up one of their longstanding traditions – storytelling: 'They're proud of their roots here. This part was very poor, sheep, sheep and more sheep. They were small mountain farmers, very much their own people with a strong sense of Irishness, though it's no longer a Gaeltacht area. You can still see their history in the Catholic-Protestant demographics. The Church of Ireland in Cushendall has only about forty parishioners. I would have been brought up Protestant myself, though I've no religion now. Hurling is the other big thing in The Glens, almost a religion here. A *camán* (hurley stick) is put into the hand of every child from about the age of two.'

And a story she tells with special aplomb on International Women's Day is how the Protestant-Unionist women of Antrim linked up with the Irish-speaking women of the Glens in a time gone by.

Liz, who chairs the Glens Storytelling Cultural Heritage Group and is director of the Glens Storytelling Fest reports: 'Storytelling is a growing interest, Even during the pandemic we told stories from different locations around here. keeping faithful to the oral tradition of The Glens.'

Just as The Glens has a draw for Liz's storytelling it earlier drew the poet John Hewitt to live here. Even though Hewit's poems tell of the indigenous knowledge of The Glens – old folk ways, customs, rituals, prayers, travelling musicians, 'wee folk' (fairies), he was well aware of his blow-in status – 'a strange bird observed about the house'. A memorial to him stands by Ossian's grave his chosen place. It is in the townland of Lubitavish, near Cushendall. (Ossian is based on Oisín, son of Fionn MacCumhaill.)

TWENTY-ONE

ASKING FOR DIRECTIONS

I'm to meet Michael Farry in the carpark near the roundabout in Collooney, County Sligo. We've no problem finding one another. We're the only two here. I'm already acquainted with him from his writing. It was by chance one day that I picked up his book in the library, *Asking for Directions*.

The sense of place that flows through his poems make me ask him for directions – to guide me around his special spot in the world, by the houses of the neighbours, the school, the shops, where he was sent on errands as a boy, the small things that turned into poetry.

'I'll drive,' he offers. That's good because I want to take notes. He's talkative, there are no awkward silences, no airs or graces, he's a fellow who puts you at your ease.

Coolaney, his birthplace, is about eight kilometres west of its near namesake, Collooney. It huddles in the shelter of 'the mountain'.

Never mind that this is the Ox Mountain range – a peekless high ground of especially ancient rock, melted crushed and folded, one billion years older than Sligo's celebrated mountain, Ben Bulben – today it's 'the mountain' because that's what it was known as in Michael Farry's youthful world. Off the beaten tourist track it may be but this, the place of his roots, is a spot with a proud sense of its own culture.

'Being from Sligo,' he claims, 'earns you no boasting rights compared to, say, scenic places like Kerry or Donegal. It has less fame, less regard.'

Maybe so. This county might not show off its landscape as haughtily as some, but, for him, the sense of kindred spirit with the places around here makes up for its lack of bragging credentials. Here with 'the mountain' standing sentinel behind, it seems like an honour to show me the spots where the three railway cottages stood in which the family had the right to live because of his father's occupation in the railway. But first, 'the mountain'.

'The mountain was an ever-present backdrop in our life,' he explains, 'fire on the mountain, rain coming in from the mountain. And the far side of the mountain was like another world.'

He links his home place with no great riches but with a pulse of a different kind. His first work was a history of his local parish, Killoran: *Killoran and Coolaney, a Local History.* He calls it 'a parish in the middle of nowhere'. I sense it's the 'nowhere' aspect of it that holds special appeal for him.

'Probably,' he answers. 'But I was always very aware of the parish too.'

He's still mindful of the liturgical boundaries and as we weave in and out of the landscape, he notes when we cross the border into a different parish. And I'm let into his former world where he went to church, walked to school, roamed freely, like the children from the Enid Blyton stories he read with relish. He loved poetry. At a very young age he liked *The Little Waves of Breffny* by fellow Sligo native, Eva Gore-Booth. He recalls the evening song of Benediction in the local churh and the rhythm of his footsteps to the school in Rockfield. This became a ready-made tempo for his poetic compositions.

We drive by Rockfield cemetery. Some of his ancestors are here – parents, a grandfather, a great grandmother, his two sisters. And now we're ready to do a circle by the houses where he grew up. He stops ceremoniously at each one.

'This is the railway cottage where I was born, the Iron Cottage, corrugated iron on the outside, timber on the inside,' he says as he pulls up alongside the small dwelling. It's in rural heartland, uninhabited now and overgrown. 'There was a strong sense of being isolated here,' he explains wistfully. 'We weren't from Collooney, not even Coolaney, but outside of it, outside of something that was itself outside. And we weren't farmers among a community of farmers. We were very far from the centre.' Maybe this was a natural condition in the making of a poet, being the outsider, seeing a different angle of his world. 'Maybe,' he agrees, 'it was something that was neither good nor bad, something given. But, though cut off, we were very aware of what was happening in the world, things like the Hungarian uprising in 1956, the Olympic Games the same year.'

We stop at the site of his second home, where this two-storey cottage once stood. Alas, that house was flattened.

'This is the one I've the fondest memories of,' he says looking at the vacant site, where he did his growing up. Although not a stone of the old home remains, the thoughtful tone of his voice brings us more into the heart of the journey of his youth than if we were looking at the building itself.

The final family dwelling, the Station House, is in the village of Coolaney. Even today it's a cut above the average design, high-pitched, typical railway company architecture.

'All three are still owned by the railway even though the trains have long-since stopped, since the late sixties in fact,' he tells me, 'the rail company still holds on to the disused railway line too. This line was built in the 1880s as a Relief Scheme. (The Light Railway Act of 1889, one of Arthur Balfour's reforming acts for Ireland, when he was Chief Secretary, established a rail system in the west of Ireland.) It used to be called the Burma line. I assume that was because it was hard for the driver, who had to cope with a great number of level crossings and bridges. There were no tunnels, no cutting through hills, so the train went uphill and down inclines. My mother used to open one of the many level crossing gates," he recalls.

Employment in the railway came with a phone. 'An open phone line, a kind of internal telephone system. The conversation could be heard by everyone within earshot. If it rang once it was for us; if it rang twice it was for someone else.'

It sounds local, idyllic. Although hardly secretive, it somehow fits in with the secret codes of a youthful world, its idioms, its halcyon days, like the adventures Farry read about in Enid Blyton's stories, with the evocative sound of the whistle of a distant train in the background – what better life could be found for a budding poet. Our chat is interrupted by the great boulder near where his old schoolhouse stands.

'This is Rockfield,' he says, pointing to the great rock, an Ice Age glacial erratic. It was carried along from its source in some distant place by a glacier, and found itself stranded in a field in the middle of nowhere when the ice melted. This outsider imposed its name on the place, Rockfield, like Farry's poetry imposes its stamp on the place where he too was an ever-so-slight outsider.

'Rockfield primary school was where I got to love learning by rote. Repeated sounds kept the mind focused. It was in tune with the tempo of life, walking to school, helping a farmer (he shows me his house, derelict now) with the hay after school, going to church on Sunday. When I began writing poetry, in my teens, I found a discovery of something in the challenge to keep to the rhyme. Looking for the right word to respect the rhythm sends you off on a different path and opens up new discoveries.'

He likes what can be done with poetry, the perseverance it takes, the limits you have to respect, I think tie in with his love of the parish – the cell-like enclosure of its borders, the natural boundaries, echoed by the chant of Benediction and the liturgical mantra of repeated sounds.

I want to see 'Coleman's flooded field' (from his poem 'Waterlogged'), the home of his adventures:

Once, I'd accept such adventures,
cruise transient seas after school
in Coleman's flooded lower field,
my boots and trouser bottoms sodden.

And there it is on our right alongside Knockadoo passage grave.

'Coleman's was where we used to get the milk,' he explains. 'The house is still there and the Coleman family.'

On our right he stops at Knocknashee (hill of the fairies), which was directly in his line of vision from his home. A Bronze Age township was discovered here in 1988 during a survey of Sligo which ranks highly alongside other European finds. But back to the parish.

'When I was researching the parish history I met people from this area who had participated in the Civil War and I found out that some around here played a big part in the anti-Treaty side of the debate in the nineteen twenties. That led me to my doctorate on *Revolutionary Sligo. The Irish Revolution: Sligo 1912-23, The Aftermath of Revolution: Sligo 1921-23'*. I think there was a guilt feeling of not having been more interested in the War of Independence, so they got involved in the civil war.'

We're surrounded by hummocky, moorland terrain, no better place to hide and fight the enemy.

As we make a sharp right turn on a fork-like bend 'the mountain' changes position and accompanies us on our left. Michael points to the pleats on the mountainside, the drills of old, or lazy beds, where any ground at all was colonised for potato growing to hold back the hunger during the Great Famine of the mid nineteenth century.

We pass by the great swathe of moorland on our right and the memory of the solid labour of work in the bog comes to him.

'Cutting turf on the mountain was a laborious job, but more than compensated for by the view over the plain. It was the whistle of the passing train that reminded us that our day's work was at an end.'

What lovely recollections of untroubled days, a life of solid work with its reward at that serene time of day, heralded by the signal of a train.

'It wasn't a place of great wealth, but we didn't know we were poor.'

No question of a dead hand of a place that he couldn't wait to be rescued out of though most of his classmates had to leave.

'I've no grievance with life. I'm grateful for the independence I learned here. I picked that up from the small farming community around here. Small farmers were brilliant at making the most of what they had.'

Onwards, by the Owenbwee river (in Irish, *abhainn bhuí*) which translates Yellow River where Farry used to go fishing with his father. It amuses him when I say that between the Burma line and the Yellow river my head is filling with the exotica of the east, of the Silk Road, the Yellow emperor, the Road to Mandalay

And now to The Hawk's Rock.

'There it is,' he points at the rock that sticks up above the surface like bones protruding through flesh. Alongside it is Tullaghan hill with its famous holy well, a hundred metres above sea level and strange enough to be described in the fourteenth century manuscript, the *Book of Ballymote* as one of the 'wonders of Ireland'. (The *Book of Ballymote* was written in 1390 or 1391, in Latin and Middle Irish and is now in the Royal Irish Academy in Dublin.) The story that gives the holy well its wondrous nature is that the tidal waters of nearby Ballysodare Bay ebb and flow and rotate salty and fresh water with the tide. Though that stretches credibility, who can beat this scheming, between well and tide, for ready-made enchantment? W B Yeats seized on it, combining the two place-names as The Hawk's Well for his play.

We have done the full circle on roads that Michael Farry remembers when they were first being tarred, and we're back in the little village of Coolaney, a landlord's town with its own mill, a courthouse, police station though, unusually, no school and no church. Before we leave he shows me where Collery's shop stood, the inspiration for his poem 'July 1958'. It was here he was sent to buy a clock and that was his moment of coming of age:

> I grew up the day my mother sent me for a clock
> with a five pound note, without dos and don'ts
> trusting my tact and taste – I had just turned ten.

Intertwining memories of his parents with the comforting sound of the ticking clock in an era when time was guided by sunsets, passing trains, the signal for the end-of-a-day's work he goes on:

> …When they died I tidied, took
>
> mementoes. Though tempted, I left the clock
> so its green fluorescent numerals could glow
> for all time as their emptied house wound down.

'I'm at home here, though not nostalgic,' says Farry. 'More rooted.' Although he's impatient of Irish poets and writers suffering from an overdose of rose-tinted vision about their birthplace, he admits that in his home in County Meath he keeps a few stones from Sligo.

It must be a Sligo trait. Yeats had the same sentiments. He wrote: 'I long for a sod of earth from some field I know, something of Sligo (his mother's home-place) to hold in my hand.' His brother, painter, Jack Butler Yeats, had a similar fixation about this county: 'I never did a painting without putting a thought of Sligo into it.'

The enchanted Ballysodare, where their mother came from, passes by as Michael Farry drives from the pivotal view of his youth, to the more mainstream tourist sights of Sligo on the road to Drumcliff. This is where Yeat's maternal grandparents, the Pollexfens, plied their trade as merchants, millers and sea traders. Though born in Dublin, Yeats belonged in his heart to his mother's home-place, it held a grip of wonderment for him. Because as a boy. Susan Pollexfen, told him stories of the magic of her girlhood growing up here. The outcome was his play *At The Hawks Well*, first performed in The Long Lounge, Renvyle House in 1917.

His mother's stories may have worked magic on the young Yeats but not on his father. John Butler Yeats described the Pollexfens as 'as inarticulate as the sea cliffs, lying buried under mountains of silence'.

Maybe it was this very inarticulateness that was the source that William B Yeats searched to find potency for his words. He would not be alone in this. D H Lawrence used to talk about the messages that rise from the depths of the earth. And Yeats's messages, no doubt, rose from the sea cliffs and the mountains of silence of Ballysodare.

We know William B liked to talk to small farmers, cottiers and fishermen around here. One of those was Paddy Flynn who lived in a nearby cabin. When Yeats asked him if he had ever seen the fairies, he answered: 'Am I not annoyed with them?'

That story sounds like someone poking fun at a believe-anything urban duffer. It reminds me of Belgian friends who were holidaying in Ireland. While they were held up by a farmer driving a flock of sheep across a small road in Kerry, my friend asked him what were they called?

'Belgian blues,' he answered. Her husband, more in tune with mischief, told her: 'Don't believe him, I saw him looking at the car registration.' (A Belgian blue is a type of cow.)

Ballysodare Bay lies under the eye of Knocknarea on our left. According to legend the mound on top, Medb's cairn, contains the body of Queen Medb, though I've heard of so many places where this warrior queen was buried that I'm no more inclined to believe it than I am that Paddy Flynn was pestered by the fairies.

Nearer Drumcliff, on the Wild Atlantic Way, Ben Bulben rises into view, over Sligo Bay. This flat-topped mountain is not your average mountain-peak. It's shaped like a loaf, like a terrain you could play a game of football on if you weren't worried about tumbling over the edge.

The resting place of W B Yeats in Drumcliff draws tourists in their droves. Michael has to do a few rounds of the carpark to find a vacant spot. The question is, would such crowds bother coming if they knew that it's actually unsure if Yeats' coffin contained the correct body. He was brought here from France, to his beloved Sligo for reburial in 1948, nine years after his death. In Roquebrune-Cap-Martin in Mediterranean France, his bones had been scattered in an ossuary when he died in 1939. The French diplomat sent to locate his remains to repatriate them said it was impossible to be sure if they were really his. But let's forget that and bend the knee above his supposed grave like everyone else here.

Over coffee, Michael talks about the many unrealities about Yeats: 'The woman he wrote so many love poems to didn't return his feelings. This one-sided love for Maud Gonne gives an unreality to Yeats's poetry. Yeats needed those unrealities. If she had responded to him there would have been no poetry. Then there was the unreality of claiming to be from Sligo when in fact he was born in Dublin.'

And if you add in the doubt about his presence here in Drumcliff, that makes for yet another fantasy.

Here in this sheltered spot nature works her enchanted ways for the poet too, providing the final round off of landscape beneath the magic slopes of Ben Bulben. To call Ben Bulben a mountain is another unreality. It's more a broad plateau. All I can see are slopes, ready to charm at a glance, its descending terrain waiting for a legend to be placed upon it. Naturally, legend makers weren't found wanting. Ben Bulben is where the mythical Diarmuid, lover of Gráinne, was killed by a wild boar. The famous tale from the Fenian cycle of Irish mythology, *Tóraíocht Dhiarmada agus Ghráinne*, in English, the *Pursuit of Diarmuid and Gráinne* describes Gráinne's elopement with young Diarmuid, escaping from her betrothed, Fionn Mac Cumhaill, leader of the Fianna.

Ben Bulben was well beyond the rim of Michael Farry's world growing up.

'Even the far side of the Ox Mountains was a different world to me, let alone Ben Bulben,' he shrugs.

People are milling around Drumcliff's souvenir shop and café. This churchyard was notable even before Yeats's body arrived (if it ever did). It was the site of the ancient battle of Cúl Dreimhne (sometimes spelt Cooldrumman) in the year 561, when Donegal saint, Colmcille, in a fit of irritation, set off a conflict when he disagreed with the high king's copyright verdict of the psalm he had copied.

When Michael drops me off to my car parked in Collooney, I leave in the glow of the glimpse I gained of this off-the-beaten-track in Sligo, from someone who knew the place from the inside out, where the family got the milk, where the clock was purchased, where the Burma line train hooted and whistled among the hummocky ground in the shadow of the Ox mountains.

As Collooney retreats into the mirror and I take the road to Dublin, I cast my mind back to the eighteenth century, to the Enlightenment, the Age of Reason, when faith began to shift from God and tradition and on to rational thought. There was a Collooney connection – William Higgins from here played a part in this stirring era. He was a chemistry expert and he developed chemical notation (some of which are still in use). He was invited to teach chemistry at none other than the court of Catherine the Great, empress of Russia. Russians, even Soviet Russians, look back on Catherine's reign with national pride even though Catherine wasn't Russian-born – she was a native of Germany. It was some breakthrough in cultural barriers (more groundbreaking than Yeats' claim to be from Sligo). She deposed her husband Tsar Peter lll and with the help of her lover, Grigory Orlov, and with the backing of the court, the people and the army, she was crowned in great pomp in Moscow in September 1762. Catherine was a big fan of the Enlightenment. Her dream was a reign of order, justice and the spreading of education. This is where Collooney steps into the picture. It was Higgins who introduced chemistry teaching to Russia.

This faraway story gives the imaginary link with Burma and the Yellow River of Michael Farry's countryside another detour. I'm sorry I can't point that out to him.

I thought the day had no more delights left when I see a sign for Michael Coleman Music Centre. I can't pass by without calling. Distinguished fiddle player and all as Coleman was, it's a sad story that I heard about him that makes me want to stop. When Coleman was leaving home to emigrate to the United States where he would spend the rest of his life, as he was about to get into the hired car that would take him to the station in nearby Tubbercurry, his father, James, asked him to play one last tune before he left. He took out his fiddle and there by the side of the road, outside his house played that tune for his father. The melancholy of that story fills my head, the haunting music in the air, the last notes of unity between father and son as the car sped towards the railway station. Those were the days when a trip to the United States was often a one-way journey.

The museum in his honour is in the village of Gurteen. When I see how elaborate it is I think if they had made half the fuss about him in his lifetime he would never have had to leave. But he did leave, as most people did from these parts. And in a neat little turnaround he would never have been heard of by so many only for he left. Because he was in the United States for the early days of recording. Between 1921 and 1936 he made eighty recordings. He also made recordings shortly before his death in 1945 and to date these haven't been released. His great technical ability and 'expressive playing' would make him the most influential traditional musician of the century.

'There's a replica of his house, opposite his birthplace,' says the woman in the museum. I'd prefer to see the wall and barn of Coleman's real house which, she tells me are still standing. She adds, 'Michael Coleman's grand-nephew, also called Michael, lives close by.'

Really? I've a great urge to call, but I'm hesitant about landing on someone's doorstep. He must have dozens of callers like me. I gain courage as I drive uphill towards the house. The barking dog on the doorstep is only half the problem. How will I introduce myself?

With my car door opened an inch I ask the man who appears at the door if the dog would bite if I venture out further, a waste of a question. Owners never know because a dog is unlikely to bite them.

'He's a good guard-dog,' he replies. I try my best to look like someone who won't put his guarding skills to the test. He speaks a few reassuring words to the barking animal and that convinces him I'm not worth expending any energy on. As he resumes his perch on the doorship I have to cross over him at the invitation to come in.

What a welcome. Over a spread of photographs and memorabilia on the kitchen table Michael and his wife bring me back the family lines. It's pure joy to sit in their cosy room in front of yellowing newspaper cuttings of a fiddle player whose music I knew since I was a child.

'There's no photo of Michael himself, though here's a picture of his two brothers. One of them, Jim, was said to be a better fiddle player than Michael.'

Tantalisingly, we will never know because Jim's music died with him.

Michael offers to show me what's left of the original house. We drive downhill on our way to the townland of Knockgrania leaving the good guard-dog's bark growing fainter and fainter.

Michael Coleman's birthplace is at a sharp bend. Walking along this road, the R294, about two miles north-west of the village of Gorteen is a hazardous undertaking as cars clip by.

I want to stay a while to soak up the hush of the old homestead, just the wall that is left, and let the story of that melancholy last tune ripple through me. I can capture the feeling, the time, 1914 when Michael Coleman was twenty three, capture the atmosphere that drove a generation or more out of this lovely countryside.

I don't take Michael up on the offer to see the replica house. I'd prefer to look at the ruins of his grandfather's home place. That brings us up a narrow laneway with grass growing on its spine. Just the barn is still standing. It's well silent now, but this once was a great dancing venue.

These were the dances where the local fiddlers played in the special style of their part of the country. That was the beauty of the cut-off world. You knew a district by its music. The downside of recording was that it made a patch of universe porous as one musician copied another. We know Michael Coleman merged pipe playing techniques with his fiddle music. His father James was a flute player and that found its way into his playing too.

'The barn looks small for a dance unless the dancers took turns on the floor,' I say, measuring it in my mind against Billy Brennan's barn in County Monaghan, immortalised by Patrick Kavanagh.

'Maybe,' he answers. 'Would you like to go to Killavil? Killavil was a place known for its music. Have you ever heard of Fred Finn or Lad O'Beirne?'

Not until now, I have to disclose. Fred Finn has a plaque erected here in his honour.

We stop for a while beside where he is commemorated, Killavil, a musical breeding ground among the hills where every note had its work cut out for it. The hands of these musicians were often rough, working hands but they became dexterous in the presence of an instrument. For this cluster of fiddle-players, flute-players, pipe-players, the tunes set them free. It was freedom like Michael Farry's roaming over his native countryside of Coolaney, a few hills from here. This carefree life would shape future memories and interlace words that flowed like the tunes. At the time there was little money in music, or words for that matter. But like Michael Farry, the musicians of Knockgrania or Killavil 'didn't know they were poor.' There was a wealth about carrying on a noble tradition.

Ahead of us rises the hill of Kesh whose caves, Keshcorran, are steeped in myth. Here I would have emerged out of Ownagat (the Cave of the Cats), that Eamon, the guide at Rathcroghan, County Roscommon, showed me if I had taken the plunge into the underworld. It's a long way from here to Rathcroghan, by car, let alone walking along an underground tunnel. No danger. I'll leave that to those of a bolder nature than me. I'll stick to the route above the ground.

The dog gets into a frenzy again at the sound of the car as I drop Michael home. But he wags with delight when he sees my passenger emerging. I'm glad I called. I was received with that glow of hospitality for which this community was renowned: dancing, playing music, singing songs, visiting one another's houses, a way of life they now commemorate with plaques and museums.

TWENTY-TWO

HOMAGE TO A RIVER

Today I'm in Athlone, a town that stands sentry over the River Shannon. I remember my first sighting of this place at the age of seven when we passed by on the way to Dublin. I wanted to stop but the adults ignored me. I sulked. Sulking was the only influence I had on decision-making back then.

That fleeting view of Athlone stayed with me – the bridge, the boats swaying and drifting on the Shannon, Custume Barracks, Adamson castle, the church. These were the places that crowded into the picture that day if only I could have named them. We got to Dublin and in my small opinion the capital had nothing on Athlone. But the adults told me to be quiet and enjoy myself whether I liked it or not. I was too spoiled, they said – as if I'd spoiled myself.

More than any other town in Ireland Athlone has a special claim to the River Shannon. Maybe we don't love our rivers like they do in other countries because we're seldom short of water, but the Shannon is worth paying homage to. It's the longest river in Ireland. From its source in the Shannon pot, a small trout stream on the slopes of Cuilcagh mountain near the border with Northern Ireland, it courses through the country. It might not speak for us like the Nile or the Mississippi represent their nations, but it gives the country a shape, dividing east from west before it spills into the Atlantic at Limerick.

Naturally, it was shown on Ptolemy's map. Lesser waterways were included in this Greco-Roman work. Since Ptolemy, it has seen many a military manoeuvre. The Irish retreated behind the Shannon in 1650 in the Confederate wars from 1641-53 against the English parliamentarians. Whether Oliver Cromwell really said 'To Hell or to Connacht' or not, it amounted to the same thing – the forced migration west of the Shannon. Later in the Williamite wars 1689-91 the Jacobites retreated to the far side of the Shannon after their defeat at the Boyne in 1690.

Every country has flood myths and river legends. The Shannon is named after a Celtic goddess, Sionann, granddaughter of Lir. Like Fionn Mac Cumhaill she ate the salmon of knowledge which swam here, and became the wisest woman on earth. The knowledge was short-lived. The well she took the fish from burst and carried her out to sea. The drowning of a goddess is a common Irish legend. It represents the breaking down of her divine powers into the water which then seeps through the land.

Farmers around the Shannon hinterland enjoy Sionann's supply of fertile power ever since. But river beauty can turn to river cruelty. The Shannon which is prone to flooding at times oversupplies the land in its path, and residents and their animals are sent packing. Politicians arrive in wellies and raincoats, looking suitably glum, listening intently and nodding sympathetically. Success or failure in flood control can make or break a political party. Flood ruin in China was enough to remove 'the mandate of Heaven'. In Ireland politicians from de Valera onwards have promised to drain the Shannon. It has never happened. Indeed, Athlone is frugal about its water. Anytime the proposition comes up to supply Dublin with water from the Shannon, Athlone is having none of it.

I'm to meet Gearoid O'Brien, local historian and librarian outside the church. This town is his birthplace and favourite spot on earth. No doubt it was this kinship with his home place that drew Gearoid to the writing of John Broderick, a daring novelist and a friend of his parents. He's going to show me Broderick's Athlone.

'Athlone is to Broderick what central Dublin is to Joyce,' he explains.

We begin our tour with the Church of Saints Peter and Paul. In his novels Broderick poked fun at this extravagant church, from wayward priests to the hypocrisy of some of the Mass-goers. Though he never named it, everyone knew his 'garrison town, given to service and cynicism...a crossroads between east and west...' was Athlone.

Equally, Gearoid has no doubt you could draw a profile of his thinly disguised characters, with names barely altered, and trace them back to the real people of the town, especially 'Sharkey's female cabinet which ran the great Bridgeford Sweepstake.' This fundraising lottery, illegal at the time, provided the money for the building of this church. Gearoid offers an extract about its location from Broderick's *An Apology for Roses*: 'He turned into the market square in front of the great heraldic church that dominated the bridge and confronted the lowering bulk of King John's castle across the way.'

Gearoid explains: 'To dominate the bridge in the 1930s, when this church was built, was important for the confidence of the Roman Catholic church. Dean Crowe (or Broderick's 'Dean Sharkey') justified getting the land from the military on the pretext that King John's (Adamson) castle had been built here in 1210 by kicking the Clunyite religious order off their property.'

Broderick is only exaggerating mildly when in his novel, *The*

Irish Magdalen, he talked about the discussion about calling the new swimming pool, The Immaculate Conception Pool. Gearoid shows me the real streets around this town, named with the same religious influence. Church Street is called after the Church of Ireland.

Along by Chapel Street, Goldsmith Terrace, by Dean Crowe theatre, Gearoid reminds me that Broderick didn't leave out a corner or a bend of the streets around Athlone. He tells me about another keen Broderick fan, a professor of Geography: 'He believed you could use Broderick's writings for a Geography lesson on the flat topography of the midlands.'

An example of this level landscape comes from his book *The Waking of Willie Ryan,* when he went on his knees to put his dogs on a lead – 'The flat land … stretched itself tautly against the rim of the sky and along this rim of the world a couple of greyhounds were racing. For a flashing moment they looked like a bas relief on an ancient frieze'.

Our tour takes us by the slightly curving Connaught Street where the family business, Broderick's bakery, run by his mother, once stood. Her son had no interest in inheriting a baker's trade, not while there were novels to be written and fun to be made of the localism of this country town. And he used the freedom of fiction to make his women and priest characters sexually obsessed.

Athlone is a town divided between east and west, the Berlin of the midlands. The River Shannon separates the County Roscommon side from County Westmeath, the province of Connaught from Leinster, the diocese of Ardagh & Clonmacnoise from Elphin, the farming tradition on the Roscommon side from the small town merchant class tradition of the Westmeath side.

In *The Irish Magdalen* Broderick traces the origins of these divisions 'to the long history of warfare between the chieftains of Leinster and Connaught in the days of the Irish chieftains, in medieval times the rows between the bishops, all fighting for control of the 'great Shannon ford'.

Gearoid adds one more distinction between Athlone's east and Athlone west, the heartfelt 'feeling of superiority of one side over the other'.

'Which side feels superior?' I want to know.

'Both,' he answers without a second thought.

He hurries me along to show me Clonown, his 'little patch of Heaven', a moorland by the edge of the Shannon about five kilometres outside Athlone. A light drizzle spoils our plan to cycle there, an easy bikeride that doesn't involve a single hill. On the way, past Queen's Meadows, Broderick's description of the level midlands becomes real, stretching all the way to the horizon. Most writers get mileage out of a mountain or a choppy scene, but Broderick's pen draws beauty into the flatness of the landscape.

Clonown is the scene of Broderick's 'purple back of the great bog arching against the horizon…which …strove with the river for mastery of the plain…' (*The Waking of Willie Ryan*). I park alongside a profusion of ferns, sloe trees and gorse. In Gearoid's opinion, 'There's nowhere nicer than here for a stroll on a fine day, nowhere better to feed the soul.'

Even today with the sky more downbeat than usual it's not at all dreary. The peaty open space against the sky mixes into a special quality of light, giving off a purple hue. It's a place soft to the touch, where time is written into the layers of undergrowth. But you have to know the bog's moods. Place a foot wrongly and you'll smartly find out its sly hazards. Gearoid cringes when I reverse the car into soft ground. As I rev safely out of danger, he explains: 'Artists are drawn to this spot and at times it's a haven of friendliness and loud banter between turf-cutters and painters.'

What strikes me about Gearoid's 'little spot of heaven' is that it's so ordinary. That's the thing about heaven, it's the small things that make people happy and remind them of paradise.

But let's leave aside heaven for a moment and get back to

Broderick's writing about this spot on the earth. He liked to call the gorse that grows copiously around here by its local name, whins. He describes the hard-to-grasp scent of their yellow flower as a 'mixture of orange and butter...' (*The Fugitives*). Broderick loved the crackling noises that the whin seeds make as they jump out of their pods: 'if you lie very still ... you can hear a little crackling among the bushes.' Gearoid too knows the joy of that sound.

'There's nothing lovelier. But you need silence to hear them.'

You have that silence in abundance here.

We leave the bog to its stillness and on the way back to Athlone, Gearoid brings me to a stop at the little bridge where the River Cross makes its way under the road – its last bridge because this little river's journey from Curraghboy in Roscomoon meets its end a few metres away, when it gets drowned in the great waters of the Shannon.

'It was here at this bridge that I used to catch trout with my father. And I brought my own children later to share the magic. We used to watch the mutes and the swans and sometimes if we were lucky we'd spot a kingfisher.'

We get out to take in the view that three generations of the O'Brien family have feasted their eyes on. I park well clear of the sheer edge overhanging the soft ground. Great and all as the fishing memories are, I don't fancy having to fish my car out of the water. From here you get a distant view of the roofs of Athlone – the dome and the two spires of Saints Peter and Paul's and the lower tower of Saint Mary's Church of Ireland.

On the far side of the bridge is the Shannon where the boats sail towards the monastic site of Clonmacnoise. That's where I plan to go next, by river, the way Ciarán, the founder saint arrived and the Vikings who came to raid the monastery. But before I set sail I have to see The Moorings, Broderick's elegant nineteenth century residence. Bay-windowed with low pitched roof, it's on the outskirts of the town and it's now surrounded by new houses.

Broderick came to live here, with his mother and stepfather, to his final home in Athlone before he left to live in Bath (10 Russell Street). The move was following a starry-eyed notion he had about this Somerset city with its baths and links to ancient Rome.

'A bad decision – he never settled and admitted it was a mistake. He died, mainly of loneliness,' says Gearoid.

With pride and gratitude Gearoid shows me the last show piece of the day, Broderick's donation to the library, the painting of Athlone by Paul Henry.

'When Broderick heard that the library had bought this work, he returned the money and presented it instead. The library also got his great stock of French novels, from Proust to Mauriac.'

It's back to work for Gearoid while I head to the riverbank. As I approach, the oily whiff of the boat greets me across the water. About a dozen people are forming a queue. We all pile in once the gangway is ready. As we pull out Viking Mike (Michael McDonnell who runs the Shannon tours) tells us that Athlone's bridge was constructed in 1846 by Thomas Rhodes, a brother of arch coloniser Cecil Rhodes who thought 'to be born an Englishman was to win the lottery of life'. I'm sure he'd have supported Brexit.

The bridge is handsome. The underside sighting of it from the water beats the view from the road. You see it slower and you see it whole. King John's Norman castle looks a little stocky but considering it has stood here since 1210, it deserves bonus points for doing its bit for the town's history. From the water the church improves too. It shows off, I imagine, as proudly as its founder, Dean Crowe, would have wished. And just as we set sail the bells start to peal. What a melodious send-off to Clonmacnoise.

Viking Mike introduces us to Timmy the lockkeeper. There are two sluice gates to be opened because of the unusual width of the Shannon. This river claims no great depth, it only reaches down four metres. This disproportion makes it burst its banks every chance it gets.

'The floods mostly last three weeks but the last flooding lasted three months. And during that time even the sluice gates went under the water,' Viking Mike tells us.

While we wait for the water level to change a bottleneck forms. People in great yachts pull up alongside us showing all the signs of a family holiday – washing hanging on the deck. It's a good day for drying. The sky has cheered up since this morning. Some clouds form like curdled milk, others roll and whip into folds. The sun makes ripples of light in the boat's pathway.

The Shannon gives the land it passes by a leisurely grace. Without the river it would be pleasant countryside. With it, it's wonderful. When the trees run out along by its banks it opens up the full scope of the flat midlands. Here an incline is an event.

The guided tour continues: 'The Royal and the Grand canals flow into the Shannon. You could cover a lot of the journey through Ireland using only the waterways. It was how people got around until the rail took over.' He points out the Shannon callows, areas of conservation. 'When the floods ebb it leaves soft fertile ground that draws birds here. The most famous is the corncrake. But the callows are drying and wildlife is at risk. The corncrake hasn't been heard so far this year. Midnight to four in the morning is their time to crake.'

This is distressing. It's one of my treasured sounds of childhood. The corncrake's haunting call is worth every minute of a sleepless night. Intensive farming has destroyed nests according to the National Parks and Wildlife Service.

People wave as we pass, even adults salute the boats. I imagine they're the most reserved of people if you were to meet them on dry land, but the passing-by effect makes people do sweet and silly things. They know they'll never meet us and have to account for themselves.

The laws of water transport have to be respected on narrow parts of the river. Drive on the right, an international navigation rule. There's no question of hooting peevishly at other boats, as car-drivers sometimes do. It's all too slow moving and out of kilter with water etiquette.

We go through such flat land that I forget there's a world beyond the horizon. As Viking Mike tells us about swans who come here from Siberia, he's interrupted by a strange appearance in these parts – hills – a sweep of little mounds.

'This is part of the Esker Riada, an Ice Age residue of sandy hills. It's a natural causeway in a boggy plain.'

The glacial ridge of the Esker Riada runs in an east-west direction to the Shannon. It was the path of the ancient *slighe* (road) from Dublin to Galway, *An tSlighe Mhór* (the Great Way).

Now for the big moment, the round towers and crosses of the monastery of Clonmacnoise on the side of a hill catch the sunlight in their slant. And our attention diverts from the river's wildlife, trade and Viking raids to rest a while. This is where contemplation joined landscape and it left its mark on the curves of the architecture, from Romanesque arches to the rounded intersections of the high crosses of Clonmacnoise.

The engine changes tone. Headstones and crosses reel uncontrollably as the boat makes the turn into the jetty. The name 'Ciarán's city fair' at this moment sounds so right. Clonmacnoise settlement was founded by the young Saint Ciarán in 544. He is said to have died of a plague in 549 at the age thirty-three.

Clonmacnoise was a triumph for Christianity over paganism. It was a seat of learning of European importance, a centre of prayer, writing and pilgrimage. Like all monasteries this was a place of pillage too. Viking Mike goes on: 'The Vikings used islands to gain a foothold on to the mainland. They first appeared in 793 on Holy Island in England, then off the Irish coast in Rathlin island on the north coast and Inis Boffin on the west.'

On dry land now we make our way up the hill, past the ninth century timber bridge and the lowing of cows. This religious centre is placed by the bend of the river. Where else would they have chosen but where the river curves, for that's a nestling spot of the earth. They were more in tune with energy points and inherited knowledge back then. More practically, it sat on the line of the Esker Riada, on the *Slighe Mhór*, giving it road as well as river access. The ruins look isolated today, but monasteries were well connected in their time, like nodal junctures, a linking geography of the spirit, from Ireland to Iona to continental Europe.

This was the golden age of monasticism, an era when they thought in polar opposites – good or bad, God or Satan, saved or damned. It was a time when the celestial was nearly as real as the terrestrial. Faith, fatalism and acceptance fitted into this world.

The monks gave the seasons, the day and the night a meaning, blending them with prayer and song. Psalms, hymns, collects and canticles changed with the seasons and the length of the day. There were psalms for nightfall, psalms for midnight, psalms for matins. Sleeplessness and self-denial were built into the ritual. Discomfort heightened the watchfulness. Communal male voices gave energy to the darkness of night, proclaiming the power of God and the nothingness of man. Their chanting must have rivalled the haunting call of the corncrake.

'Ciarán's city fair' was a victory for Christianity over paganism, much like Dean Crowe's church further up the river gave King John's castle a run for its money.

'You can watch a video or do the tour,' the lady at the reception tells us. 'The tour guide says exactly what the video covers.' I feel like asking her if the video makes jokes like tours guides. He's a jovial fellow too, the guide. He's finishing with the previous group when we arrive. Before they disperse he answers a few questions about each of the eight churches on the site which are all assigned a different cure.

In the cathedral you pray for backaches, in some other chapel, headaches, stomach aches somewhere else. There seems to be endless pains to cover.

'Is there a chapel for migraine?' asks an anxious-looking woman.

'I suppose that would come under the general heading of headaches,' laughs a man in the crowd. She's not pleased at him making fun of her.

'Don't leave the site without seeing the original crosses. The Cross of Scriptures is one of the best in Ireland. They're well taken care of here. They're kept inside,' says the guide.

In other monastic sites the crosses are left in the open air to take whatever the weather drops on them and they grow white spots of lichen that make them look as if they need a sand blast. The cross here depicts The Last Judgement. They were very anxious to emphasise the point in those stark days, that the end of life would involve a verdict, a severe one at that. As in all sculptures like these, the righteous are segregated from the damned (otherwise what would the point in being good?). Here the saved are behind a flute player. And on the other side is a figure driving the wicked away, no music to accompany these poor sods on their doleful journey.

The Nun's Church is said to be a gem, but I haven't time to go and see it because the bus is due to leave. If only I had spoken to the driver I could have gone at my ease. He's an easy-going chap. He would have waited no problem. On the way back to Athlone I'm tired. I want to let the day run into a dream and let the droning voice of the driver lull me as he chats with the woman in the front seat.

Slieve Bloom is on my right. In my half-trance I wonder where would the midlands be without it, the only mountain range that gives the centre of Ireland a lift out of the vast Bog of Allen. I think of a line from Broderick's *The Waking of Willie Ryan*': 'Except for the short blue line of the Slieve Bloom mountains, there was no part of it (the landscape) that did not end with the sky.'

This lone mountain range was given its rightful heft in Irish legend. Fionn MacCumhaill was raised in the woods in the Slieve

Bloom mountains, in secret, by two women, before his mother found him. Where more fitting for a warrior than the only crest in the centre of a western island?

My next trip is to explore this flat expanse of bog, the Bog of Allen.

TWENTY-THREE

FOOTSTEPS OF A SINGER

What caught my attention as I watched a programme on singer-songwriter Christy Moore, was not his singing, not even the social causes he promotes; it was how he talked about his mother's attachment to her home place Yellow Furze by the River Boyne. That spot, he said, stayed with her for the rest of her life. People only notice traits in others when they mirror their own. And when I ask him to tell me about his own home place, Kildare and the Bog of Allen, he's more than willing.

'I'll always carry a deep love for my place of origin, Newbridge, where I grew up with my three sisters and two brothers and our parents Andy Moore and Nancy Power. The place exists very clearly in my mind. Voices of old neighbours and friends still resound. And though Dublin is now my home, where my heart beats, I still love to walk down by the Liffey banks, across the Curragh Plains, on the bog and around the Hill of Allen. All these places and things matter deeply to me. And I love to visit the old churchyard where Andy and Nancy lie.'

These tumbling memories of home place comes through a

song himself and his brother Barry (Luka Bloom) wrote: 'Where I Come From':

> I come from The Bog of Allen, beneath the seat of the ancient King,
> Listen for the distant Corncrake, hear the Lark and the Curlew sing,
> And the refrain: 'I'm a bogman, deep down, it's where I come from.

'People and places have found their way into many of my songs,' he says 'visions of my own, singing songs from other writers. When I sing John Spillane's *Gortatagort* I see the fields around Baronstown in County Kildare.'

It's this threading of people and places, causes and principles that makes his songs ring true. I'm going to let their harmony propel me as I wander around Kildare.

I begin my journey in search of Clongorey, his favourite spot in the Bog of Allen. Though getting there takes a bit of effort – it's neither on GPS nor map – it's pleasant hardship. It brings me along by an array of hills far into the east. These are the Wicklow mountains, rolling along in a perfect shade of blue, keeping watch over the flat plains of Kildare.

Anyone I ask assures me that Clongorey is easy to find. I try to enquire in a house but I'm blocked at the gate by a gang of Jack Russell terriers barking up an appetite to snack on me. I'm harmless, I want to reassure them but they aren't in the mood for listening. Their owner hears their yelping and comes out to rescue me. He gives me directions, adding the usual local send-off: 'You can't miss it.'

Believe me, I can.

He sees me across the busy road as if I'm a child. With great effort, waving, warning oncoming motorist and interweaving perilously between cars coming in both directions, he gets me safely to my car.

When I finally reach Clongorey I make a note of where it is, off the Milltown-Allenwood road, so that I'll never have so much trouble again finding the place. I can see why Moore has good memories of it. It's the ideal spot where a young lad would like to be out messing around with his mates, free to wander on the commonage of the moors

Milltown church, his next heart-place, is a whole lot more straightforward. The village itself is on the R415 from Kildare town. Chapel is a more apt name for places of worship like this one. I'm glad that the plaque on the wall backs me up. It reads: 'This chapel was erected in 1817.' At the door a whiff of burning candles and incense greet me. It's a simple building, unembellished, a place where a local community gathered to pray. And there was plenty to pray for in 1817 and the years that followed its foundation – on-and-off famine, evictions and poverty. The altar is of timber with a plain tabernacle on the wall behind it. An oldfashioned Stations of the Cross runs on either side of the aisle. Simplicity is its name, the kind of place of nostalgia I remember chapels to be – one-roomed buildings, no side aisles and a modest gallery at the back.

The adjoining graveyard is the resting place of Moore's parents, Andy and Nancy and that makes it special. Because roots define Christy Moore. Maybe roots define us all but Moore knows it more than most. His family is brought into every conversation.

'My grandfather was Jack Power. He came from Hayes near Navan in County Meath. My grandmother, Ellie Sheeran came from The Cotton Mills near Navan. The Cotton Mills still exist though the old mill is a ruin. The row of workers' cottages are still occupied. They're beautifully situated beside a weir on the river Boyne. My Granny often spoke lovingly of her young life in The Cotton Mills.'

Standing here beside Milltown chapel you can imagine some of the things that appeal to Moore, the humble things in life he says make him happy and find their way into his songs.

'I love the sound of an evening chanter, the smell of turf, dinner in the middle of the day, the pagan sound of the Angelus bell, the clash of the ash.' The resonance of his voice propels these small things into a place of importance in his world.

Pollardstown Fen, the next place he guides me to, brings me past the substantial homes of studded Kildare, of racehorse wealth, manicured hedging and forbiddingly high gates. This is jeep, horse-box country and beware-of-dog dwellings. Though I can see no sight of any, I've no doubt that if I made the slightest advance towards a gate, a pack of these hounds would appear. And they would be a whole lot bulkier than the little Jack Russells that took me on earlier.

Maybe it was here, alongside the great wealth of the equine world that Christy Moore learned to look out for the not-so-lucky in life. He says himself that keeping an eye out for the concerns of others was something he picked up from his mother and father.

'Both my parents were involved in social issues. Going right back to childhood, I learned of society's inequalities, evictions, church hypocrisy, the Rich, the Poor, army life in the Curragh which also boasted an internment camp of republican prisoners. Thirty years earlier Newbridge boasted a large British army garrison.'

He has an advantage over his forebears in that he can sing the forgotten ills of society to life. That's why he's sometimes called a modern-day bard.

There's something delightful about walking in the footsteps of others, picking up the pulse of the feet of those who tread their way before you, loving the place as they do. I feel like this about Moore's other loved-place, Pollardstown Fen. It shelters quietly in a dip in the landscape by the water's edge. A singer would especially like it here because of the bird song and the musical sound of the rustling reeds. I take a stroll on the boardwalk over wetlands. It feels thrillingly safe to look down between the solid boarding into the swamp where a foot could lose its way and disappear from under you. A strong scent of whitethorn fills the air but this is July, too late in the year for that so it must be some other plant that's wearing the same perfume.

Going into the final turn of the boardwalk, I look behind to see where the Hill of Allen peeks. In the flatlands of Kildare this mound has something to say for itself. Naturally, it was given a mythical job to do, carry a legend on its volcanic back. It was said to be the seat of the hunter-warrior Fionn MacCumhaill and the Fianna. In a peep through the clearing, a rich golden cornfield, typical of this county, comes into view, representing the other side of Kildare, its rich lands where horses develop strong bones and racing skills.

The time isn't right for Moore's 'pagan sound of the Angelus bell' to toll across the landscape. Pity.

There's no one here to ask where to locate Donnelly's hollow and the Gibbet Rath, two spots not to be missed on the Moore trail. Back in Milltown village I get the lowdown from a pair chatting on the footpath.

'The Gibbet Rath?' he says to the woman alongside him. 'That's over near you.'

'Near me? I never heard of it.'

'It's near the monument, near that pub, what do you call it. I can't remember the name but if you park at that pub,' he says, turning to me, 'you can walk up. You turn right, go past the Hanged Man (he doesn't explain that this is a pub but he says it in a tone that doesn't elicit any alarm), over the bridge, then by Father Moore's well, you can't go wrong. Then take a left at the traffic lights.'

'No that's a roundabout,' she corrects him.

'No it's traffic lights, then down by the Curragh racecourse and on to traffic lights and you're there.'

Where? I've lost my way already. I don't know where I'm

supposed to be, Donnelly's Hollow or the Gibbet Rath. But one thing is sure. Both are hideaway places.

Then the man launches into another conversation.

'I knew a fellow once, he used to live over there, he trained horses.'

Where's this story leading I wonder? Does it help me to find the places I'm in search of? But the thing that strikes me is that racing comes into every conversation around here – gamblers, trainers, chancers, the tilt of the hat, the cryptic nod of the bookies, the tang of the chase.

'Listen here to me, you can't go wrong,' he says as a final sendoff.

Place-names and directions are buzzing around my head: Brownstown, Maddenstown, Pollardstown, Ballymany, Baronstown, the Hanged Man, humpback bridge, traffic lights, no roundabouts, no traffic lights.

I know when I drive over the grids that I'm in the cattle-free zone of the Curragh, uniquely horse territory. The stands are within sight now, the fences of the gallop runs.

Curragh is an old Irish word for racecourse, it also means marshy bog. This stretch of land was an Ice Age godsend. Gravel was dropped here, sixty metres deep, filtering and creating a well-drained plain with a springy turf that racegoers have rejoiced in ever since. A race course was established here in 1727 though it had been used for races before then, well before then. We're told that Fionn and the Fianna trained here. And the ground has never been disturbed, probably not since the mythical time of the Fianna.

Kildare is a strange county. On the one hand it's dominated by the flat Bog of Allen, on the other by the green track of the Curragh, kept in a state of flat perfection. There's nothing flat about the roar of the crowd on a race day here, but all is quiet today. No racing. I spot a train in the distance ahead and I try to find my bearings from the railway track.

I arrive, I know not how, at Donnelly's Hollow. It's worth all the effort. I'm back in 1815, two years before they built the chapel in Milltown, listening to the roar of a crowd of 20,000, overflowing the limits of the Curragh. It was like artillery going off. So people who heard it said. And that was a sound with a big future in this neck of the woods because the first military camp, established in the Curragh forty years later during the Crimean war, began the Curragh's long link with the army. But in 1815 what inspired this roar was neither military manoeuvres nor racing. It was boxing. It took place in this hollow on November 13. Bets were buoyant on the main attraction, boxer Dan Donnelly, the first Irish-born heavyweight champion.

Though Donnelly's Hollow is a natural amphitheatre, a glacial kettlehole, I can't imagine how they squeezed in 20,000 people. Donnelly's great steps are still here, etched into the side of the hill, made when he carried his defeated opponent, Englishman, George Cooper, out of the ring and up the hill. He must have been a giant of a man, if you believe these are his true footsteps. While all this was happening in Kildare in 1815, news of another defeat, Napoleon's, was doing the rounds of Europe.

Within about half a mile of Donnelly's Hollow, a story unfolds of a different hollow, where in the mid to late nineteenth century dwelt the Curragh Wrens. There may be a lightness about the name, but that belies the real story.

'They were prostittues and they lived in holes in the ground on the hills of the Curragh. They were brought in to service the soldiers in the camp. Some of these women would have been orphaned or displaced by famine,' explains Moore. Though the last official record of the wrens' presence was 1880s, Moore believes they went on till later than that. 'Growing up in Newbridge when I was young, people used to talk about them as if they were within living memory. They talked too about how unwelcome they were anytime they came into Newbridge.'

The people of Newbridge weren't alone in their distaste for the wrens. Though the army supplied them with water and they were allowed to shop in the camp market three times a week, complaints were plentiful – a rate-payer objected to his money being used for these sex workers, a Presbyterian army chaplain penned a letter complaining about them to The Times in 1857. When the Pall Mall Gazette did a report on them, it led to some recognition of the problem, and a lock hospital to treat sexually transmitted diseases was established. The reporter, a James Greenwood, recorded their lifestyle too. And that was a curiosity in itself. They lived together, leaderless, sharing belongings, food, money and home remedies. The older wrens looked after the children while the younger women went out to 'work'. Some of them knitted and sold their wares in the local market. The name wrens came from their living set-up, like wrens' nests, in a hollow sheltered by furze bushes, which they had to crawl in and out of.

From wrens to Gibbet Rath. I park at a pub which must be the bar whose name the man in Milltown couldn't recall. Before I walk to the monument on the side of the hill, a few clients come out to show me the way. Three of them give me different guidance. I take directions from the one who seems to have drunk the least.

The commemorative stone on the side of the hill remembers the priest who lost his life here: An t-Athair Ó Fearghail, on June 29, 1798 during the rebellion of the United Irishmen. The rath itself is further uphill from the monument. The 1798 insurgents defied British rule, taking their lead from French and American revolutionaries. This rebellion is linked to Wexford, but here in Kildare the uprising of the United Irishmen was strongly supported.

'All the men and young boys of the town of Kildare agreed to surrender and they were slaughtered,' esplains Moore.

The revolutionary nationalism of 1798, was notable in that it began a series of uprisings against British rule in Ireland. The Young Ireland rising (more of a skirmish) was next in 1848, the Fenian rising (an equal fiasco) in 1867 and finally the 1916 rising.

As one rising would fail, the taste for violent revolution would retreat in favour of constitutional politics. 1798 was followed by the great parliamentary movement of Daniel O Connell who believed one live repealer (repeal of the Act of Union) was better than a graveyard of dead ones. Again, after the Fenian rising, history lurched in the direction of the powerful constitutional movement of Parnell. But the thing was the supporters of violent means of evicting the British didn't see the various uprisings as the flops they were, but of important events in keeping the flame of revolution alive.

It's evening by the time I walk down the hill. Towards the north the sun is lighting up the slopes of the Hill of Allen, the racecourse stands east of the hill, the Wicklow mountains and a steeple from the local town of Kildare squeeze into the picture. The warm pink-edged glow of sunset spreads a quiet mood over the view, a long way from the commotion of boxing, rebellion, slaughter, surrender or ostracised wrens.

My Christy Moore-guided trail is at an end. It was a scattered look at Kildare held together by one thing, simplicity. That's fitting. It ties in with his unfussy take on life.

'I like knockin' about Ireland, whether it's the Wild Atlantic Way or the Ancient East. holidaying, working. I've been invited to play the Opera House in Sydney and Carnegie Hall in New York, but I feel more contentment playing the Hall in Knocknagoshel or The Mayflower in Leitrim.'

Yes, he likes his concerts like that, an audience small and attentive more so than a roaring crowd that would fill the Curragh racecourse. The smooth delivery of his songs contrasts with their slamming social message, turning up wherever injustice beckons, giving it a bar of a song.

TWENTY-FOUR

THE BOG

There's more to explore in Kildare, in the Bog of Allen, and before July is out I go to Mount Lucas, where I join a group on a field trip in search of bog flora. We're to meet in the eastern car-park of Mount Lucas Wind Farm and Amenity Walk. Eastern carpark appears on neither screen nor map.

I ring to find out which carpark is eastern. I've got some poor directions in my time but this takes the prize.

'Go to Portarlington, turn left.' The woman is so pleasant that I don't like to tell her that she hasn't asked me where I will be coming from, that left and right depend on which way you're facing. 'You can't miss it,' she goes on. Then she changes her plan. 'Go to Clonbullogue, that's a better way,' but before she finishes her sentence she has found an even better approach. 'Go to Walsh island, go by a railway, by a bog, by a bridge. You can't go wrong.'

I will seriously need to find some other means of finding my way. A bog is bewildering even with good directions. The next time I ring the guidance is more straightforward.

'Take the road from Portarlington towards Rochfordsbridge. Follow the sign for Mount Lucas Wind Farm Amenity.'

It's a day in good form, with fluffy clouds patrolling the sky as I drive along the R400, an isolated narrow bog road, constructed at a higher level than its surroundings ground. The inconvenience is that if you meet a vehicle which doesn't fit side by side with yours, you run out of width to pull in. At least you pull in at your peril. You just might plunge into the bog which if you're not interested in a somersault, could be quite a jolt or a one-way journey.

Despite the worries I enjoy the drive. The bridges remind me of my teenage years when a cousin used to drive a gang of us along a bog road and rev up just before the bridge, putting us leaping off our seats. All great fun. No chance of playing games today. In any case it's not the same on your own.

This countryside is mostly barren but in places trees form canopies over the road. There is, as promised, a sign for Walsh Island so at least I know I'm vaguely where I should be. I travel on for miles with no sighting of house or person. When I finally spot a collection of wind turbines on my left I know I must be nearby.

At the end of my long straight drive I spot a car-park and two people. To see someone in this isolation is a reason to stop even if you have nothing to say to them. One of them turns out to be Fiona Devery, today's co-leader, the Botanical Society of Britain and Ireland recorder for County Offaly. I park alongside them and soon a crowd gathers. They're all very gracious and knowledgeable. Two men are having a chat about bird-watching. They're discussing crested gold finches, meadow pippets, skylarks and a host of others. I feel tongue-tied. I must do a birdwatching course so that I won't find myself retreating into such silence again. I can identify some birds, no problem, a crow, a magpie, a robin, a pigeon. Put a hoopoe, a lapwing, a skylark or a buzzard in front of and I'm stumped.

We follow Mark McCorry, the other co-leader, through the gate.

'There are two and a half thousand acres of bogland here,

which has not been in peat production for nearly three decades, so it's left to go its own way, into natural colonisation,' he tells us.

I wonder why some people have come along at all because they've so little to learn. Every now and again someone bends and picks out the minutest of flowers, and says the name of something ever so unpronounceable that I would have passed by or probably trampled on. Though I was raised on a farm, I'm really at the they-all-look-the-same-to-me stage of plant life. To me a thistle is a thistle that sits there waiting for a blow of a slash-hook, but today I learn about so many varieties – march thistle, spear thistle, field thistle – I will never again look on them with such prejudice.

We assemble around London rocket. As Mark touches it lovingly he tells us that we could add it to our sandwiches. It would certainly sharpen up my cheese rolls. We eat sitting on a sandy ridge within sight of a crop of twenty eight turbines. When some people look askance at them, a man in the group says he believes turbines aren't harmful to health, that people who report feeling unwell when they're placed near them, are afflicted by worry. However, since they arrived more sensitive birds, like swans, lapwings and skylarks come a lot less frequently. Who knows, maybe it's worry in their case too?

When a dead bird showed up recently, they took it very seriously. They just about stopped short at bringing down the state pathologist to look into the cause of death. The verdict was good. The turbines were found not to be guilty of the bird's passing.

There's a loveliness about eating in the open air, and you won't find a place more open than Mount Lucas. Sitting on dry ground in this wilderness I feel snug as the wind plays mild artillery sounds with my rain coat. In the midst of the flat expanse of land, a far-off field climbs into a fertile incline. I'm sure it wouldn't prompt a comment if it were in normal terrain, but here among its flat moorland neighbours it looks like a sight with something to say for itself.

Fiona shows us silverweed which I know well from my childhood days, though I never put a name on it. I'm familiar too with the horsetail she picks up. It tears away in sections, like perforated paper where 'Tear here' is written. I loved 'tearing here' when I was growing up but I didn't know back then that it was horsetail that I was tearing into.

A rarer plant is round wintergreen. Mark, an ecologist whose job is the rehabilitation of the bog, tells us,

'I was full of excitement the day I first found round wintergreen leaf in County Offaly. I thought it unique. Then I found another and another and the delight wore off.'

Delight is catching. Between the enthusiasm of the guides and the others in the group, I feel an urge to know more. By the end of the day I'm tripping off names like pink redshank, wild carrot, fragrant rosebay willow-herb, and a whole range of orchids. But despite my new-found knowledge, my favourites remain two I had long since befriended, bog cotton and bulrushes. The bulrushes are my Minotaurs of the bog and the sight of the wind blowing the bog cotton stirs in me lazy days of youth.

The Bog of Allen is the largest area of raised bog in Ireland, 115,000 hectares of moorland. It's not one continuous expanse but several neighbouring bogs. It stretches into eleven midland countries, including Kildare, Offaly, Meath, Laois and Westmeath. While I'm still in bog mood I want to look into Lullymore in County Kildare.

The approaching roads are narrow. But it's no hardship to drive slowly. The leisurely pace keeps you in tune with the bog that appears through the breaks in the hedges. Peat grows at a dawdling rate, one millimetre a year. Raised bogs took a dizzying amount of time to form, over 10,000 years. Bogs are often called archives in that whatever falls on them – pollen, dust, insects – are stored in neat layers and in chronological order.

I come by Rathangan, a town of curling bridges, over two waterways, the River Slate and the Grand Canal, and on by signs pointing to Barnaran and Drumsru. Next up is the sign I'm looking for: 'Welcome to Lullymore.'

I didn't know that Lullymore was an island until I meet Katie Geraghty who works for the Irish Peatland Conservation Council (IPCC). And there's no reason why I would know because today almost half of the peatlands have been drained from mining turf. And so dry land like Lullymore is no longer the unique foothold in the bog it once was. Katie talks of the potential to return the harvested bogs to their natural wetland state. This is the aim of the environmental group for which she works. The IPCC doesn't encourage the use of peat, and leads by example in its organic garden where they use no peat moss.

'Peatland habitat survives today within the Bog of Allen,' she says, 'and they need to be conserved for nature's sake and for future generations to enjoy.' To undo the damage, the IPCC restores bogs which have been lost by drainage and peat mining over the past four hundred years. Drains are blocked with plastic dams to restore the wetness that's needed for the bog's wildlife to survive.'

Forgetting for a minute about its usefulness, it's easy to love the bog. Maybe it is its great expanse of land without boundary that is its appeal. It's like the beginning of time here, when land belonged to everyone, before someone had the idea of fencing it off and saying, This is Mine.

The journalist Con Houlihan once wrote about how people fall in love with the bog like they fall for the desert. In an article entitled *Bogged Down* he wrote: 'Friends of mine who served in the North African desert in the war fell in love with that vastness of sand.'

Even before Katie says that in many ways the bog is like the desert, I'm thinking of the early hermetic monks who took to the desert in Egypt to turn down life's pleasures. Saint Anthony of

Egypt was the first of the hermits, and he withdrew from the world in 270. It fulfilled the need stated in Mathew's Gospel (6.6) 'not to pray in public but to enter into thy closet and when thou hast shut the door pray to thy Father which seeith in secret shall reward thee openly'. Anthony spanned two centuries, the third and fourth and lived to 105, a long life without fun.

Abba Moses was another who turned his life around. He gave up his banditry, inspired one day when he took shelter in a monastery in a colony in the desert near Alexandria. 'Sit in your cell and your cell will teach you everything,' was his advice.

In Ireland monks did the next best thing and set themselves up in the rare piece of solid earth within a bog. In the days when Lullymore was truly an island, it housed a monastery that dates to the fifth century. Here among the wild orchids, Sphagnum mosses and multicoloured butterflies of Lullymore, you still feel that monastic remoteness.

Thomas Foran was the last of the monks here, and Foran's Wood takes his name. The story goes that during an attack on the monastery in which all his fellow monks were massacred, he managed to escape and take important records with him.

Watching the night sky was one of the many things monks spent their time at in the 'Dark Ages', according to a book by Seb Falk. And back then they didn't have to contend with the constellations offering broad and broader band service that confuse the stars nowadays.

Falk claims that the popular idea that nothing much happened in the dark years prior to the illuminated fifteenth century is nonsense, so he called his book *The Light Ages*. Astronomy was well developed in the monasteries. They reported sightings like eclipses, comets, aurora borealis. These communities, he argues, worked through the scriptures to understand a God-given, living cosmos. And they were, he believes, blessed with something that modern scientists lack – humility.

Here's a story that fills me with pride though I hardly deserve it personally. In Durrow Abbey, about thirty kilometres south from Lullymore in July 1054, an entry into the *Annals of the Four Masters* recorded that the monks there saw an especially bright star. This sighting from Durrow seems to have been the only European observation of the Super Nova of 1054 (though it was seen in China and Japan).

A tray of tea is waiting for me in the greenhouse when I come back from my saunter around the 'island'. I love every sip of it, as much for the hospitality as for the tea itself. When I admire the thriving parsley, Katie gives me a large root which I can report hasn't died despite my ungreen fingers.

'Even though a lot has been lost in drainage, Ireland still is special when it comes to raised bogs. It's protecting about half of the bogs of the European Union,' she tells me.

It's not that Ireland was especially endowed with moorland, it was more by default that it got preserved here. Turf was cut with hand implements and so it lasted longer than in countries where they rolled in the big machines and sliced their boglands out of existence. Now we're left to mind what remains. They're worth taking care of. Peatlands cover only three per cent of the world's terrestrial surface but they store two-thirds of the earth's terrestrial carbon.

Katie shows me what to watch out for in the bogs that the IPCC has turned into wildlife sanctuaries: the orchids, butterwort, lichens, snorklers and the varying shades of butterflies. The sundew with its sticky petals designed to trap insects, sounds like a neat trick. I thought it was only in the tropics where plants eat flesh, but it's a lot closer to home – like a turn of revenge for all the times it happens the other way around. This adds one more exotic touch to this land of ancient prayer and contemplation.

Katie says a footprint made on Sphagnum mosses takes years to disappear. It's like a mobile phone in tracing someone's whereabouts, at a much leisurely pace admittedly. These mosses have one up on the cell phone – they are antiseptic. During the first world war dried Sphagnum from here made its way to dress the wounds of war from India and Egypt to continental Europe. The depots were located in various places around the Bog of Allen. As I leave Lullymore I look out for them but I see no trace of any.

Shee Bridge brings me out of the island. Shee (*sí*) means fairy and where better could they roam at their ease than here in this wilderness.

TWENTY-FIVE

THE RING OF KERRY

In County Kerry I'm standing at a viewing point called Dooneen, on the Abbeyfeale-Castle Island road. It's worth stopping here to view this scene – mountains, hills and lowlands swirl and curl over the plain, fields of green and greener wander away as far as the eye can see. The near enclosures are shaped in rectangles but the distant ones level and shimmer into straightened lines. Farmhouses sheltered in clumps of trees spread through the picture and blue mountains stand protectingly behind – the MacGillicuddy Reeks, Mangerton, Stoompa, Crohane and the Paps. This is Kerry on one page. From this spot, its other name – The Kingdom – suits better.

I remember stopping here on my way to do my very first tour of the Ring of Kerry just months after my nineteenth birthday. It hasn't changed at all.

I was to cycle the Ring with my friend, Cathy. But she fell ill at the last minute. When I got news that she was out of danger I headed off and I made the 179 kilometres round journey from Killarney to Killarney on my own.

The month was May. Fluffy clouds clipped along the sky. The wind was in my face as I cycled past rough grasses, rushes, bracken, a dog's bark from behind a fence, and a distant lake sparkling in the morning sun. The scent of wild buttercups, whitethorn and heather gushed at me. A bike was the perfect pace to see the countryside, and being alone allowed me to go at my own speed. Poor Cathy, lying in a hospital bed, it didn't feel right to be thinking it was going so well without her.

When I think of all the safety stuff you have to take care of nowadays before setting off on a cycling trip and compare it to how I was prepared. I wore no helmet, brought no emergency kit, wore no special gear like today's cyclists. And the bike didn't have about sixty gears either.

Not until I reached Glenbeigh, after thirty-five kilometres of peddling, did I take a rest. I stopped at a pub for a sandwich. A pair of jokers were seated on high stools at the bar. They looked like they were waiting for something to happen and I walked in, just the ticket for a bit of teasing. I wasn't acquainted with Kerry wit back then.

'Are you touring on your own?' asked the older of the two. 'I could get a man to go with you,' he offered with a glint in his eye. 'There's a nice fella living just up the hill from here.' (In such hilly country that hardly narrowed him down.) 'He'd suit you.'

Like performers, they chatted and joked with choreographed winks as they mocked me, poor outsider, who didn't understand the local devilment that ripples lightly into every conversation here. It was good to meet them. I needed a laugh. But I hadn't all day to spend chatting. The bike was rented for a week. So I made tracks, leaving the two of them to their pints of Guinness.

At the end of the first day I was pleased to have covered more than eighty kilometres. I thought I had put my legs to enough exertion for one day, so near Cahersiveen I booked into a Bed and Breakfast. It was called Stella Maris (Star of the Sea) to advertise the waves of the Atlantic which were within hearing distance. An old couple from Limerick were holidaying there (who, come to think of it, probably weren't so old). They liked to finish their breakfast with Cornflakes, not start with them like the rest of us. An English couple and their two young boys were staying too.

'Touring on your own?' asked the Englishman. That made me feel odd but before I had time to explain that the friend I had lined up to come, was laid low, he had gone on to his pet subject. 'This is a holiday of dreams. We go driving every day and in the evening we come back and write down what we've seen. Monday, a hedgehog, Tuesday a fox, Wednesday a deer, Thursday... We bring back a sample of each herb every day.'

They listed them off (anything he forgot, his wife filled in) though they stopped short of offering us a tour of the specimens. I could hear mild snores coming from the man alongside me.

'Did you know that haws are the best cure for heart disease?' asked the Englishman who told us to call him Richard. I didn't know that, nor did I care. I was hardly aware of my nineteen-year-old heart so I presumed it was managing well without haws. The dozing man alongside me stirred to life.

'Haws for the heart, did you say?' he said, straightening himself up on the sofa. 'How do you take them?' I felt like suggesting that he take them with his Cornflakes after breakfast.

Later that evening a middle-aged, well-dressed man with stubborn-looking grey hair that would give a cartoonist a field day, joined us in the sitting room. As the evening wore on, his gaze made me distinctly uncomfortable. After some warming-up conversation about the weather, the state of the roads around Kerry and a few other comments, he asked if I would join him for a drink. I was just answering that I wasn't interested when the landlord walked by and interrupted the flow but he quickly went back into the kitchen.

Next morning the landlord explained, 'I noticed I was interrupting a bit of romance last night,' he said. 'You could do worse,' he added, with a mischievous grin.

Then his wife came in to clear off the tables and confirmed with a frown that I could indeed do worse than Mister Hayes. 'He comes from a fine family, and you'd fall into the clover.'

But fine family, wonderful and all as it was, wasn't what I had in mind back then. And as for clover, I wasn't eager to fall into it, not with Mister Hayes anyway.

The English couple arrived for breakfast and seated themselves at the table alongside me. They wanted to know about Daniel O'Connell, the Liberator whose nearby house they had seen a sign for the day before.

'Who was he and what did he liberate?' asked Richard. My knowledge of O'Connell was hazy but I did rhyme off all I could remember from my school history. He fought for Catholic Emancipation and that put an end to the Penal Laws, I told them.

'What were they?' they asked.

My goodness, didn't they know? Then as I went to tell them all about the Penal Laws, I found that I didn't really know myself. All that came to mind were fleeing priests, red-coated soldiers hot on their heels, dropping chalices in flight, the story that my elderly neighbour had regularly put great energy into telling me about. Then I thought of something more concrete and told them about how education and the practice of religion for Catholics were banned, and that they didn't allow Catholics to sit in parliament.

Soon Mister Hayes appeared and he was able to fill in the gaps in my emancipation knowledge. He told them that the reason the O'Connells, who were Catholics, managed to become rich was by smuggling goods to and from mainland Europe. He went into great detail about the wines and brandies that were hidden in the hold of the ships that moored in the choppy harbours around O'Connell's residence. There was glee in his voice as he told them how O'Connell electrified the country with monster meetings in his agitation for Catholic Emancipation, how he won 'handsomely' a seat in parliament, the first Catholic to sit in Westminster in modern history.

'But I thought you said Catholics weren't allowed sit in parliament,' said Richard, frowning towards me. I was relieved when Mister Hayes confirmed that this was the case, beaming as he told them of O'Connell's cunning.

'He found a loophole in the law. The law forbade him from sitting in parliament but it didn't forbid him from standing for election, you see,' and he gave a light thump to the table as he said it. As well as coming from a fine family, Mister Hayes had an impressive knowledge of history.

'Would anyone like more toast?' the landlady called as she popped her head around the dining room door. But Mister Hayes hadn't even eaten the toast on his plate.

'O'Connell was catching attention all over the world. He was the first European leader to pull off such a feat peacefully (Catholic Emancipation in 1829), but his biggest gain was convincing the Irish people the power in their numbers. He died at the height of the Great Famine.'

Richard looked relieved to hear The Liberator was dead at last so that he could get on with stories about herbs and wildlife. All he wanted to know was what he had liberated, which I imagine he thought he would hear in one sentence. And he launched in about the treasures of the countryside, red clover, chickweed, shepherd's purse, yarrow. Now it was Mister Hayes's turn to be uninterested.

Later that morning as I pedalled towards the southern side of Kerry's ring, two cars passed me in quick succession, waving as they went. They were Mister Hayes and the English family.

The years have totted up since then. The roads have improved. The cars have increased. I can cycle these days around the Ring of Kerry and back without having to fight off men like Mister Hayes. My heart has taken its knocks for which I know haws are the remedy. I know a lot more about Catholic Emancipation and O'Connell now.

I have developed some eccentric habits along the way, but I still don't eat my Cornflakes after breakfast.

What interests me as I stand once again all these years later at Dooneen viewing point, is to be able to locate the mountains that come into view, to name them one by one, the MacGillicuddy Reeks, Mangerton, Stoompa, Crohane, the Paps – which, come to think of it, is not too unlike what the English family was doing on that holiday long ago.

I have arranged to meet a man who rang me a few weeks ago asking if I needed anyone 'to wander around Kerry with'. He knew my neighbour and she told him I was looking for some company on the trip. He said he thinks of Kerry like the Sound of Music, and I reckoned he was exactly the companion I needed. We're to meet in the Tourist Office in Killarney. I smile when I remember how he said I'd recognise him.

'Watch out for the good lookin' chap, tall and dark. I'm often mistaken for George Clooney.' Then after a pause he added: 'Actually, I'm small and bald and I could do with losing a few stone.' I'm hoping I'll know him. There's no shortage of people who answer to that description.

In fact, it's a woman who approaches me.

'I'm Ada,' she says. 'You were to meet James. He's my brother and he asked me to come and meet you. He was taken to hospital with a pain in his chest. (Oh no. I must put a jinx on anyone I'm to do the Ring of Kerry with.) The good news is that he's doing well. I'd go with you myself but I really would be no help. I don't have near as much knowledge about the place as James.'

She shows me photographs on her phone of herself and James as children holidaying in Kerry taken with their grandparents. She offers to send them to me. We both laugh at the idea but on second thoughts I decide to take them as silent comrades for my journey.

James's original plan was to start with the Ring of Kerry and then come back and take a look at Killarney.

'There's a ritual about starting off with a circle. It gets you off to a spinning start,' he said jauntily.

I'll stick to that plan, follow the route as a kind of pilgrimage to him, to get the energy trundling round that will bring him a speedy recovery.

I bid goodbye to Ada and drive off, once again on a lone tour, from Killarney to Killarney, taking the same road as I took on that journey on the bike long ago: by Killorglin, Cahersiveen, Waterville, Sneem, Kenmare. By car it's faster than a bike and before I know it I'm in Glenbeigh where I met the two men who took pity on me for touring on my own. I can find no trace of the pub where I met them or the man who lived 'up the hill' with whom they wanted to pair me.

I stop at Coomakista viewing point, beyond Waterville. To the left of where I look down over the sea is Derrynane House, home of Daniel O'Connell, though the trees have made it invisible. I can see the choppy coastline, that smuggler's haven on which the O'Connells made their money.

Invisibility is apt. That some old Gaelic houses like the O'Connells managed to escape the ravages of three centuries of Penal Laws and the confiscations of the sixteenth and seventeenth centuries, depended on outwitting the authorities. They took the best option natives could take at the time – they kept the head down. The thing was that the lawyers and boundary officials in Dublin had only a vague notion of the demarcation lines of the lands they were seizing and re-bundling out to their supporters. So local knowledge was the saviour of the few Gaelic families who managed to survive.

When a historian, a Doctor Smith, visited Derrynane and offered to give the O'Connells a mention in his forthcoming work, they presented him with a pony that he had admired, on condition that they wouldn't feature in his history book of Kerry.

Up the ranks, they were not above bending the rules. In 1782 when a Captain Butler from headquarters in nearby Waterville did an early morning swoop on the O'Connell's smuggling business, he and O'Connell struck a deal over breakfast in Derrynane House. Butler agreed to take a cut of all contents of the smuggling craft that came ashore. So this Officer of the Crown had every reason to be pleased as he passed this very spot in Coomakista, on his way back to Waterville.

It had to be this way that Butler came, on this spectacular cliff road from Derrynane to Waterville, because there's no other way to get past the mountain.

I recall something Mister Hayes left out of his long smuggling list from these shores that morning long ago in the guest house – young men rustled out for Holy Orders. They left from shores like the one beneath this viewing spot and made their way to study in the Sorbonne, Rome, Salamanca and Louvain. My own ancestors, Nicholas and Charles Lovelock, went to the Sorbonne to become priests. I used to think that this was singularly courageous in the eighteenth century when they faced the rigours of the Penal Laws. But an event in Galway in 1747 that I read about made me realise that it was quite a mainstream thing to do.

The commander of Galway, Governor Colonel Stratford Eyre made a complaint to Dublin Castle about how Galway erupted in celebration on hearing the news of the defeat of England by the French on September 16, 1747, at Bergen-op-zoon, during the Austrian War of Succession,. Candles burned on every window, including convents.

The French had cut through a fortress in Dutch Brabant believed to be impregnable, never successfully sieged before because of its natural marshland defences. And here's the Irish connection – it was Irishman, Lally and the Irish Brigade who were given the task of reducing the outlying forts which held out. This triumph involved massacre.

It's a story that brings home how close continental Europe felt back then. The Wild Geese who had left Ireland after the serial defeats and confiscations of the sixteenth, seventeenth and eighteenth centuries to fight in the armies of France, Austria and Spain, used to make stealthy visits home and they brought the news from mainland Europe. A constant stream of recruiting friars also made their way into the most remote parts of Ireland. Disguised as laymen, they were scouting for workers to join the Roman Catholic Church at a time when the price for belonging to any faith other than that of the Anglican religion was severe. So to head for the ecclesiastical centres of Paris, Louvain, Salamanca and Rome was quite a mainstream thing to do.

Continental education widened the gap between native Irish and Planter and it made mainland Europe feel closer than London or even Dublin.

My ancestor Charles Lovelock came back in the first batch of teachers appointed to Maynooth College, founded in 1795, when the British decided it was preferable to concede an Irish seminary for student priests than to have their heads filled with French revolutionary ideas that they could use to strike against them.

Daniel O'Connell was educated in France. He was smuggled there to get the schooling he was denied at home. But he never followed the violent example of the French revolutionaries. Passive resistance was his thing. And he later inspired great pacifists like Gandhi. But in his own country his legacy didn't endure. The year after his death, 1848, 'Young Ireland' a nationalist movement who had criticised O'Connell bitterly for his limited version of Irish independence and for his alliance with the Whigs in Westminster, burst into an ill-prepared shambles of a rebellion in Ballingarry, County Tipperary. It was led by its spokesman William Smith-O'Brien. Like revolutionaries all over Europe that same year, the rebellions were organised by middle-class intellectuals and they all failed. The rebels hadn't enough in common to hold them together.

The light over Coomakista is heady today – the mingled effect of sea, rock and sky and the patchwork of fields underneath. A fog obscures Sceilig Mhicíl from view. Like its two similarly-named sites, Mont Saint Michel in France and Mount Saint Michael in Cornwall, this island-rock is dedicated to Saint Michael the Archangel. Saint Michael was the typical belligerent saint that scared the wits out of medieval man. He held sway when crusades and militancy were prized. Both the French and Cornish sites are easy climbs compared to Sceilig.

I can't report first-hand from the summit of Sceilig because I'm cowardly about heights. I never saw the beehive huts the monks built in the sixth century at the very top though I've been there several times. Each time I failed to budge beyond the lower platform of the rock. Courage is not my strong point.

Monks lived in Sceilig for five hundred years, living on fish and birds' eggs and they even grew vegetables on the small space at the peak of the mound. They must have had a better head for heights than mine.

The most enchanting time to approach Sceilig is when the coast is wrapped in a cloak of fog, a regular event. As the rock comes at you out of the vapour, it's like an otherworldly sight that makes mythical beings feel close. It's a reminder too of the Celtic rounds of navigation for which Irish monks like Saint Brendan were known. Brendan the Navigator and his crew left home and took to the ocean and witnessed scenes of fear and delight along the way – the Island of Sheep, the Paradise of Birds, burning mountains, crystal pillars, raging struggles between sea serpents, fire from the nostrils of a monster. Later came more down-to-earth descriptions of these scenes – icebergs and volcanic activity.

I drive on towards Killarney by Sneem. In Kenmare I stop briefly to see the Druid's circle, fifteen stones on a slight hill overlooking the Finnihy River. This is the best example of a stone circle in the south west of Ireland. They're rarely found elsewhere. They date from the Bronze Age but, I can say without doubt, that they show no sign of their generous age. The stones erected were for ritual on solar and lunar events, but you would never see the sun or moon now with the row of sheltering palms that surround them.

Soon I'm back in Killarney, my circle complete. Near Muckross Park, I spot an American woman on a stubborn-looking horse. She tugs the reins but the horse won't budge, like a child pushing his luck when he's dealing with an amateur.

'How do I get this animal to move?' she shouts to a man who is sitting on a wall.

'Yerra girl, you just put 'im into first gear there and he'll be off.' I hide my smile and leave the woman to her difficulty.

A jarvey canvasses me for a trip around the lakes in a jaunting car. I turn it down and head for the shore of Lough Leane which is within sight of Muckross Abbey. If there's one place where ethereal Ireland breathes at its strongest, it's here. I stop to distill the experience, the colour of purple, in strong and stronger shades. The philosopher, Bishop Berkeley said of this spot, 'The King of France might lay out another Versailles but… with all his revenues he could not lay out another Muckross.'

Scott, Tennyson and Wordsworth too sang Killarney's praises.

We have the Herbert family to thank for this ten-thousand hectares of national beauty. But we have the Elizabethan Plantation of Munster to blame that it was seized from the natives in the first place. The Queen needed to reward the men who fought to control the unruly Irish and this was one of her gifts.

I'm looking at a map near the lake when a cyclist rounds the corner.

'Hello, are you lost?' he shouts over his shoulder, his bike at an acute angle. His jauntiness and friendliness are typical of Kerry. Their forebears around here may have been Elizabethan planters, Cromwellian settlers, or tourists who came to visit and then stayed but Kerry has shaped them all in its own image and likeness.

Even more recent arrivals working locally, have taken into their personality a bit of Kerry levity.

I have to step out of the way of a jaunting car. The jarvey, reins in hand, a leprechaun hat on his head, is giving a guided tour. I can hear the lilt of his approaching accent against the trotting of hooves. I can't make out what he's saying. His guests are laughing. No doubt he's telling them a well-embellished yarn. A Kerry joke is different each time it's told.

The roofless ruins of Muckross Abbey lie beyond the field near the shore of Lough Leane. Its square tower contrasts nicely with the curving edges of the lake, and the grey limestone stirs one more tone into the mix. I climb the narrow steps and look down on the yew tree in the centre of the cloister. It has outgrown its space. Small wonder – it's been here since 1344. The yew gets the name 'tree of life' because of its longevity, so it's used as a symbol of the immortality of man. But this one must beat all records. It's dizzying to think of some of the events it shared the centuries with – the decline of the Normans and the burgeoning Gaelic resurgence, the Black Death, the Hundred Years' War, the Great Schism in Rome.

The lettering on the stone plaque showing the names of the four Kerry poets who are buried here in the abbey needs retouching. The difficulty in reading it is like a symbol of the sad fact that few people nowadays know who these poets are. The two who interest me most are Aodhagán Ó Rathaille and Eoghan Rua Ó Súilleabháin. They came from the same spot, and I'm going to visit their birthplace later, that enigmatic part of east Kerry, Sliabh Luachra. But for now, I'm heading for Ross Castle where a little boat is waiting to leave for Innisfallen island. We all pile in. Our bulky lifejackets take up the room of at least another person.

Three generations of the boatman's family have worked on Lough Leane.

'Leane (*léann*) is the Irish word for learning. The learning was provided by the monks who lived on this small island until the fourteenth century. It was an important place of scholarship,' he tells us.

As Ross Castle retreats from view, the mountains loom larger lining up in great hulks. The boatman names them.

'Shehy, Purple, Twomeys. Nearer the island there's Torc and Mangerton. These two are nice walks for the the not-so-fit. Torc has cardiac steps all the way up by the great Torc Waterfall. Mangerton, is a harder climb, but the pathway right to the top doesn't put too much pressure on the heart either.'

When the boat prepares to moor at the island harbour, the boatman's little dog twists her nose as if she's sniffing the air of the old monastic ruins, or sniffing the length of time she's going to be waiting. We have half an hour to explore the twenty-one-acre Innisfallen island – thirty minutes within a day, on an island within a lake, within a group of mountains. It's like being in the nucleus of a cell, the perfect pause, the perfect sanctuary, no destination, no road, no journey.

This island monastery once housed the treasures of the surrounding area for safe-keeping, relics, precious altar plate and the likes. Though it no longer guards valuables, it still holds the same quality of treasure. No evidence remains of the sixth century monks who lived here. Their dwellings were made of wood, unlike those of the Augustinian canons who arrived in the eleventh century. They used stone, and the ruins are now the only traces of that hermetic presence. I don't know if it was in a wooden or a stone buildings that Brian Bórama was schooled, but it's said that he was brought here for his education. He did well out of it. He became High King of Ireland and he defeated the Danes in 1014, a big date in Irish history.

It's easy to spot the church, but a few signs would be nice to mark out the dormitories, the refectory and, most of all, where the monks wrote their famous chronicles *The Annals of Innisfallen*. These scripts are one of the earliest Irish historical records. They contain over two and a half thousand entries, written in Latin, the news of a thousand years (433AD to 1450) as well as a short history of pre-Christian Ireland. The Bodleian Library in Oxford now houses them. They can no longer be opened because of the delicate state of the animal hide on which they were written. Copies were made before they clapped them closed forever. A look at them online is all that's available now.

Kerry is full of peninsulas and sea lanes, and next day I drive to Dingle, another place of treasure on the most western point of Kerry. On my way to see the greatest of them all, Gallarus Oratory in Ballyferriter, the roadsides blaze with orange coloured montbretia and red fuschia. The red yielding flowers of the fuschia are called locally *deoir Dé* (God's teardrop). And God feels very present in this stretch of land where beehive huts give the clue that it once sustained a large population.

In that reflective time of eventide when the sun lowers itself, making a double image in the sea, it looks like the heavens are brought down to earth. This fits well with the Celtic mythical idea that Paradise was located on islands in the western sea.

Gallarus Oratory looks perfect fourteen centuries after it was constructed. It's a corbel-built structure in the shape of an upturned boat and that goes well with Celtic seafaring or *immrama* (sea journeys) going back to when early monks set sail in their curraghs doing the ocean rounds. That it doesn't smell even slightly damp after all those years is like a hymn to the design and skill of its builders.

From this spot you can see the top triangle of Mount Brandon. And to the left, towards the sea, the Three Sisters peak in a row behind a cliff. The biggest of these three hills confronts the water, sheltering her smaller siblings like a good sister should.

A local man is telling an American woman about the distinction between the beehive huts atop Sceilig Mhicíl and Gallarus Oratory. The mention of Sceilig sets her off.

'Oh Sceilig, What a place. What a wonderful sight, it's mystifying, simply unbelievable. The day I was there they weren't sure if they would be able to take the boats out because of the thick fog. Then as we approached the rock it was in a cloud of mist. We didn't know what to expect because it was all a haze. And out of nowhere it came into view, this great rock…'

'That happens,' he replies, comically unmoved. 'I live within sight of Sceilig, I was born there, lived there all my life. I knew it long before Star Wars made it famous. My force awakened a long time before the film crew landed.'

'Do you not waken up every morning and exclaim how beautiful it is?'

'Yerra I don't,' he drawls.

I leave and head for the rock promontory Dún an Óir and Smerwick Harbour, but though they're perfectly visible from Gallarus, I can't find them now. There are initial signs, but follow-on directions are nowhere in sight so I drive into roads that get thinner and thinner, finally dissolving into someone's back yard where a little black Collie is intent on barking hysterically at the wheels of the car.

Going astray is not all in vain. From these small roads you feel nearer the peaks that are shaped like motionless tidal waves, frozen after the assault of an angry sea.

Anger is fitting. Dún an Óir was the scene of a terrible massacre of the six hundred or so Spanish and Italian soldiers who came to help the Irish during the Elizabethan wars. Serving at the Siege of Smerwick along with Lord Deputy Grey on that July day in 1580 were Walter Raleigh and his poet friend Edmund Spenser.

Elizabeth 1 gave Spenser vast tracts of confiscated land in Kilcolman near Doneraile in County Cork. With this amount of loot, Her Majesty was worth serenading and he wrote 'The Faerie Queene', an epic poem celebrating Elizabeth and the Tudor dynasty. Spenser's brutal treatment of the Irish even horrified his fellow planters. He despaired of his own class falling into native ways, and even adopting the local language.

Raleigh was given Myrtle Grove near Youghal in County Cork, a similar size estate, for combatting the Irish. He played a crucial role in England's empire at a time when it was not so sure of itself. In 1584 Elizabeth granted him an exclusive patent to colonise north America.

Raleigh brought tobacco from the new world. When one of his servants in Youghal saw him smoking – or smoldering as she thought – she swiftly took action with a bucket of water. It might have been more foresightful than it seemed at the time but it sure spoiled that smoke anyway.

Raleigh probably brought potatoes to Ireland too. He is said to have first grown them in his vast acreage in Youghal. From the discovery of the potato by the Spanish in Peru's Andes in 1570, it had to fight for its place on the table. For a long time it was the poor relation of grain, fit only for pigs and the poor. The potato got a boost when a German chemist, Parmentier, survived on nothing else when he was taken prisoner during the Seven Years war 1756-63.

Favourite and all as Raleigh was of his queen, for his opening up of the world, she had him sealed in the Tower of London for secretly marrying her lady-in-waiting. He was locked in the tower, three times, once by Elizabeth 1, and twice by James 1, on a charge of treason. He didn't waste his time there. He wrote a history of the world and experimented with making medicine (which people swore by). It was part of this same sense of investigating things that made him ask, on the morning of his execution, to take a look at the axe. When the executioner hesitated, Raleigh asked him, 'Dost thou think I am afraid of it?' Then the axe man agreed and Raleigh ran his fingers over the blade. 'This is a sharp medicine but it is a physitian for all diseases,' he smiled. On October 19, 1618 he was led from the tower. Along the way he smiled and joked. Seeing a bald man in the crowd he offered him his hat. 'Thou hast more need of it now than I'. Two blows it took to decapitate him.

The following morning before the noise rises above the surface of day, I go to Brandon Creek where Brendan the Navigator set sail with his crew, on a seven-year Atlantic voyage. The picture is complete with a little boat moored in the narrow space between the cliffs.

It was a fellow monk who suggested to Brendan that he should go and see the wonders of God. In the story of the Brendan voyage, the Christian message weaves neatly onto the classical legendary tradition. Christianity by the sixth century wasn't yet so confident, and the story fuses the new Christian message with the pagan past. Brendan and his crew leave home (like the mythical heroes before him) and lead us through the mysteries of the gospel. The seafarers are trying to find Paradise from which they have been barred by the sin of Adam. And before they depart, they 'leave all' (as recommended in the gospel) confessing and fasting for the three previous days. The boats, currachs, are described in true-to-life detail. Once across the boundary and on to the sea, all becomes possible and the marvels unfold. Their faith clashes fiercely with fear, like the fight between body and spirit. Sea serpents and monsters stain the sea with blood but end up becoming their friends.

The explorer Tim Severin also left from this spot, Brandon Creek in the 1970s, re-creating a replica of Brendan's boat (including using oak, ash and tanned leather from twenty-five oxen) sailing from Ireland to Newfoundland, to re-enact the voyage. Severin wasn't trying to prove that Saint Brendan discovered America nine hundred years before Columbus, but to test if the story of the Brendan voyage could be true.

From Brandon Creek I go to look into another voyage, Roger

Casement's, on Banna Strand. I take the northern exit from Dingle by the Conor Pass, Ireland's highest mountain route. It's showing off its great spread this morning. It was a stroke of geological luck to have erupted, and then settled in such a lovely form. It's another stroke of luck to be able to see this sight without its usual veil of fog.

Pedlar's lake, a gouged-out corrie, lies beneath the viewing point where I stop. This provides the first evidence of Ireland's Ice Age. I get this information from the map in the car-park. While I read it I have to steady myself against the strong breeze that has forced a group of passing cyclists off their bikes.

I head westwards, then loop back on myself at the far side of the water to get to Banna. I need sunglasses to reduce the glare bouncing off the white sand. This is a beach for bare feet.

Surfers are out in full force though there's precious little surf to ride. A colony of students in navy uniform file down towards the shore. Having approached in such ant-like order they suddenly begin to run in all directions, as if they get a signal from this wilderness that rules are off limits. They get down on their knees and begin digging with their hands. This is what children get up to when their parents' backs are turned, burying themselves in sand in their good uniforms. I cringe. But that shows my small knowledge of Banna sand. It brushes off like star dust, leaving not a trace for even the most fussy parent to spot.

It was here that Irish nationalist Sir Roger Casement (whom we met in The Glens) arrived on April 21, 1916, dropped off from a German U-boat. He came to warn his fellow plotters to call off the Easter Rising against British rule because the help Germany was offering wasn't enough. He must have cut a fine figure on that Good Friday morning. People who knew him described him as the finest looking man they'd ever seen. He was without his recognisable long black beard that day. As part of his conspiracy he shaved it off before he set out for Germany.

I can get no sighting of the primroses and wild violets that greeted Casement. And it's afternoon, not the time of day to hear the skylarks as he did when he landed at three in the morning.

Casement had been knighted for his work as British consul, for showing up injustices in the Belgian Congo. He gave the British colonial state officials news of the terror when locals were forced to collect rubber and ivory for export, of the retribution when quotas fell short and of the practice of paying for every human head collected just to strengthen the resolve of the collectors. He thought Britain should lead the way in opposing these abuses, like they had in the anti-slavery movement.

Just what was the British Foreign Secretary thinking when he recommended him for a knighthood? Did he not know that the next logical step for Casement would lead him to take a stand against all colonial wrongs? Casement himself said it was his Irishness that gave him an eye for injustice in the Congo.

As for receiving a knighthood, he had a problem about an Irishman kneeling before the king to accept such an award while his own country was in bondage, so he pretended he was ill on the day.

It only took hours for the authorities to pick Casement up from Banna. I can well believe it, you'd be spotted instantly here on such an expanse of beach. He had been careless with the details too, leaving a rail ticket for the journey from Berlin to Wilhelmshaven (a German submarine port) in his pocket. The job of charging him with high treason was easy, though such an accusation against a knight of the realm was a rare event in British history. He was lodged in the Tower of London.

I would like to know where exactly they found the three Mauser pistols, ammunition, binoculars and maps that Casement buried in Banna's sand. These accessories were in line with his new thinking, that 'the only rule John Bull respects is that of the rifle.' At his trial, his plea that self-government was a right – 'not something to be doled out or withheld by another people, where men must beg for leave to subsist in their own land, to think their own thoughts, to sing their own songs' – cut no ice in a country caught up in war. Casement had plotted with Germany, Britain's enemy, and they were unlikely to be swayed by his argument about thinking your own thoughts or singing your own songs. In faroff India, two men were listening – Mahatma Gandhi and Jawaharlal Nehru.

The trump card of the trial came when Scotland Yard got hold of Casement's diaries in his lodgings in which he had noted details of his homosexual experiences.

Twenty years earlier Irishman Oscar Wilde had been tried on charges of sodomy. More recently in 1903, the most highly decorated Major General Sir Hector Macdonald was exposed as homosexual and due for court martial, but saved himself by taking his own life. (Consensual homosexual acts were not legalised in England and Wales until 1967; in Ireland in 1993.)

Casement's diaries gave the trial its final punch. Photographic copies were sent on their impelling rounds – to the king, to MPs, to journalists, and a set of copies for Washington. He was doomed.

Such were the times. Even for deserting the army you were court-marshalled and shot, let alone scheming with the enemy. The hangman called Casement the bravest man he had ever executed.

I leave Banna and go northwards by the coast. Staying on the map of Kerry, my next journey is to Sliabh Luachra, a place of poetry, music and dance.

TWENTY-SIX

SLIABH LUACHRA

There's debate over where Sliabh Luachra (mountain of the rushes) begins and ends. On a map it stretches east of Killarney, from Rathmore, by the Quagmire River, south to the River Flesk and to the source of the Blackwater. But in the mind, Sliabh Luachra stretches back to the seventeenth century, when the severest of times overlapped with the sweetest of poetry.

Two names stand out: Aodhagán Ó Rathaille and Eoghan Ruadh Ó Súilleabháin whose graves I stood over in Muckross Abbey in Killarney. The woman I meet in Meentogues Primary School calls them by their first names, Aodhagán and Eoghan, as if they never died to the people of Sliabh Luachra.

I need not ask at all, because a little further on is a sign for Sliabh Luachra's cultural trail. This leads me uphill, rising over an array of fields, brown moorland and rivers. The sun folds and unfolds across the hills like a searchlight peering into every dip and curve of the uplands, looking for outlaws. The whole array is overseen by the Paps of Danú, two mountains in distant blue that pleat into one another like a pair of breasts.

The high ground of Sliabh Luachra might not match the tectonic credentials of Kerry's bigger names – Mangerton, Mount Brandon, Carrauntoohil, Shehy, some I can see in the distance. But this landscape of gentle hills holds within it a milder wonder. It's as if the night sky dipped down to earth and left its imprint on the hills.

Rolling beauty blends with noble past. This once was the heartland of scholarship, where a Bardic school thrived, where poems crossed uplands, rims of valleys and streams. It's easy to fancy yourself in another era, watching traipsing scholars covered in dust having walked for hundreds of miles to get to the Sliabh Luachra's famous school to learn the skill of being a poet.

It was worth the effort. Fully fledged poets enjoyed the rank of a privileged caste. As well as learning the craft of poetry (style, structure, metres, composing in the dark) their seven years of tough schooling covered Brehon law, chronicling, and how to preserve the Gaelic way. Genealogy was highly prized. These scholars would be the future bards for the old Gaelic families, and they would sing their praises in return for patronage.

The Bardic schools weren't like the universities that sprung up in mainland Europe around the twelfth century. The universities grew out of the cathedral schools with churchmen in charge, and Roman law and language became their standard, but the Bardic schools were secular and fostered the local.

I find Aodhagán Ó Rathaille's birthplace, to the nearest field at least, perched at the top of a hill. Scrahanaveale is the name of the townland, in English that means 'riverside place of the honey'. The view from here is suitably sweet. The whole array of Sliabh Luachra lies beneath.

There's no place to park unless I go into someone's back yard. That would definitely be cheeky, so I park on the road to read the plaque to Aodhagán. I have to move to let a farmer with a brimming trailer of hay drive past. He isn't cross with me for parking in his way. They don't show irritation in the country like pressed-for-time urban folk.

Ó Rathaille was the last of the old school poets. Like a lot of people who hit a transition that makes their skill redundant, he took it badly. The Bardic schools went downhill around the time of his birth, 1670, though they were kept going informally when poets who felt responsible for preserving the Gaelic way, assembled in groups called the 'Courts of Poetry'. These true-believers kept up some of the teaching of the Bardic schools, discussing poetic techniques and copying manuscripts. By then, they had taken the great tumble from intellectual aristocracy to penury, living as *spailpíní* (wandering labourers), farming a few acres or on-and-off teaching in hedge schools.

The caretaking of Gaelic genealogy when the chiefs of their ancient patrons were either in exile or poverty-stricken amid their former possessions, was about as useful as teaching someone today the skill of the hod carrier.

I'm enjoying the day. I'm on high ground in all senses. I don't feel brought down by the theme of overthrow that I'm looking into – the echo of defeat that wails through the verses of the sixteenth, seventeenth and eighteenth centuries as one wave of dispossession followed another – the Plantation of Munster, in the 1580s (the first mass Irish confiscation), the suppression of the native language, the Flight of the Earls, 1607. the Cromwellian conquest, 1649 to 1653.

The wasted effort of the poet's trade was summed up in a pithy poem by Mathghamhain Ó hIfearnáin. It was written early in the seventeenth century *Ceist! Cia do cheinneóchadh dán?* (A question! Who Will Buy a Poem?) Many a skilled craftsman has crooned the same bleak question since.

The thing is, Catholic Ireland backed the wrong horse, King James, during the Glorious Revolution of 1688-89. The Irish had little choice but to back James. He was the Catholic king but so much history followed from that decision. They lost on the Boyne, in Aughrim and in Limerick (the stone of the Treaty of Limerick, signed on October 3, 1691, is still there). The Catholic King James was replaced by his Protestant daughter, Mary and her husband William of Orange (William lll of England).

After the unhonoured Treaty of Limerick, Patrick Sarsfield and nineteen thousand followers, the Wild Geese, left Ireland in 1691 and, by then, Irish Ireland had collapsed, its leaders either in prison, in exile or, like Sarsfield, fighting the wars of the Sun King, Louis XlV of France. What was there to sing about? And if someone did break into song the notes should have been dissonant. But here's what happened. The poets sang out sweeter than ever, turning misery into greatness.

The writer Daniel Corkery calls Aodhagán Ó Rathaille the Dante of Munster. His poems cry out of this dark grief, reproducing the local rivers, fields, the anguish, and gave birth to a new genre in Irish literature – the *aisling* (vision poem), perhaps the greatest native art form. Sweet and pure it is, flowing, dazzling, bewitching.

'Gile na Gile' (Brightness of the Brightness) is one of the first *aisling* poems ever written, acting as a tuning fork for all that followed. (Translation by Frank O'Connor.)

> Gile na gile do chonnarc ar slí in uaigneas,
> criostal an chriostail a goirmroisc rinn-uaine
> binneas an bhinnis a friotal nár chríonghruama,
> deirge is finne do fionnadh 'na gríosghruannaibh.

> Brightness of brightness lonely met me where I wandered,
> Crystal of crystal only by her eyes were splendid,
> Sweetness of sweetness lightly in her speech she squandered,
> Rose-red and lily-glow brightly in her cheeks contended.

Corkery compares Ó Rathaille's poetry to the music of Mozart who said, 'He who understands my music is lifted above the sorrow of the world.' There's a Spanish saying: 'Hunger sharpens the wit,' and maybe that explains this literary outburst amid such gloom.

I drive about a mile downhill where Eoghan Ruadh Ó Súilleabháin was born in 1748, twenty odd years after Ó Rathaille was buried. While Ó Rathaille feels distant, aristocratic, bitter about his loss of rank, you fancy you could enjoy a laugh with the red-headed Eoghan Ruadh. He was carousing and reckless, and left a trail of stories in his path, as a playboy, prankster and womaniser. There's hardly a road that doesn't recall tidings of him. Typical of him is the poem he wrote to his friend James Fitzgerald, in mock heroic style, asking to put a handle on his spade.

> *A chara mo chléibh 's a Shéamais ghreannmhair ghráigh*
> *d'fhuil Ghearaltaigh Ghréagaigh éachtaigh armnirt áigh,*
> *maide glan réidh i ngléas bíodh agat dom rámhainn*
> *'s mar bharra ar an scléip cuir léi go greanta bacán …*

> Make me a handle as straight as the mast of a ship,
> Seamus you clever man, witty and bountiful,
> Sprung through the Geraldine lords from the kings of Greece,
> And fix the treadle and send it back to me soon …

The poem goes on, if the steward chides him for poor spadework, he will relate the adventurous wanderings of Death or the tale of the Grecian battles at Troy where the princes fell.

> *Mar is fear tú mar mé do chéas an seana-thart lá,*
> *racham araon faoi scléip go tabhairne an stáid;*
> *is rabairneach ghlaofam ale is dramanna ar clár,*
> *is taisce go héag ní dhéan d'aon leathphingin pá.*

> For you're a man like myself with an antique thirst,
> So need I say how we'll give the story an end?

We'll shout and rattle our cans the livelong night
Till there isn't as much as the price of a pint to spend.

Another of Eoghan Ruadh's tricks was to ask foolish questions and pretend not to understand the answers, or let on to a priest he didn't know the Ten Commandments, only to break out into impromptu verse mocking the clergy when the priest had gone to great trouble to teach him.

You still have to watch out for Kerry people who fake that same fiendish modesty, the don't-mind-me kind, that pose as half foolish only to outsmart you punchily when you least expect it. A friend of my cousin is a semi-professional bridge-player. In a tournament his club met a group of Kerry players. 'Don't mind us,' they told them. 'We wouldn't beat beginners.' But, when the results went up, the semi-professionals found out that they'd lost, badly. So there's some of the residue of Eoghan Ruadh's tricks left.

Eoghan Ruadh's stormy life had spun itself out at thirty-six. He had sung through the good and the bad times. He was the greatest of lyric poets and master of the *aisling*. Some compare him with Robbie Burns, Pindar, or Rudyard Kipling. Yet Lecky's *History of Ireland in the Eighteenth Century* lists him as a farm labourer. And there was no reason why Lecky should have known him as any other, because at that time neither his nor Ó Rathaille's poems ever saw the light of print.

Irish was not just poorly thought of, it was feared. Words have power and so the official aim was to suppress the native language. Colonialism could never relax while its subjects spoke a different tongue. And that was a success because, today, if you mentioned these poets, few would know who they are.

Eoghan Ruadh wrote in English too. One famous poem came about after his employment on the Nagle farm near Fermoy in Cork came to a hasty end. He was brought in from the fields to tutor the children of the house when his master discovered he could speak four languages: Latin, Greek, English and Gaelic. But his charm and womanising got him entangled with one of the women of the household for which his master showed him the door – with a shotgun, for emphasis.

He fled to the British navy, to the West Indies, where he partook in one of England's most famous sea battles, when they routed the French fleet under Admiral Rodney on April 12, 1782. This was a victory unmatched until then in British naval warfare.

Far away in the West Indies Eoghan Ruadh longed for his own hill country and he wrote 'Rodney's Glory,' an ode to flatter his way out of the navy, ahem, an ode to celebrate Admiral Rodney's victory.

> Give ear, ye British hearts of gold,
> That e'er disdain to be controlled,
> Good news to you I will unfold,
> 'Tis of brave Rodney's glory,
> Who always bore a noble heart,
> And from his colours ne'er would start,
> But always took his country's part
> Against each foe who dared t' oppose
> Or blast the bloom of England's Rose,
> So now observe my story.

It went badly wrong. For his poetic efforts he got promotion. So, he tried a better trick, blistering his shins with spearwort so that they would think he had some contagious disease and allow him go home. It worked.

Back home he planned to set up a hedge school. For that he needed money so he repeated the ode trick and wrote a flattering poem to the newly-appointed colonel of a body of yeomanry, Daniel Cronin of Killarney. The colonel didn't acknowledge the song to Eoghan Ruadh's liking and so he turned his words the other way and wrote a satire.

Cronin's men caught up with Eoghan Ruadh in a tavern in Killarney and the Colonel's coachman hit him a blow to the head with a tongs. This was the head from which the most enchanting lyrics had flown, earning him the name, *Eoghan an Bhéil Bhinn* (Eoghan of the sweet mouth). He would sing no more.

From the height of his birthplace you can see the route they took as they shouldered his coffin across the River Blackwater, to Muckross Abbey. As if special background sound was laid on to escort this man of ready wit, a thunderstorm bellowed and flooded the crossing so the cortège was halted and the bearers had to make a hasty grave where he could overnight before making the rest of the journey to Muckross.

This was the route he had taken in his youth on his way to the hedge school in Faha where he first became acquainted with the Gaelic sagas, poems and the stories of Greece that sparked his imagination.

It's a struggle to leave Sliabh Luachra and return to the world of bustling traffic, of highways and timetables while the spell of the place still envelopes me. That fleeting delight that makes you fancy you could live here. Maybe if you did, it would spoil the spell, let the light of day flood in on the magic. Fleeting delight is delightful only because it's fleeting.

If I feel like this after a few hours, no wonder Eoghan Ruadh felt the pangs of loneliness in the West Indies. I play some of the local music to lessen the transition.

Sliabh Luachra, like many a hill country, grew its own style of music. The fiddle and accordion playing of Pádraig O' Keeffe, Denis Murphy, Julia Clifford, Jerry McCarthy and Johnny Leary matched the fair landscape and the fragrant words of its past.

It was great dancing country too. Dancers stepped it out in their own way, floor battering footwork combined with smooth body movements. Though the polka made its journey from Bohemia, it took on a local name here – the slide – and that ties in with the terrain and the high-spirits of the people.

Before I leave Kerry I'm going to look into another corner of this county, the region around Listowel, where locals contributed more than their share to literature.

TWENTY-SEVEN

A PLACE THAT BREEDS WORDS

Ballylongford, Listowel, Duagh, Ballydonoghue, Castle Island in the northwest curve of County Kerry, hemmed in by the Shannon River to their north and the Atlantic to their west, bred so many poets, writers, dramatists, journalists that there's a mild suspicion that there's something in the air around here that inspires words.

Today I meet one of them, poet Brendan Kennelly in his home-place, Ballylongford. This town, 'Bally', is his 'centre of the universe'.

Maybe he notices my unease. Awe makes you nervous. I met him years ago in Dublin at a talk he gave. It was a knockout. It wasn't just his smooth delivery, his lack of airs and graces, his output (he has written about fifty books of poetry since the publication of his first, *Collected Poems* in 1959), it was the demeanour of the evening, his mischievous take on life, on literature. Today, as I sit alongside him and listen to his charming voice, I can see he has lost none of his gifts. He tells me a roguish joke while we're waiting for his sister Nancy to arrive. She's going to drive us around their native place.

Nancy Kennelly-McAuliffe is a few minutes late. When she arrives, she steps from her car with the sprightly air and ready smile that runs in the family.

'I met someone who delayed me,' she explains.

Under her arm is the pictorial account of her home-place that she produced, *Ballylongford, a Photographic Memoir*. As she sits down she explains: 'I dedicated the book to Ballylongford people, the people I love. My love of people is even greater than my love of place, especially those of my birthplace. Growing up in a pub gives you a special insight into people.'

Brendan agrees: 'It's that freedom of conversation that marks a good pub. I remember how after a few pints they sang their songs and told there stories. They enjoyed their drink and appreciated each other's company.' That became the inspiration of one of his poems, 'Living Ghosts':

Richard Broderick celebrates
This winter's first and only fall of snow
With a midnight rendering
of *The Bonny Bunch of Roses O*

Nancy tells me: 'A lot of the locals are related to one another around here and Ballylongford people love their place, Bally as it's called.'

Her words begin the journey with a flourish, of a spot on the earth where everyone is kin, of a people who are always up for a song. Naturally, Brendan has slotted his 'centre of the universe' into his poems, mostly treating it as something more of a personality than a place, where humour is a way of life.

Nancy's book gives Ballylongford the same status, in pictures. Whether it's showing the town's signature buildings, its niche on the River Shannon, its glory days, the town in a smoking ruin after the reprisal by the Black and Tans, it's the people who shine through the book – historic figures, people of bravery, people of importance, people of little importance (there are no such people in Nancy's world) and the picture that captures best for me the spirit of the time and place – Eddie Kelly bringing home the cows for milking through Main Street. The photo was taken in 1953. You wouldn't zigzag cattle around all the cars in this Kerry town today.

Like every 'centre of the universe,' Ballylongford has a universal edge. We stop to read Brendan's lines. They're etched on the wall of the Kennelly premises on the corner of Main Street where their brother still runs the family pub:

If life in little places dies greater places share the loss;
Life, if you wish, may not be worth
One passing game of pitch and toss;
And yet a nation's life is laid
In places like the Crooked Cross.'

(The crooked cross is the intersection in the centre of Ballylongford).

The Kennellys trace a Bardic lineage. Nancy explains: 'Our great grandmother was Sarah Langan from Tarbert, a niece of Tomás Ó Langáin, who was a poet to the Knight of Glin in nearby County Limerick.' Brendan might be the most famous now, but he's not the only poet in the family.

Family means a lot to both of them. As we go outside the village, they point to their mother, Bridie's birthplace and a nearby hill where their father, Timmy, came from. The father was a great man to sing and he had a fine collection of songs. That, no doubt, was the Bardic poetic legacy turning up whenever a bar of a tune was needed. I reckon it's from him the rollicking wit that breaks through Brendan's poetry comes from. Brendan gives a clue into his nature: 'He wasn't a rigid parent. He would let you go your way. That kind of tolerance is wisdom, it's respect.'

Kennelly senior had enchanting stories for his children too. At a curve on the road they point to a house on a sloping site. The dishes in this house, he used to tell them. slid off the table. These two still nurture that magic. Even today as they pass the house, they say they picture sliding cups and plates.

Bally sits on a plum spot. The River Shannon flows by and offers this spot a cradled corner of its estuary, before it empties itself into the Atlantic. The siren of ships once echoed around here and made this harbour town the hub of north Kerry. The development of the nearby pier at Saleen on the Shannon became the trading point that received the goods that supplied this surrounding countryside where the dairy cow provided the wealth. Nancy recalls: 'In those good old days, ships came up here with coal from Poland, grain for the local bakeries, and all the other goods it took to stock these parts. There were seventy-two businesses here in this town – hardware, creamery, timber yards, pubs, shops and restaurants (though one of Brendan's poems 'Paddy Scanlan's Ating House' gives one of them a more homely name). O'Sullivan's hardware once employed forty five, Jim Hanrahan's bakery had about twenty staff. Heaphys (which sells food and household goods) is the only surviving business since our childhood.'

O'Sullivan's is singled out for a pictorial chapter in Nancy's book, as well it might. Its business interests once ranged from shipping, milling, timber yard, travel agent, public house to a piggery. It closed in 1990 after a little over a hundred years in business.

Some houses of substance in the centre of the town are a reminder of that flourishing time. Further up we pass by a group of cottages, built when Ballylongford was thriving, that hold memories for Nancy and Brendan. All the roofs are slated now but they were thatched in their youth. From here we go by Tay

Lane, Sand Quay, Moneen, Rusheen, Doctor's Cross. But Bally was a place with a much older story to tell.

We drive towards the battered ruins of Carrigafoyle Castle and Lislaughtin Abbey, the original centre of the place. Brendan's sequence of poems on Cromwell, where he mixes comic lines with buccaneering history, makes it feel that these incursions happened in living memory.

On the way Nancy points out where they swam as children, and Bambury Wood further out the road where they played among the trees and which Brendan preserved in a poem. Their childhood, like their home town, is bound up with the waters of their rivers, the great Shannon and the smaller River Line.

Carrigafoyle stone castle has stood on a rock here in this small bay on the Shannon estuary, since the fifteenth century. Its height – five storeys – and its cut-stone corners gives it a sharply gaunt look. It was a century old when it suffered the battering which knocked gaping holes in two of its walls. This attack, the siege of Carrigafoyle Castle, took place during Easter 1580, when Elizabethan forces knocked chunks out of it. Since then daylight beams through the gaps and it stands as a record of the plunder.

For the Kennelly children the ruins provided height for the scaling they got up to when adults were out of the way.

'We used to go right to the top, on the spiral stairs, up to the battlements,' says Nancy.

With my poor head for heights I shudder at the thought of chancing my luck on Carrickafoyle's rickety skeleton.

This ruin was once the proud residence of the O'Connors, the chief ruling dynasty of this area from the mid seventh century. They lost their footing after the Norman invasion of the twelfth century though they continued to live in Carrickafoyle until 1666.

It was an O'Connor who founded the nearby abbey of Lislaughtin in the 1470s and named it after Saint Lachtin, the saint who brought Christianity to this area in the seventh century. My cringing mispronunciation of Lislaughtin isn't let hang in the air. Brendan promptly intervenes with the correct one, Locals don't like their place-names miscalled. I feel like apologising for defiling the word, adding to the abbey's long history of irreverence.

The abbey walls are covered with growth now and the ivy emphasises the shapely passing of time. The most famous of the thirty windows is the Gothic one facing east. A processional cross (one of the finest examples of fifteenth century Irish art) was donated to the abbey with the inscription in Latin: *Cornelius, son of John O'Connor, captain of his nation, and Juliana, daughter of the Knight* (of Glin), *caused me to be made by the hand of William, son of Cornelius, June 4th, 1479.*

It has a gripping story to tell. In that 1580 attack by Elizabethan forces under Sir William Pelham, they looted the abbey, routed the monks and their land was granted to Sir William Herbert. On the day, just to bring their work to a heroic end, Sir William's forces slit the throats of three elderly friars, – O'Hanarahan, O'Shea and Scallan – in front of the high altar. One plucky monk ran away with the processional cross. Maybe it was he who buried it in a field in the townland of Ballymackessy. It would never be heard of again only for a ploughman unearthed it in 1871.

Brendan's poem 'The Lislaughtin Cross' follows the lead of the inscription, of putting words in the 'mouth' of the cross. He gives the transfer to its new home in the National Museum in Dublin a comic twist when the cross reveals that it felt more liberated underground in '...the lightless place/Where I understood the dead/And the blunderers above my head' compared to where it is now: a Prisoner behind glass.

That would be him – I reckon he was using the cross as his own personal story. Like himself, it felt rooted in its native place. Not in highbrow places like the National Museum, but back to where it belonged, until the blades of the plough – unhelpfully – turned it up to the light.

I remember a story Brendan once told about when he first began teaching in Dublin's Trinity College. An American woman came to him at the end of a presentation to complement him on 'a very charming lecture. Will the next one be in English?' she asked. That was one of the events that made him modify his Kerry accent, though not abandon it. Heavens, no. He would never give up the folksy idioms of North Kerry. It used to delight him when often, strolling down Dublin's Grafton Street, a call would lob across busy shoppers from the opposite side of the pavement: 'Up Bally!' That transported him back to his roots, to the world that inspired him most. And he lapped up this momentary break from stiff academia. No doubt, he did much for Trinity too (where he became Professor of Modern Literature in 1973), and let in the Kerry jovial air into the oak-framed institution of Elizabeth 1.

Brendan Kennelly had to get church approval to enrol for his studies in Trinity College.

'McQuaid (Archbishop of Dublin) was opposed to Trinity,' he explains. 'I had to go to the Bishop of Kerry, a Doctor Moynihan, but he gave me permission without a problem.' Permission was only half of the difficulty. Trinity at the time was a daunting place. When this college was first founded in 1592, its aim was to turn out an educated Protestant clergy. Roman Catholics could study in Trinity too provided they renounced their faith, a ban that was lifted on May 1, 1794. From 1871 to 1970 Roman Catholics needed permission from their bishop to study there.

Amid all this my-God-is-better-than-yours, comes a little beam of light – the Reid Sizarship, still in existence. It provides part-funding for natives of Kerry of limited means, regardless of religion, to study in Trinity College, based on their public examination results. Brendan won a sizarship. It was one of his teachers in nearby Tarbert, Jane Agnes McKenna, who spotted his talent and encouraged him to apply for it.

'She was a Limerick woman, small, with a great passion, a great love of truth. She looked out for your strong points. I loved words and she saw that and encouraged me.'

This endowment was originally associated with Sandes, a local Kerry landlord. Nancy explains: 'Sandes settled in Kerry as part of the Cromwellian plantation. In 1592 when Trinity was founded, he made a contribution to the new university. For his generosity, a sizarship was established for natives of Kerry. That endowment still exists. Brendan and two of his brothers benefited from it. (The sizarship is linked to a more recent bequest too. In 1888 a local Kerry landlord, Richard Touhill Reid, endowed £6,200.)

'A lot of places around here are called after Sandes. Moyvane (a local townland) was once called Newtown Sandes and Collis Sandes House in Tralee,' she says.

Sandes makes a change from tales of raids and pillage. The year 1592 when Trinity College was founded was only a little more than a decade after Carrigafoyle and Lislaughtin were sacked.

Nancy takes up her historical guide of Bally as we drive by the graveyard: 'After the O'Connors lost their private chapel (which stood beside their castle at Carrigafoyle), it became a Protestant church. Here's where the local gentry were buried – the Sandes, the Crosbies, the Colts, the Popes and the Ponsonbys. It's no longer an entirely Protestant graveyard. Protestants got absorbed into the population and very few remain.'

And now to the place of baptism of that keen coloniser, Horatio Herbert Kitchener, who distinguished himself in Sudan, Egypt and the Boer War. He also won fame – or infame – for organising his blockhouses and concentration camps to wear down Boer resistance. And what young man in 1914 could resist the excitement of war, with Kitchener's recruiting poster pointing the finger straight at them? 'Your Country Needs You'. He was born on June 24, 1850 here in Ballylongford, the son of Lieutenant Colonel Henry Kitchener. Now colonising prowess, however much valued it was in Britain, wasn't a big hit in Ireland so Kitchener needs an antidote. One is to hand.

'Ballylongford was the birthplace of nationalist, The O'Rahilly.'

The O'Rahilly family house stands on the town's crossroads. The story of Michael Joseph, who called himself The O'Rahilly, has a tragic edge. Like many in the Irish Volunteers in 1916, he didn't want the organisation used by a group of extremists who were intent on going headlong into a hopeless revolt. He thought it should stick to the aim for which it was founded – launching an attack only in self-defence. He tried to convince the hardliners, like Pearse and Connolly, to stop the Easter Rising, and when he couldn't he felt a duty to join them. Many years later W B Yeats captured the essence of the heartbreak of his position in a poem, 'The O'Rahilly':

Am I such a craven that
I should not get the word
But for what some travelling man
Had heard I had not heard?

The O'Rahilly was killed leading a charge against a British barricade in Moore Street, around the corner from the GPO in Dublin, the building the rebels had abandoned.

We stop at the school where the Kennelly family got their early education. Barely audible above the gaggle of the pupils, Nancy points out one of the remaining features of a time gone by – the dividing wall between the girls' and the boys' playground. More of these traces of division are coming up as we leave Ballylongford and drive to the seaside resort of Ballybunion. With sea on our right and the delicate sweep of the Knockanore mountains on our left, we pass by the coast, by Ladies' Beach, Men's Beach, Nun's Beach, reminders of these set-apart years. It ties in with the segregated school playground, the segregated education in a university to which Brendan Kennelly was allowed to go to only with the bishop's blessing.

Ballybunion is a seaside town, once famous for its late-night drinking and revelry. The pubs stayed outside the pale of rules and trading hours during the carousing summer months, adding another segregating feature.

Nancy parks near the beach which is tucked in the shelter of the sheer cliffs of its two promontories. Like other parts of the Kerry coast, Ballybunion takes the full blast of the Atlantic wind when occasionally it rages and rants, overturning all in its path, like a drunken lout coming home to a sleeping family. At other times, like today, the wind blows gently, in a fit of making-up for its outburst, smoothing the sands again as skillfully as a craftsman with a trowel.

Sitting in the car by the lapping waters, Brendan recalls a tragedy he witnessed here on the beach and recites the poem he penned to remember 'A Drowned Girl'.

Doctor, priest, civilian prayed and probed and tried
To find one reassuring remnant of breath,
As if they couldn't see why a girl in a green swimsuit
Should be so irretrievably stretched in death.

He credits a teacher of his, Johnny Walsh, for giving him a special love of the spoken word.

'He encouraged us to learn by heart and I really liked that.' That affection for the oral tradition brings him to his other great love, his roots.

'I love Kerry, the place I was born in. I think that rooted feeling to your homeplace makes it easy to absorb other identities. Dublin became a second love of place. When I was in Trinity I lived in Cork Street and it was great to walk around there early on a summer's morning. I loved the Dubs. I became a kind of Cul-dub.' (Culchie means a rural person. Brendan affectionately blends it with Dubliner.) And Dublin returned that love for Brendan Kennelly.

Later in the day over tea, in a moment as relaxing as it's casual, in Nancy's house in Duagh, about four miles from Listowel, she tells me stories of other sibling poets. She hands me a copy of a poem by her brother Paddy Kennelly 'Knockore Church' (a fictional name for the church in Ballylongford). Touched up by the Bardic family wit, this small church takes on a voice to tell its story:

Suppose Andy Boo is right.
Suppose those who come here to pray
Are the blackest transgressors of all,
Whose sins, in the light of the day,

Would draw blushes from Satan himself;
Suppose that among those who come
Is the gossip with words that can kill
With a rattlesnake flick of the tongue;

And the vulgar man, common and loud;
And the randy man, bent on his thrill;
And the sly one whose sins are unknown,
Being hidden with devious skill;

And the openly scandalous man
Ever ready to boast of his fall;
Suppose only these come to pray;
Still, I welcome them all.

And I welcome the vain man, too,
Who assumes a posture of prayer;
And the proud one who struts down my aisle
With a haughty, superior air;

And I welcome the judgemental one

Who pronounces what others should do;
And when the imposter shows up,
I welcome him too.

Yes, I welcome the children of Eve,
Sad victims of sin and the Fall,
For, were I to wait for the saint,
I'd have no one to welcome at all.

Belonging to the poetic Kennellys wasn't enough. Nancy acquired more literary links by marrying a relation of dramatist George Fitzmaurice who came from nearby Duagh House. Fitzmaurice was born in 1877 and died at the age of eighty-six. She lives in full view of the countryside of his youth, the landscape that gave him the spur to pen his plays of fantasy of a land bewitched, of a people enchanted, of changelings, faith-healers, strange music, gods and the like. These otherworldly characters were made real by speaking in the local sayings and dialect of this part of North Kerry. (This magic tied well in with Timmy Kennelly's dishes sliding off tables.)

The Enchanted Land, The Pie Dish, The Dandy Dolls, The Magic Glasses were some of Fitzmaurice's plays. Even though his work was produced by the Abbey, he fell into that lonely list of the under-appreciated. One critic, Joseph Holloway, wrote of *The Magic Glasses*, when it was produced in 1913, that it was 'the maddest of the Abbey's madhouse farces'. But stained-glass artist, Harry Clarke thought differently. He used it for a panel in his Geneva Window which was commissioned by the Irish government in 1926. Each panel would show off the best of Irish writing from 1900 to 1930. Alas, displaying over-daring Irish writers, like George Fitzmaurice, Liam O'Flaherty and James Joyce, was too permissive for its time and never graced the spot for which it was meant – the Irish office of the International Labour court in Geneva. The window was bought instead for Mitchell Wolfson's Museum in Miami Beach, Florida. Actor, Micheál MacLiommóir saw the value of Fitzmaurice's works. He called him 'a kind of literary Rousseau le Douanier, who bridged the worlds of fantasy and reality in a manner that is only today (1949) beginning to find real appreciation.'

Maybe Fitzmaurice's influence breaks out in the buzzing brilliance that is one of the wonders of this area around Listowel. A taste for yarns and word spinning touched this spot with some force.

During a radio interview on RTE, Bryan MacMahon, a teacher from Listowel, who himself contributed to this yield, offered an explanation to the often-asked question, what inspired so many from the same locality?

'First of all, we're a plain, and the hills are above us and the hills pour into the plain. North Kerry is a square and two sides of it are bound by the Shannon and the Atlantic. That means that everything that happens in North Kerry has to pour into Listowel… We try to keep the little candle of the imagination alive here as a policy. And of course we have a background of classical learning from Saint Michael's College. We learned Latin and Greek. The old humanities are still vibrant among us. The size of the town is very important too. It has under four thousand people. If it was any smaller you couldn't harness it. If it was any bigger it wouldn't be worth harnessing, so it's about the right size to get people to connect as a unit. We have no social strata here. This is something we frown on. Every man has some gift and we try and bring his gift out.'

It was playwright John B Keane who came up with the idea for Listowel's Writers' Week. He was a publican, and like Nancy and Brendan Kennelly, where better was there to cast an eye over the proverbial 'human condition' than from behind the counter of his pub in William Street, Listowel? He transferred his observations on to the page and that gave his plays heft. But let me give the best description of Keane's skills to Brendan Kennelly – 'his surgical insight into feelings'.

Keane's play, *Sive*, hit with a bang in 1959. It was earth-shattering. But like Clarke's window in the twenties, Ireland in the fifties wasn't ready for its stark message. Sive, who is 'illegitimate', is to be married off to an old, but well-off, man. She takes her own life rather than go ahead with it. The raw truth of the play meant it would have to take its time delivering its blow.

Keane's later play *The Field* he himself claimed would never have seen a stage were it not for Brendan Kennelly. Brendan loved it, and thought The Bull McCabe was a magnificent character.

Bryan MacMahon was a contemporary of Keane's, and he put his own interest in literature down to the inspiration of Listowel bookseller, Dan Flavin. Flavin saw the value of a book beyond the shut-down censorship years that dominated the first half of twentieth century Ireland. It was he who put a first-edition copy of the banned *Ulysses* into the young MacMahon's hands, with the warning, 'Read that and don't let anyone see it'.

Maurice Walsh 1879-1964, from nearby Ballydonoghue, lived at almost the exact same time as George Fitzmaurice. Fitzmaurice was born two years after him and he predeceased him by one year. Walsh's short story *The Quiet Man*, was destined for a bigger world than North Kerry when filmmaker John Ford saw how well it would work on the big screen.

Every May Listowel hosts Writers' Week. Crowds attend the talks and workshops in the hopes of picking up some of the homegrown energy that shot their local mentors to fame. The author Roddy Doyle thinks 'no other writing gathering compares with Listowel (Writers' Week) in warmth and in madness.'

I think Fitzmaurice's otherworldly writings must have some say in the proud madness of Listowel Writers' Week. The charming vision of his home place: *The Enchanted Land, The Pie Dish, The Dandy Dolls, The Magic Glasses* accompanies me on my left as I leave Nancy's house and go towards Abbeyfeale on the R555. Even the road is suitably numbered. It looks down on the River Feale and at the far side of the river the ground rises again to the same level as mine.

Empowered by the local mood of the day I drive to Castle Island, a place brought alive in the writings of journalist Con Houlihan. I want to view 'the great saucer of land' that he wrote about with such intent, the Castle Island Gap, which spreads like a symphony to his memory. I want to put a shape on 'the middle stretch of his heartwater, the Gleannsharoon (or Twomey's river) which springs from under Crinna Hill'. Here alongside 'the deep mysterious river' was where the 'bitter apples grew' (crab apples), where he experienced the joy of a spot of fishing, from 'netting' to fishing with a rod.

Place-names made Houlihan's heart sing and within them bubbles a great spread of social history. Lambs Island was called after a man called Lamb, a criminal who took to hiding here. A 'non-human' place, Houlihan called it, because no one had ever tilled or grazed it.

I met Con Houlihan once when he gave a talk on writing in The People's College in Dublin. He was a sports writer, but literature, biography, philosophy and life observations streamed into his writing. He was born to write you could say, beginning, according to himself, before he reached 'double figures in age'. The authorities in his boarding school were none too fond of his talent. When he became editor of the clandestine *College Courier*, he was expelled and taken to the train station, as he himself put it, 'at dawn in an unmarked car'.

That evening, in the People's College, he talked, wittily and shyly, half covering his face with his hand, about writing, the challenges of sports writing, how to make every goal as if it was the greatest score ever, the fundamentals of writing (every sentence had to have a subject and a predicate), the importance of polishing.

And he cited D H Lawrence as a man whom he could have chastised for leaving so much of his work unpolished. It didn't do DHL much harm it seems to me.

The intimacy of Houlihan's writing changes the view of Castle Island, especially an article where he wrote about the bog near his home place. He painted its portrait in the same heartfelt way as his favourite artist Cézanne painted Mont Sainte-Victoire. He brought to life the camaraderie when everyone turned out to cut turf during wartime fuel shortages. He recalled the piercing sadness of raking the embers of the fire and quenching them with water from the kettle on his last day with his father in the bog as he was about to embark on a new life.

I stop among the curving hills, seen and written about by Houlihan, and more tantalising still, the places unseen, where it all happened. I drink in the raw localism and it feels like balm. Alas, I can't see all of his loved places in detail. You would need the guide himself who could make the most obscure place sing. The words he strung together like the landscape they match are breathing life into the place I would have otherwise sped past.

He once wrote. 'Working out the meaning of place-names is cracking the pre-Celtic code.' Indeed, the memories rise from deep beneath the soil around here. Their soothing nature will soon disperse as I join a motorway that cleaves through the countryside.

Highways get you from A to B, those two terrible non-places but they scatter the spirit of place into the air, like the exhaust fumes of competence. Even the GPS doesn't register them as you pass, but shows generic names – Tralee Road, Killarney Road. Great for delivery services, but they lack a sense of wonder. Of course, satellite navigation never claimed to create an enchanted journey where you could tarry. To get you there with added speed, that's its job description. To each its place.

TWENTY-EIGHT

FAR FROM THE CONVERSATIONS OF MEN

This morning looks especially laid on for my Australian friend, Karen. She asked me early on to delay my visit to Kilkenny until she was available to come too. And we form the same trio as we did in Galway, she, Treasa and I. We're driving from Dublin, through a landscape flooded with fog, on the route of Ireland's Ancient East. The livestock in the fields look like photo negatives, horses wrapped in a haze, sheep fleeced in dew, cows with heads down munching the moistened grass. Only the tops of the trees are visible. This scene ties in with Ireland's otherworldly folklore. Fairies and goblins are easy presences in this ether – they left their silken web behind them before they fled the night.

Treasa suggests that we turn the car around towards the east and enjoy the sunrise. It's worth it to watch the landscape grow with the dawn. The streaky red sky is making its way through the mist. Colour is changing by the second, pink streaks mingling with the inky blue clouds that sit motionless above.

'Early Christians believed that heaven was in the east, where the sun rises,' says Karen. 'I think they could be right.'

When the fog slinks out of the way and clears the day, we move on. Trees are growing visible now. I think winter trees are nicest of all. Like a face without cosmetic help, they've no coverage to hide behind and their arteries show off their intricate mesh.

The Blackstairs mountains stretch to our left along the Wexford-Carlow border. Treasa points out Mount Leinster, the highest of them. We follow a sign for Mount Leinster Heritage Drive, going left at Borris. This brings us by a narrow road. Even meeting another car could put us to the limit of width, much less a tractor.

Mount Leinster is an easy-climb hill (says I from the comfort of a car), fertile all the way to the top. From a viewing point high up in the hills we take a look into the valley. Quilted green fields tumble downwards, and above rise the Blackstairs in swells and rounds, overlaid with a blue wash.

Signposts point to the Hidden Sky Road, *Turas Columbanus*, to villages I've never heard of – Rathanna, Fenagh, Garryhill. Their unfamiliarity makes the day all the more beyond meaning. We enjoy being lost in the little townlands of County Carlow.

Finally, we emerge onto the main road and on through County Kilkenny. At the ring road around Kilkenny city we take the turn for Thomastown. We're on our way to the ruins of the old Cistercian monastery of Jerpoint. The winding roads that lead us here hold the memory of when monastic sites were located in the wilderness. Saint Bernard, founder of the Cistercian Abbey of Clairvaux in France and mentor of the order, stated that monasteries must be placed 'far away from the conversations of men'.

I'm not sure that Jerpoint fulfilled his requirements. The medieval way (*slíghe*) connecting Dublin and Waterford passed by Jerpoint. The River Arrigle flows through what was monastic property and joins with two of the Three Sister rivers, the Nore and the Barrow. Given the lively use of roads and waterways at the time, Jerpoint may not have been far enough from the conversations of men for Bernard's taste.

It's not just because this is the county from where her ancestors left for Australia that excites Karen, but for the historic feel of a monastic site.

'Nothing moves me so much as these tours,' she says, 'even the stones of such old buildings thrill me.' More than likely, her interest is heightened because she comes from a country that has no examples of the distant past, no trace of a Middle Ages. All the medieval mythmaking and folklore that Europe is steeped in has eluded Australia. What a gap.

The locals, the aborigines, didn't write and so 'real' history only began when Captain Cook sailed up Sydney harbour in the *Endeavour* in 1770. The new arrivals, coming mostly from the congested land of England, could scarcely believe their eyes to find such emptiness. Empty, except for the natives. But they were a small problem. They were a passive people. They refused to fight back, and that made them all the more strange in white men's reckoning.

It was the ideal place for a penal colony, for the thieves and bandits that made the prisons of the British isles bulge at the seams. They were put to work exploiting this hostile soil in chain gangs, spurred on by rum. Karen loves that her ancestors were members of this chained-up labour.

'How many times have you been to Jerpoint?' she asks us. Treasa has been twice. I only once. I know she's about to say something but I'm saved the rebuke by the signal that the tour is about to begin.

We follow from the visitors' centre to see one of the best preserved Irish Cistercian monasteries. Some stragglers, three women and two men, don't make any effort to hurry, and a few in the group are getting tetchy. The guide starts without them. Then, as they join, they don't mind asking questions that have already been covered. A man in the group is throwing scowls in their direction.

'This monastery was founded here on the banks of the Arrigle river, in 1160. The date is disputed. It might have been 1158 that the Cistercian monks came to Jerpoint,' says the guide.

Who cares? When we're talking about an event so buried in the past, we're not going to argue about two years. Whichever date it was, the monastery was founded about a decade before the Normans arrived in Ireland.

There was no shortage of people eager to give land for a Cistercian foundation, like modern-day sponsors. The guide tells us about the motive of one patron. He donated 'for the love of God, the health of his soul, that of his wife and children and the souls of his ancestors and successors.'

'Successors?' exclaims an American man. 'That took in a large amount of people. Maybe some of his progeny are right here in this group,' he quips. No one claims to be related.

The Cistercian rise was rapid. The order grew to forty-two houses within 130 years of their first Irish foundation in Mellifont in 1142. This strength-to-strength was in line with what was happening elsewhere. In France it became cool to join the Cistercians. In 1145 King Louis VII's brother, Henry of France, entered the order in Clairvaux. By the mid twelfth century there were nearly four hundred Cistercian monasteries in Europe and a Cistercian pope, Eugenius III, in Rome.

The guide explains that a delegation was first sent to check out the suitability of a donation of land for a monastery. She invites us to take a quick look around. This was a fertile spot, not like stony Corcomroe Abbey in County Clare. The limestone countryside of the Jerpoint plains slopes through the heartland of Kilkenny, running along the fertile boundary of Leinster and Munster, lying in the shelter of the Walsh mountains to the south, stretching to the Castlecomer uplands and, on their west, to the Slieveardagh hills. The boundaries of their 1,903 medieval acres (about 14,000 statute acres) were formed by rivers, uplands and other natural landscaping.

'It's hard to exaggerate how much the Cistercians changed the landscape,' the guide tells us. 'They shook up farming, turning bad land into good. As well as a changeover in land ownership, they changed social and cultural mores. They cultivated good relations with the locals, a lot of them were locals themselves.'

A negative note for me is that they brought the old monasteries into decline. These *parvenus* from Clairvaux brought down places like Kilmacduagh, Clonmacnoise, Monasterboice, Kells, more effectively than the plunder of the Vikings. I like the old monasteries, their interlaced crosses, manuscripts and round towers. The guide explains: 'It's thought that the Cistercian monks were purposely installed in contested places to encourage peace. This was a time of great strife. Not long after the Jerpoint foundation Diarmait MacMurchada, King of Leinster, travelled to Bristol and France to invite military support from the Normans to regain his kingdom.'

Help arrived between 1167-1171, ushering in the next ground-breaking event in Irish history – the arrival of the Normans. Nothing would be the same again.

The Normans never managed to control the whole country. Local knowledge was the trump card of the Gaelic Irish and they drew the unwitting Normans into battle on bog-land, mountains and woodland where they couldn't defend themselves.

'Only abbots of Norman origin were installed in Jerpoint after the arrival of the Normans, The new lords of the monasteries enjoyed the inherited power of exemption from things like tolls, ferry dues, passage, pontage (bridge building), lastage (place for storing goods in a ship), like present-day industries are lured with tax breaks,' says the guide.

When we're told about the little comfort the Benedictine Rule allowed the monks I feel the chill of that early morning mist that we had passed by earlier, going through my bones. I promise not to complain for the rest of the day.

'Only one room of the monastery was allowed heat. The fire was lit on the first day of November and put out on Good Friday. And all of this on a single meal a day, for the most part vegetarian (though their "vegetarianism" just excluded four-footed animals).'

On that little food they did the heavy work of their farm, which provided them at least with some heat. One of the requirements of the Benedictine Rule was self-sufficiency.

In the monastery's heyday this manual labour made the outside areas hum with industry. As you moved towards the centre, away from the workaday world, it grew quieter because the rule involved a vow of silence. I expect little of the 'conversations of men' could be heard above the praying and chanting of the monks, just as Bernard wished. A day's prayer contained nine offices and one hundred and fifty psalms.

A woman in the group says, 'At that rate of praying what chance have the people of our secular age of getting to heaven?' The guide offers no answer. Instead she leads us towards Paradise – to the church in the northern side. It faces east, in the direction of heaven. She points out the dormitories and more importantly, the guest house.

'The rule of Saint Benedict stated that anyone seeking refuge was to be welcomed as if it was Jesus who had dropped by.'

She points out the changing architecture from Romanesque to Gothic, by the decorative cloister and the procession of saints in sculpture. It's clear that this is her favourite part of the tour. But this must surely mark the time when they lost their way. Bernard of Clairvaux specified that the monks were not to indulge in paintings, sculpture or other artwork that could distract from their real aims: prayer and rejection of the world. It was, after all, the gaudiness of the Benedictine monasteries that had led to the foundation of the Cistercian order it the first place. They seem to have got over these limits by the fifteenth century. Maybe the pressure to keep their sponsors sweet got stronger. Their big egos had to be satisfied with colourful effigies and family coats of arms.

'These are the wall paintings,' she says as excitedly as we were in an art gallery. I find it hard to even see them, though little by little the eye becomes accustomed to spotting the bits of paint that remain.

And now, after the excitement of the artwork, on to the harsher side of things, to the row of early martyrs. This would smartly sober you up. If you think the life of the monks was harsh, consider the suffering of these unfortunates. A walk by the two mensa tombs (flat tombstones) tells their severe tales. Saint Bartholomew, skinned to death; Saint Thomas, speared to death; Saint Jude (shown with an axe), beheaded; Saint Andrew, shown with an X because he was crucified on that shape of cross, not feeling worthy to meet his maker on the same form of cross as Jesus was hung on. And then, Jesus's favourite John, beardless, to symbolise his youth. (It surprises me to hear that Jesus was so partial as to have a favourite.) Saint Christopher is here too, shown in the decorated cloister, as a ferryman navigating people across a river. Now we're told he never existed, just when our faith had been built up to make him the prestigious patron saint of travel. He doesn't look too put out by his demotion. He probably lost his footing in the age of easy jetting and low-fare airlines. There was no further need of prayers to him.

Monasteries were vulnerable to attack and monks though they were, they didn't mind using a machicoulis against intruders. This was an unusual weapon in an abbey. The machicoulis poured burning oil on intruders. (*Coulis* is French for molten metal.) So much for treating visitors as if it was Jesus himself who called.

This reception for the unwelcome got Jerpoint over all the usual assaults on a monastery until the big one – Henry VlII's order of dissolution in the sixteenth century. Not even the burning oil could do battle with that. The abbey still bears the wounds of that terrible era – their roofs were knocked off, like the heads of the men and women who stood in King Henry's way. And there's no plan to restore the roof.

'Why not?' asks the American man.

'That would spoil the history,' explains the guide. 'Better to leave it as it was to explain what happened.'

Great swathes of land were turned over to the crown and the king was hugely enriched. This new wealth would finance his personal indulgence. Not for long. Within his lifetime Henry had sold off almost two thirds of the monastic lands.

Dissolution brought about a big social change. People had etched out, many in bare feet, the pilgrim trails that converged in places like Jerpoint because they saw them as a place to purge themselves of their sins, a patch of heaven on earth, where longings were fulfilled. Henry saw them as fulfilling a longing too. He needed their works of art, precious altar plate, and most of all, their fertile acres to fill the crown's dire need of money. He would have dissolved Rome along with them and taken its wealth if he could have got hold of it. As in England, while the monasteries stood, they were an obstacle to his power and the spread of Protestantism.

Artifacts, relics, libraries, manuscripts, much of the chronicling toil and mystical works of the medieval monastic tradition got blown to the wind. No more chanting melodies crossed the fields, no perfume of holy incense, But most of all, a continuity was broken. The monasteries had marked out landmarks, because they were placed on pre-Christian sacred sites, strong energy points on the earth.

The Butlers of Kilkenny, the Earls of Ormond, relations of Anne Boleyn (second wife of King Henry), got a lot of the monastic lands of Kilkenny – Jerpoint, Kells, Duiske in nearby Graiguenamanagh, the Augustinian Friary of Callan about ten kilometres to the west.

This added roughly 14,000 acres to their property. They held it for about a century.

We round off the day with a concert in Saint Canice's Cathedral in Kilkenny. We haven't much breath to spare by the time we climb the hill to reach this great building but we aren't going to be singing, so no worries. The crowd is already surging in. There's the usual commotion of people trying to find their places. No need, the pews are carefully numbered and soon everyone is installed – not a single space left. Holy fervour would never prompt such enthusiasm these days.

With everyone in place, we wait for the musicians – The Gloaming. In the twilight effect of stained glass and great rafters, the eagerness of the crowd is catching. The music gets off to a rousing start, scaling arches and surging through the stonework of sandstone, dolomite and limestone. All these materials were found locally when they laid the foundation stone here in 1215, on an older monastic site. The Round Tower still stands as a reminder.

Everyone is here this evening, the young, the old, the neither, traditionalists, modernists, swaying to the same rhythm. I'm sure the cathedral has some sobering off to do to get back its composure for the next praying session. The reason this building didn't lose its head with King Henry's dissolution was because by then it had been taken over by the Church of Ireland.

We should be tired after a long day when we come back to the hotel but we can't resist chatting into the early hours. Karen starts the conversation with the story of the Min Min lights, an Australian mystery.

'They're said to be like balls of fire of white, blue and yellow and they light up the night sky, like car lights,' she says, 'Aboriginies believe they're the spirits of the ancestors coming back. Some councils in Australia have made a tourist industry out of them – you're in the land of the Min Min lights. Scientists explain the Min

Min lights away as optical illusions but why then are the Aussies the only ones stricken with this illusion?'she asks.

Karen says she never saw them herself but she knew people who did. Not quite as good as a firsthand account. And here's where my story scores. I remember as a child seeing the will-o'-the-wisp, something science explains as the oxidation of natural gases – methane, phosphine, diphosphane – igniting as they mix with the oxygen in the air. When I was growing up in Galway we lived beside a wetland which we called the lake. At night my brother used to watch for the will-o'-the-wisp. He'd call us out when he'd spot it. It was like a bike light, a more anaemic version of the Min Min lights, moving along by the edge of the lake. But we knew it wasn't a bike unless the cyclist was very irrational, going back and forward over the way he had come (and I only say he because it was usually a he who would be cycling alone at night). What we loved was to frighten ourselves by looking at it and then charge into the house when the spookiness got too much, to the safe cover of adults.

Next morning, I wish we hadn't chatted into the late hours. A hot shower usually sees me right ater a late night so I climb in. The water is taking its time to warm up. After several minutes I realise it's not going to heat at all so there's nothing for it but to get under the cold flow. I think of the monks of Jerpoint but it doesn't lighten my suffering. So by the time I turn up at the reception desk I'm in the right mood for a row.

What's your room number, says the receptionist. Her calm demeanour doesn't match my irritation. She avoids my glance and fixes her gaze on the computer. Ah yes, I get it. The shivers of my cold shower are going to be re-enacted on the screen. She does reduce the bill, a little. But a smile and a Sorry might have calmed me down. Neither are proferred. And the computer isn't programmed to smile or apologise. I hope that will be the next discovery.

I come back to tell the others there's no chance of warm water until the maintenance team arrive. Karen's reaction makes me have a rethink about mine.

'What's a cold shower once in a lifetime? What's a bit of hardship? And it heightens the adventure of my trip. We can warm up with breakfast.'

Breakfast turns out to be disappointing too. Karen complains to the manager. I'm surprised she puts even that limit on her sense of adventure.

TWENTY-NINE

DOUBLE SOLSTICE

I'm in County Kilkenny again for the winter solstice, at the Neolithic Knockroe Passage tombs, known locally as 'The Caiseal'. The double solstice here makes this site rare in archaeology. With its two aligned passage tombs, east and west, it has an advantage over more celebrated sites, like Newgrange.

South Kilkenny Historical Society is organising the winter solstice trip. When I ring Eddie Synnott, the chairman, he offers to meet me in some place more easily found than the little village of Owning, where the crowd is to assemble. No need. Owning, though tiny, is well mapped and I'm outside the church way before the meeting time of 2.30 in the afternoon.

I'm not the first here. We acknowledge one another one by one as we arrive. We chat in the way people engaged in a common purpose gravitate towards one another. There's a generosity of spirit around. While I'm eating a sandwich in the car, a couple pass by and slip a bar of chocolate through the window. I've never seen them before. It could contain anything. I chance eating it and to date nothing has happened.

The church has an outside toilet, very handy for events like this one. But the door doesn't budge for the woman who gets there before me. She turns to me with a look of distress. As luck would have it there are plenty of yew trees around the graveyard. She asks me to keep watch. She'll do the same for me, she promises. It's all very co-operative.

When Eddie arrives he asks us to double and triple into cars because of the limited car-parking space in Knockroe Neolithic site. Tony is the driver of the car assigned to me. He and his wife Margaret make me feel very welcome even when I suddenly remember on arriving in Knockroe, that I've left my carefully-packed wellingtons in the car in Owning. The news hasn't yet come that this is the wettest December on record but the grimy signs are all around us. I cringe when I think what state my boots will be in when I come back to their impeccable car.

Though Knockroe is smaller, it has a lot in common with the World Heritage site at Newgrange on the Boyne valley. It's more hidden from the sightseeing world and it's this unsung part of it that makes it special. Like Newgrange, it dates from around 3000 BC. While Newgrange receives the sun only at sunrise, Knockroe's two passage tombs, aligned east and west, were constructed so that sunset illuminates the western-facing chamber and sunrise lights up the smaller eastern-facing chamber.

As we arrive the sunshine warms the moment and the conversation hums among the crowd. The surrounding patchwork of hedged fields rises into the hills and dips down to the level of the flow of the River Lingaun. Grazing cattle munch on the hills. To the west towers Slievenamon.

I've never seen it from this angle and it gives me goosebumps to hear I'm at the foot of this mountain that has prompted such homage in myth and song. A streaky sky of pink caps it, shifting a glow on to its cairn on top. Gentle mosses and grass lichen drop down lazily from its slopes.

Slievenamon translates as Mountain of the Women. The women were the gang that the legendary Fionn MacCumhaill, the most sought-after man in Ireland, put to the test of running up to the summit and back, to see which one he would marry. I can see that this run required a fair level of fitness.

According to a tale from the Fenian cycle Fionn loved the beautiful Gráinne, daughter of the High King of Ireland, Cormac MacAirt, and told her the best way to win the race. She did win but double trouble – not only did she balk at marrying a man of such advanced years as Fionn but she eloped with his handsome warrior, Diarmuid. Fionn spent seven years following them and the story, *Tóraíocht Dhiarmada agus Ghráinne* (The Pursuit of Diarmuid and Gráinne) looks as if it was written as a device to describe the Irish landscape.

All around me today are seasoned solstice attendees. Some were already here this morning for sunrise which by all accounts was no loss to miss because the sun didn't do its magic trick. The conversation is all about what a great day it is, the best they can remember in their many years coming. As well as solstice adepts, many are keen dolmen spotters, dawn-chorus adepts and cairn sighters. I hear about more stones, dolmens and sacred places than I've time to make a note of – the dolmen in Mooncoin, the Piper Stones near Blessington and a host of others.

People are having a chat about the dawn chorus which they never miss. Clearly few here shy away from getting up in the small hours of morning.

As the sun ambles towards its setting point the chatter quietens and archaeologist Muiris O'Sullivan addresses the crowd. He tells us about the discovery of this megalithic tomb a quarter of a century ago (he led the excavation work), its uniqueness in having east and west passage tombs, the illustrious unknowns who built them, the cremated contents here of about a hundred people. And the enigma that preoccupies him:

'There are about 1,500 or so megalithic tombs in Ireland. Around a third of them are astronomically aligned, another third align to mountain tops, but it's the other group, the third that have no evident alignment, that I wonder about. We don't know a single name, a story, what language these people spoke, yet we can look at the same landscape as they did, unchanged since their time.'

He cuts off as the sun is about to sink into the horizon, to allow the astronomers of old to take centre stage and display their accurate calculations, their skill in measuring the gathered-up light of the setting sun and trap it in the chamber. A silence descends on the crowd and about a hundred gazes turn westwards, eyes shaded with flattened hands. Alas, it doesn't work. As it lowers itself on to the horizon a cloud parks in the way. What a party pooper. Still we stare intently, hoping it might move to one aside. Not a budge. And soon the watch of the crowd tapers off and a murmur of chat rises again over the tomb.

Scattered around the site are quartz stones, once believed to have been transported from Wicklow or Lambay. Muiris O'Sullivan doesn't go along with this theory. There was no shortage of quartz here in Knockroe, in his opinion.

The decoration on one of the stones on this site is similar to the design on the passage grave in Gavrinis in Brittany and that far-off link stretches the imagination further.

I lose sight of Tony and Margaret. I'm afraid they've gone back to the car so I rush up the hill to the farmyard carpark, kicking up the loose mud that the crowd has made muddier. I don't want to delay them. It's enough to have to put up with my dirty boots. They haven't arrived so I go back, walking against the crowd. I locate them, craning their necks in search of me.

As we drive out of the farmyard and head back to Owning, the day is cushioning itself into the still glow of eventide. Clouds, ragged-edged and stationary have seen off the sun on its journey downunder. The sky is reflecting different blues – inky blue, pale blue, turquoise – like a paint colour chart. The after-light of day is sending a red hue upwards from the rim of the earth.

Tony suggests a quick look at the nearby Ahenny high crosses. We have to walk through a field in the fading light to see them, making squelching sounds in the soggy soil. The graveyard is walled off. All we can see in the fading light as we approach are the white spots of lichen on the old stone. It's too dark to examine the ringed high crosses in detail, the north cross and the south cross. They are known for their skillful carving and geometric Celtic design. Darkness has other compensations though. The surrounding villages of Counties Tipperary and Kilkenny are sparkling and glinting in the distance. How I'd love to locate them one by one, put names on them. Low in the sky the waxing moon is rising, filling up for full circle, due on Christmas Day.

Tony and Margaret see me to my car at Owning and I drive over the hill on the narrow road. There's hardly a house on the way. I fancy pulling in and looking backwards to see the black calligraphic outline of Slievenamon against the night sky. But on second thoughts, I keep going. I don't want to ask for trouble on this quiet road all alone. But I know this mountain is there, escorting me on my way, like a motherly presence. When I connect to the motorway and join the other speeding vehicles in the direction of Dublin, mountains and passage tombs leave me to fend for myself.

THIRTY

ATONEMENT

Today I'm on a pilgrim trail to Lough Derg in County Donegal. And what a privilege it is to have the exact route that medieval pilgrims stepped on, though unlike them I'm not making the pilgrimage on foot. This record of the journey was kept by someone who walked it in 1430, Guillebert de Lannoy, chamberlain to the Duke of Burgundy and knight of the Golden Fleece.

The Middle Ages were lively times of pilgrimage. They came here in their droves to Lough Derg, or Saint Patrick's Purgatory as it was also called. By the twelfth century there was a steady stream of arrivals from all over continental Europe. What gave this spot the edge over other pilgrim places like Rome, Jerusalem or Santiago de Compostela was, not only did it hold out the promise of salvation, but it offered a peep at the afterlife.

De Lannoy, arriving at the port of Drogheda, took his first stop at Mellifont Abbey. From there he walked along by the River Boyne on to Slane, to Donaghmore to Drumbane and then to Enniskillen. At Enniskillen his walking ended for a while and he sailed up Lough Erne, stopping at the monasteries of Devenish Island, Inismacsaint and White Island.

I set out to follow his path on a typical Irish day, not too hot, not too cold. I know our climate confuses outsdiers, and I wonder if it had that effect back then. I have a French friend who wonders,

'Why are Irish people so fond of looking at the weather forecast when they know it's going to be sunshine and showers?'

I remind her of the upside of our climate: Ireland doesn't have venomous creatures. The story goes that Saint Patrick banished snakes from the country. Probably the worst attack you can get here is a bee sting. No small matter admittedly, but nothing compared to what a scorpion or a snake can do to you.

A new crop of people are finding an interest in pilgrim walks these days. Maybe they think that our easy life is out of tune with nature. Or maybe it's for a bit of nostalgia. My motives are to recall a moment in time without that dreadful fear of the afterlife that so terrified our forebears. Who knows, it might be they who will have the last laugh on Judgment day, but like everyone else I'm taking my chances.

Following Guillebert de Lannoy, I begin in Drogheda in County Louth. Back in these early centuries this was the busiest port on the east coast. The Boyne cut a deep channel into its long estuary. Norsemen had a trading post here and it was from this port that the Black Death first made its way to Ireland in 1348. This plague, which killed from a third to half the population of Europe, got more pilgrims on their feet. They did what people do when they get a whiff of trouble – pray.

Not all medieval pilgrims did the journey voluntarily. As well as the pious who thought some penance would earn them points for paradise, criminals were sent on pilgrimage to make up for their misdeeds. Religious communities were thought to have the power to absolve them.

Following Guillebert de Lannoy's lead, I take my first stop at Mellifont Abbey. I reckon this stopover was for pilgrims like staying in a five-star hotel, because the ruins and a drawing on the wall of a fifteenth century reconstruction look very elaborate.

It's sited between a ribbon of waterways, north of the bend of the River Boyne, near the Devlin River and the smaller River Mattock which flow alongside the edge of the monastic grounds. Saint Bernard's chapel looks down from a hill as if staring severely on the site. Bernard of Clairvaux, the central figure of the order, considered a saint even in his lifetime, looked severely on everything. He was an unrepentant killjoy. He thought you should banish all pleasure from your life if you wanted to get to Heaven. If he lived in this age, he would despair of us. But even in his own day he clashed with the spirit of enquiry of the twelfth century Gothic age, when they started to look into things like classical learning, philosophy, law, and horror of all, analysing God

The most handsome building on this site is the eight-sided lavabo where the monks washed their hands. We're told it's a masterpiece of Romanesque architecture. Washing hands was not just a hygiene practice for the Cistercians; it was an important ritual. It ties in with the hundred times a day we wash our hands since Covid struck.

From this view it's hard to believe that when the Cistercians were first founded, in 1098, it was to shed the worldly ornamentation and adornment of monasteries. Sparseness was their policy, but even through the ruins (which Henry Vlll's policy dissolved it into in 1539) you can see how groundbreaking their architecture was. It was altogether on a grander scale than the monasteries of old. Mellifont Abbey (*Mainistir Mhór*, the big monastery) was their first house in Ireland after their arrival in 1142, from Clairvaux in France.

Monks had always been involved in land clearances and taming of land but the Cistercians reclaimed on an altogether grander scale in the twelfth century. In their monasteries in France – Citeaux, Fontenay, Clairvaux, Pontigny – they established plains and grasslands in areas where the forest had taken over. They drained low-lying marshy lands that had been abandoned and they built bridges and dams. Later in the fifteenth century the popes established them in the Roman countryside to drain and combat malaria with the same success that they had in France, especially in Burgundy.

When you read the names of the bunch of luminaries who turned up in Melifont for the consecration of the abbey church in 1157 you know how welcome the Cistercians were – Murtagh MacLoughlin (the High King), Donough O'Carroll (the founder of the monastery), Dervorgilla of Breifne (the wife of the King of Meath), the papal legate, groups of archbishops, bishops and all the abbots of the land. They brought gifts of substance – land, cattle, money, gold.

Mellifont was well endowed – 3,874 medieval acres. It included in its farm the heritage site of Newgrange, the new grange of the abbey (*grange* is French for barn).

I'm not the first to arrive. Neither is the man on the bench who looks as if he has come for some peace and quiet to read his book within earshot of the Mattock River. He's out of luck. Children are bounding around. One boy wants to go down the steps, which look as if they're there since the monks' time, to the lower level of the river. His mother won't allow him. He can't go anyway. Someone has anticipated his wish and put a barrier there.

I have to get on with my pilgrimage so I go back to the Boyne Valley drive to replicate Guillebert de Lannoy's footsteps as much as possible. His next stop was Donaghmore. This monastic site sits on a hillock. It must have been one of the earliest church foundations; a notice reads it was founded by Saint Patrick.

Just the Round Tower and a single wall of a much later church remain now.

The place feels homely. Hills and hillocks around it bump in a haphazard flow. Some look fanciful, as if they're having fun, like children out of a storybook playing a circling game until they get a swirling head and fall sideways.

Even though de Lannoy didn't mention the big ecclesiastical settlement of Kells as part of his journey, I can't pass by without calling. I get there as the woman who looks after the church, which doubles as a visitors' centre, is turning the heavy lock of the church door.

We go upstairs to the gallery where she shows me drawings of what Kells used to be like in its heyday, when it was a religious centre of European importance. She points to a picture of beehive huts surrounding the Bell and Round Towers and illustrations of the monumental high crosses for which Kells is famous. Kells high crosses are often overshadowed by their more illustrious possession, the *Book of Kells,* one of the treasures of medieval Europe. She points me to the facsimile edition of the *Book of Kells* in its special corner.

A lobby group makes the case that the original book rightfully belongs here in this monastery which was burned by Oliver Cromwell, and not in Trinity College where it has been kept since the 1650s. They question the university's right of ownership of the book's copyright. They disagree with how the book was rebound in 1953 and divided into four, a book for each gospel. If they had their way it would be put back to its original single form.

It's an argument with a little irony, a modern-day 'battle of the book', which the lobbyists use to make their case. Colmcille was the founder of Kells monastery, the saint we met in Donegal who caused the fuss that led the High King to declare the first ever verdict on copyright.

Throughout the *Book of Kells'* lifetime, of over eleven hundred years, it has had many names: the *Book of Colmcille,* the *Great Gospel of St Columba* (to confuse matters, Colmcille is also known as Columba). Some think that the manuscript was written in Colmcille's other monastery, Iona in Scotland and was smuggled to Kells for safe keeping as Iona was more exposed to Viking raids. It was found hidden in a bog near Kells, put there, it's thought, for safe keeping in the bog's natural preserving composition. Just the cover skin was damaged and the rest of the book survives.

Beside the Round Tower stand the crosses. Their intricate carvings are like the interlacing of the capital letters in the *Book of Kells.* The depictions engraved into the stone are stories of Moses receiving the law, the miracle of the loaves and fishes, the miracle at Cana, the massacre of the Innocents and in the intersection, the crucifixion.

The guide interrupts her conversation with a group of visitors to apologise for the distance I have to walk to see Columba's cell.

'It's outside the walls of the site. There's the entrance where you could have gone that would be about half the walk, but it's locked up now. Security is a lot tighter these days.'

I assure her it's no bother at all. It only takes a few minutes to get there and it's a small inconvenience compared to the suffering of the saint himself. He used to use a stone for a pillow. I'm fond of my night's sleep and the thought of a rock battering into my skull while I sleep is giving me a headache.

Columba's cell is locked but an address hangs on the door where I can pick up the key. When I get there there's no one in, so I leave Kells and go back to the next stop on de Lannoy's journey: Drumbane, in County Cavan.

Cavan is a county of drumlins – tiny hills – and that's a view I know for sure I share with the pilgrims of old because they have been there since the Ice Age retreated. That makes them all the sweeter. They remind me of the landscape of the Black Forest, the heartland of the stories of the Brothers Grimm. They look playful, mysteriously hiding what's behind them, maybe Little Red Riding Hood or Rumpelstiltskin spinning straw into gold.

The pilgrim journey is becoming so real that the sign to Drumbane monastic site comes like a light out of the darkness. I have to remind myself that my weary legs are not weary at all, chiefly because I haven't used them apart from a gentle push to the accelerator.

The approach has a tenderness about it, a narrow road twisting and turning. It was put there in the days when pathways fitted in with the terrain, formed to follow the feet that treaded on them. That was before road builders straightened out hills and hacked into rocks.

Summer growth verges along the way – hedges, ferns and interlocked foliage and they tickle the metal of the car as I pass. Then, as I emerge over a little bridge, a water-land opens up. Water was an essential highway for every monastic foundation. Drumbane, like all monasteries, was part of a busy maritime hub.

Uphill by a narrower road I see beneath me two lakes on either side of the old monastery. Hills toss and turn above the water. There's good grass right up to the summit of these drumlins and a herd of Friesian cows are enjoying it. The only human in sight is further uphill, a farmer pulling out bales of hay.

The loneness of this retreat is a far cry from the hive of activity it was in its heyday. Founded in the sixth century, they're unsure by which saint, Colmcille or Maodhóg. The buildings you see today, apart from the Round Tower, date from a lot later than either of these two men. The church is wrapped in scaffolding and the safety netting is making a flapping sound in the breeze. The place is dripping after the rain and that makes the buildings look grey and dreary. More clouds are banking up, shaping themselves up to drench me so I don't delay. Getting wet of course is a small distress compared to the self-denying rules that I'm commemorating.

Sometimes I think that the criminals who were sent on pilgrimage suffered more than those who did it willingly. Forced penitence had neither faith nor hope to carry them through.

Now to Enniskillen, where de Lannoy took to the waterway. I'm just in time for the 12.15 sailing of the MV Kestrel to Devenish, the biggest of the lake's islands. The sun comes out to see us off. There's no trace now of the clouds that were making threatening shapes over me in Dunblane.

From the swaying boat you can see the buildings of Enniskillen. A handsome block of flats overlooks the water, topped by the two steeples of the Catholic and Protestant churches and Cole's (the founders of Enniskillen) monument. It's not obvious that Enniskillen is built on an island. Onlookers are seated on the pier side of the lake. Some are feeding the ducks that are gathered with their broods in tow. Was a diet of bread ever meant for a duck? The good-doers don't seem to be pondering this particular question.

The tie with land is broken and the boat pulls out. The guide-skipper lightens the trip with that northern humour that often finds itself a few steps ahead of you – while you're laughing at one joke you've missed the next. Safety instructions are none too serious: 'If you see some guys in red (he and the bar attendant are wearing red T-shirts) abandoning the boat and heading for the shore, know you're in trouble. You can either follow us, or else stay. If you decide to stay you can help yourself to the contents of the bar. By then drinks will be complimentary.'

The lake is calm, no looming danger of having to lull ourselves to our end with all the drink we fancy from the abandoned bar. Willows along the banks dip their heads into the water like thirsty animals bending for a scoop. You can see why this is a place where kingfishers like to hang out. We get a fleeting glance at the blue and orange plumage of one disappearing into the trees. The next bird of note, a cormorant, gives us more viewing time. He's perched on top of a directional signpost. These sightings shorten our twenty-minute trip to Devenish. We pour out of the boat as it pulls into the jetty – no hanging around because we're given a limited time to look around the island. There are no roads though sightseers have carved out pathways from the Round Tower, the visitors centre and the old church ruins.

Full white clouds, with edges of flimsy curls float overhead. A rainbow behind a drumlin colours up the sky, like a view from a storybook. I wouldn't be surprised to hear the blow of a woodcutter's axe or to see the white pebbles of Hansel and Gretel.

The Bluestack mountains in Donegal fix themselves in my line of vision between two islands on the lough. I wonder if the pilgrims or criminals got a chance to see them or were they allowed that much enjoyment?

People are taking pictures of the church ruins and the fifteenth century cross which claims to be without parallel in Ireland. I can well believe it. It is intricately carved with plaiting cables and vine leaves.

Wine might seem out of line with our climate, but Ireland had plenty of vines according to the eighth century writings of the Venerable Bede (an English Benedictine monk who died in 735, one of the greatest scholars of the time). A regular supply was needed to celebrate the Eucharist and from the many references to wine in Irish sagas it seems there was no shortage. They didn't depend on local wine either. There was plenty of trading contact with France, especially the Loire Valley.

I go into a building where depictions of monastic life line the walls. Devenish Island consists of 120 acres. It produced a nice spread of cultivation for the usual things that monks grew – medicinal flowers, vegetables, fruit, herbs. Through gardening monks could seek a closer link with God and atone for the disobedience of Adam and Eve. I think of the modern version of gardening. We think little of Adam and Eve as we fill our baskets with vegetables in a supermarket. And as for atoning for the misdeeds of others, that has fallen into disuse entirely.

The monks needed the produce of this land to feed the great throngs who arrived here. With their strong tradition in learning they received scholars from all over Europe between the sixth and the eighth century. Local children of high-ranking families got schooling here too. Patrons gave money and often placed their relations as abbots. They taught Scripture and Latin. In Ireland Latin had survived in a purer form than in the rest of Europe because it never was colloquialised by the vernacular Roman presence.

In the annals this island is described as 'Devenish of the Assemblies' as it was used as a place of conference by the chieftains of Ulster. Like all monasteries, it was a hive of industry with its own stone masons, builders, carpenters. And of course, there were the scribes. They commented on the scriptures, books and prayers, documented the lives of the saints and dealt with church legislation.

Devenish is still a farm. The cattle have been moved for our convenience but you can see from the fresh hoof marks that they were here not too long ago, exploring around the Round Tower and the fancy cross.

After we're dropped back again on to the mainland I can no longer faithfully follow the pilgrim path of this lake-full of holy island sites – Devenish, Inishmacsaint and White Island. I settle for second best and drive by the southern shore of the lake.

At Beleek, in County Fermanagh, I stop at a meadow gate to look down on the other side of Lough Erne. Clumps of trees and intermittent houses surround the water's edge. The sunlight is shining into every curve of mountain and the mountain in turn is responding like a cat curling up to the warm glow. A perfume is drifting from the wild honeysuckle that winds itself around the meadow fence. It's joining its scent with the purple clover. Birds in flight are making swooping sounds and their chirping companions are patrolling the long grass. The air feels heavy with the drone of bees and dragonflies. In the distance comes a hum of a different kind, a tractor. Later it will confront all the song, scents and racket when it rounds on them with blades attached.

On with the pilgrimage. What made Lough Derg a major European destination for pilgrims in the Middle Ages was the Treatise on Saint Patrick's Purgatory (*Tractacus de Purgatorio Sancti Patricii*). It was written in 1184 by a Cistercian Anglo-Norman monk. It gave an account of a journey to Lough Derg and it became popular throughout the continent. It still survives in over a hundred manuscripts.

As early as the fifteenth century Saint Patrick's Purgatory was shown on maps all over Europe, the only Irish site shown on some. There were some fanciful tales about it. One story told of how Saint Patrick asked God for a sign that would help to convert the doubting Irish to take on the new Christian faith. God obliged with the very thing that would strike terror into them, a pit leading to Purgatory.

People who tell stories in hindsight can be careless with details and this tale gets caught out in a serious error – Purgatory hadn't been invented in Saint Patrick's time. Not until 1274 was the dogma of Purgatory defined at the Second Council of Lyon. As Lough Derg grew in popularity, as a place of pilgrimage, Purgatory got a boost as well.

In Saint Patrick's Purgatory not only did a pilgrim get the promise of salvation but a vision of the afterlife. A major draw for coming here on pilgrimage was that there would be no further need for purgation but there was a risk – the pilgrim might never return. The vision of the afterlife was of terrifying scenes, making the hair stand straight on the head of one who told about his experience, or putting hearts into an uncontrollable flutter. I know the feeling. I get it on a plane, a journey that for me carries the threat of oblivion too.

I approach 'Purgatory' across hills untamed, through withered whitened mountain grasses and wild countryside. Nearly all the way to the border village of Pettigo there's hardly a house. Then in spots where the land is fertile, the landscape comes alive with animals, farmhouses, hay-sheds and stables. Finally, I arrive, driving downhill and through the gates. Arched lettering over the entrance reads *Purgatorium Sancti Patricii*. There's no sign of pilgrims. Maybe they're in the group that met its end.

The boat which ferries people across to Station Island, the 'Saint Davog', is swaying at the pier. The young woman at the reception is the only person around and she has no knowledge of the history of the place. I don't mention anything about the 'no return' reputation of the island. I can hear the music escaping out of her earphones and I remember enough old bores who held me captive in my youth with their tedious information, to avoid making the same mistake myself.

Looking across the water, Station Island looks desolate. I can't dredge up anything inspiring about it though it has impelled nifty words from poets like Yeats, Kavanagh, Kennelly and Heaney.

W B Yeats wrote in 'The Pilgrim' of praying at all the stations 'upon my marrow bones'. And in 'Station Island' Seamus Heaney wrote about its mystery: 'nobody ford or plumb its deepest fathom'. Patrick Kavanagh gave Lough Derg another twist when he brought up about the beseeching made here: 'Solicitors praying for cushy jobs/ …/Shopkeepers threatened with sharper rivals/…Wives whose husbands have taken to drinking'. Brendan Kennelly's verdict on Lough Derg is that it's a place 'where sorrow for sin goes to town'.

But this pilgrim spot had been written about by writers from much further into the past. Saint Patrick's Purgatory got a mention in Dante's 'The Divine Comedy', Francois Rabelais made a bawdy reference to it in *Gargantua* and Shakespeare alluded to it in *Hamlet* It was known to Petrarch too who first read about it in *Topographia Hibernica*, an account of Ireland written in the mid 1180s by Gerald of Wales (Giraldus Cambrensis). Gerald was a big fan of Ireland's conqueror, Henry ll, whom he hailed as a western Alexander. In *Topographia Hibernica* he described Ireland as a land of marvels, of rich pastures and meadows, where crops abound, wild animals roam the woods, where milk, honey and wine flow, a land of miraculous wells, a climate that knows neither thunder nor earthquakes.

Then came the down-side. The people are entirely unworthy of such bounty. They're lazy, preoccupied with eating and leisure. They dress (or don't dress, more like) improperly, they fight, and their sexual habits are not up to standard. Their saints are malicious.

Naturally, that makes a good case, indeed a duty, to tame the Irish. For those people need help, he believed. They need civilising. And, the best means of civilising is colonising.

Renaissance humanists, like Petrarch, Boccaccio and Dante, 'born-again Romans' as Eric Haywood calls them in his book, *Fabulous Ireland Ibernia Fabulosa* were only too eager to agree with the 'help' theory. They, after all, greatly admired the civilising process of Rome. In their time, which was also the Age of Discovery, the world was mapped. Maps were no neutral onlookers. The strong interest in geography was done with an eye to expanding.

The Church in Rome was keen to take up the geography cause too. Without maps it was impossible to spread the Christian word. Pope Celestine thought it a major coup that the Irish were converted in the fifth century, because it meant that the Christian word had reached the remotest 'others' of the world. That was then. By the fifteenth century there was a whole new world of 'others' to contend with, and to conquer.

Petrarch read Gerald's *Topographia Hibernica* with some relish and he gave it to his friend Giovanni Boccaccio. But Petrarch didn't read *Topographia* in the spirit in which it was intended. In fact, he loved the Irish unwillingness to civilise because he thought life in the woods was far preferable to a civil life. Besides, Ireland was a land that knew neither thunder nor earthquakes; and because he was very scared of thunder, he thought this was another point in its favour. I wonder did Petrarch understand that the tradeoff for thunder is all-year-round sunshine and showers.

'Penance' over, I'm ready to leave. And happy I am that I can, knowing the threatening tale of oblivion that hangs over this place. But I doubt if a single sin is forgiven me. It would be an unfair God who would absolve me for such a soft journey.

On my way back across the wilderness I stop to breathe in the elevated air and take a look on the enchanted eyeful. It's rare to be in Donegal without some mountain or other coming to treat you to a view. Beneath, roads ride off great distances into the heather, water glows in pools and lakes. The red roof of a barn carved into the side of a hill catches the sunlight. Two fellows in a van pull up.

'Are you lost?' they ask.

'No, I'm not lost. But thanks for asking.'

With a salute they pull off. Their friendliness charms the scene further. I wonder did the pilgrims of old notice that we are a hospitable people?

ACKNOWLEDGEMENTS

I wish to thank the following for permission to use copyright material in this book:

The poems by Patrick Kavanagh are reprinted from *Collected Poems*, edited by Antoinette Quinn (Allen Lane, 2004), by permission of the Trustees of the Estate of the late Katherine B. Kavanagh, by permission of the Jonathan Williams Literary Agency.

The poems by Brendan Kennelly are reprinted from *Familiar Strangers* (Bloodaxe Books, 2004) by permission of Bloodaxe Books.

'Knockore Church' is reprinted by permission of Paddy Kennelly.

The poems by Siobhán Ní Luain are reprinted by permission of Maura Ó Loan and Paula Tumelty

The poems by Michael Farry are reprinted from *Asking for Directions* (Doghouse, 2012) by permission of Michael Farry.

The quotations from John Broderick's novels are reprinted by permission of Lilliput Press.

INDEX